Designing the Global Corporation

Designing the Global Corporation

Jay R. Galbraith

JOSSEY-BASS
A Wiley Company
San Francisco

Manufactured in the United States of America on Lyons Falls Turin Book. This paper is acid-free and 100 percent totally chlorine-free.

Library of Congress Cataloging-in-Publication Data

Galbraith, Jay R., date
  Designing the global corporation / Jay R. Galbraith.
      p. cm.—(the Jossey-Bass business & management series)
Includes bibliographical references and index.
  ISBN 0-7879-5275-3
  1. International business enterprises—Management. I. Title. II. Series.
  HD62.4 .G348 2000
  658'.049—dc21

                                        00-008430

FIRST EDITION
HB Printing 10 9 8 7 6 5 4 3 2 1

The Jossey-Bass
Business & Management Series

Contents

To Sasha, the most globally skilled person I know

Preface

This book was conceived after I completed my chapters for *Tomorrow's Organization* (Mohrman, Galbraith, and Lawler, 1998), the Center for Effective Organization's latest book. I was considering several alternatives for my next project and sought advice from my colleague, Ed Lawler. I said, "I could do a book on global organization or . . . " Before I could mention any alternatives, Ed said, "Do the global book." Ed has always been a good reader of the book market and he knows me quite well, so I moved the global book to the top of my list.

I have always wanted to do a book on organizing international business; I have addressed the topic several times in my previous work, but it was never the primary focus. I wanted to do a book that would pull this work together. In *Designing Complex Organizations* (1973), I included a summary of the groundbreaking work of Stopford and Wells (1972); I have followed their approach to strategy and structure ever since. Summaries of the research have been reported in Galbraith and Nathanson (1978) and Galbraith and Kazanjian (1986).

A previous approach to analyzing multinationals was taken by Anders Edstrom and myself in the mid-1970s. We were both expatriates at the time; I was at the European Institute for Advanced Studies in Management in Brussels; Anders was at INSEAD in Fontainebleau, France, on leave from the University of Gothenberg. With support from Shell and British Petroleum, we studied how rotational assignments across borders built personal networks and shaped managers' values (Galbraith and Edstrom, 1976; Edstrom and Galbraith, 1977). I have always wanted to return to this work; the emphasis today on networks and shared values provides an excellent opportunity to do so.

In the early 1990s, Ed Schein and Dick Beckhard asked me to revise my original 1973 book in their Organization Development series. Instead of writing a revision, I focused solely on the lateral-coordination chapters of the original book, expanding them into a book-length treatise on coordinating across organizational units like functions, business units, and subsidiaries (Galbraith, 1994). This work again emphasized multinationals but only as one type of lateral coordination. I now wished to focus entirely on the organization of multinational enterprises. But what was the best framework to use in addressing the subject?

In January 1995, I began a professor's visit to the International Institute for Management Development (IMD, formerly IMEDE) in Lausanne, Switzerland. As it turned out, IMD is a great place to gain perspective on international business and multinational enterprise; here my framework of the challenges and the organizational forms to meet them crystallized.

I first became excited about the topic that would become this book's focus in the summer of 1995, when Thomas Gasser, deputy chief executive of Asea Brown Boveri (ABB), came to IMD to address the MBA class. I had done a lot of work over the years with matrix organizations and was curious to hear about ABB's experience. I was amazed, however, when he discussed the managerial issues resulting from ABB's *five-dimensional* matrix; most of my experience was with companies who were struggling with either the dual structure of businesses and geography or the three dimensions of functions, businesses, and countries. Here was Mr. Gasser saying that regardless of whether you have mastered the two- or three-dimensional matrix, the business world is imposing additional dimensions on your organizations!

This view was reinforced in the summer of 1996. My colleague Ulrich Steger surveyed the priorities of CEOs from companies in IMD's Partner Network and constructed from their responses a "CEO's agenda." A couple of their short-term issues were not surprising: cost competition and constant change were clearly on everyone's agenda. The two most important long-run issues, though, were enlightening for me. One was "How do we handle geopolitical uncertainty?" Today, an increasing number of investments are going to countries in which the government actively participates in the economic process; although companies have always tried to separate business and politics, many governments—like the Chinese government—specifically tie them together. Once a government does combine business and politics, a company cannot untie them. The CEOs saw the creation of a company political strategy as a new challenge.

The other long-run priority was managing organizational complexity. It was not just ABB experiencing an increase in the number of business dimensions; this was the experience of a majority of IMD's Partner Network companies, and it is the major focus of this book. Complex organizational forms like matrix structures, which have always constituted a large portion of my consulting and research, became necessary elements.

My experiences at IMD led me to observe the emergence of a new organizational complexity above and beyond the balancing of the standard three dimensions. The focus of this book, therefore, is, "How does management master the old complexity of businesses, geographies, and functions and prepare to meet the new complexity of global customers and solutions?" Before proceeding, however, let me state my personal views about complexity.

I am an agnostic concerning the design of organizations. Despite the fact that I wrote a book entitled *Designing Complex Organizations,* I have always tried to present the dual options of either simplifying the complexity or building the capacity to manage the complexity; both options have costs and benefits. My advice has always been to articulate both the good news and the bad news; if proponents of an option can articulate the bad news of that option, they will make an informed choice.

This balanced perspective was easier when people were open and often enthusiastic about matrix organizations than it is today. Today most people are biased against complex organizations, instead embracing the bias to "keep it simple." As a result I spend most of my time trying to present the case for complexity, which I do in this book as well. Managers know how to manage clear, simple structures; what they know less about is managing complexity.

Most companies do not have the capabilities to institute the multidimensional organizations that are required by their strategies and necessary to serve their global customers. In one memorable conversation, Harvard Business School professor Chris Bartlett summed up the situation well, stating that companies pursue third-generation strategies using second-generation organizations staffed with first-generation human resources. When first-generation managers attempt to institute third-generation multidimensional organizations, they fail and attribute the failure to the organizational form, not to their lack of capability. They then call for a return to simple, first-generation organizations. These simple organizations will work if the companies follow first-generation strategies in clear and stable industries. However, if a company wants to enter complicated countries like China, create value for the global customer desiring solutions, and be competitive in converging industries, it must pursue a third-generation strategy.

This book is intended for those who wish to design the third-generation organizations required by third-generation strategies, for managers and students who want to create the capabilities required by these organizations. Significant difficulties have resulted from trying to implement advanced organizational forms without first building the required capabilities. This book identifies the necessary capabilities and describes how they can be built as a company evolves from a national to a global firm. It also briefly addresses the development of third-generation human resources to staff the third-generation organizations; a full treatment would require a focus on global human resources. This book is written to aid those practitioners who must design and work in these organizations, to increase their understanding of why these organizations need to be complex in some cases and simple in others.

I believe in "keeping it simple" but with two twists. First, I believe we should keep it simple for the customer; a company should work toward being easy to do business with. Second, I believe we should keep it simple for front-line employees—those people with direct customer and product contact. The problem with previous prescriptions to keep it simple was that the intent was to keep it simple for management. The new mandate to keep it simple for customers and front-line employees makes management's job difficult and complex; how to organize in order to manage this complexity is addressed in this book.

Some firms see opportunity in managing the complexity. The opportunity arises because managing complexity creates value for the customer, who, after all, created the complexity by requesting integrated responses from suppliers. But managing complexity to create customer value is difficult, and therein lies the other part of the opportunity: by doing difficult things, firms create advantages for themselves. You get no competitive advantage from doing simple things; by definition, anyone can do them. Firms create competitive advantages by surmounting challenges that their competitors cannot.

Some firms, like ABB, IBM, and Citigroup, believe that the winning companies are going to be those that can manage global complexity. It is for these firms that this book is written.

May 2000   Jay R. Galbraith
Lausanne, Switzerland

Acknowledgments

There are always many people who contribute to a book in addition to the author, whose name goes on the cover. For this book, two people were indispensable and acknowledgment falls far short of what they deserve. My words never quite express the gratitude I feel. The first person is my partner, Sasha Galbraith. As always, she was simultaneously my best critic and my strongest defender. On this book she also provided extra support, which I needed. In the final push to meet the deadlines, she put my work ahead of hers. She was unwilling to have my poor graphics be submitted. I am more than grateful for her skilled and timely efforts.

The second indispensable person is Scott Wagner. Scott helped make the last couple of books I have written more readable. He too contributed extra effort at the last minute. He questioned me, argued with me, and then apologized for being "picky," only to argue again. This book is better because of his persistence under the time pressure. Thanks, Scott!

The Author

Jay R. Galbraith, an internationally recognized expert on organization design, divides his time between Switzerland and the United States. He is affiliated with the International Institute for Management Development in Lausanne, Switzerland, where he was on the faculty from 1995 to 2000. He is also professor of management and organization and a senior research scientist at the Center for Effective Organizations at the University of Southern California (USC). Prior to joining the faculty at USC, he directed his own management consulting firm. He has previously been on the faculty of the Wharton School at the University of Pennsylvania and of the Sloan School of Management at MIT.

Galbraith's principal areas of research are organizational design, change, and development; strategy and organization at the corporate, business unit, and international levels of analysis; and international partnering arrangements, including joint ventures and network-type organizations. His current research focuses on organizational units that are rapidly reconfigurable to suit the quickly changing demands of customers and markets across multinational boundaries. Prior studies looked at the formation and development of joint ventures between Indonesian firms and other Asian or Western firms. Galbraith has had considerable consulting experience in the United States, Europe, Asia, and South America. He has written numerous articles for professional journals, handbooks, and research collections, and is the author of four books on organization design and coauthor of four additional books.

Designing the Global Corporation

Chapter One

The Challenge of Organizational Complexity

Organizing a company to do business on a global scale remains one of the most complex managerial responsibilities. Organizational skills and capabilities simply have not kept pace with the ability to expand into new countries and markets. Today it is hard to find a company that does not claim to be global; it is equally hard to find a company that has mastered the ability to organize and do business globally.

Before a firm can organize globally, choices must be made, challenges must be met, and mind-sets must be transformed. The organizational choices that are made—which will be detailed in the next chapter—are directly related to the challenges that must be addressed; the greater the complexity of the challenges, the deeper the complexity of the required organization. These challenges are discussed, with a full examination of the problems and their solutions, in subsequent chapters. The first obstacle, however, is the mind-set of the managers who are asked to use these strategies.

Simple Versus Stupid

At the heart of the issue is the manager's difficulty embracing the complexity of the organization and building the capability to manage it. Most managerial mind-sets have been shaped by past experience with either clear country-subsidiary or business-unit structures. They may also be influenced by the so-called management principle of "keeping it simple." Yet serious students of cross-border organization have arrived at the position that keeping it simple is stupid; the world is complex, and a simple organization in a complex world becomes less and less viable.

A company's organization must be as complex as its business (Ashby, 1952). If the business environment contains fifteen constituencies that can affect a company's performance, the organization needs at least fifteen responses to manage those constituencies. If the business is simple, the organization can be simple. Take the example of Lykes Brothers, one of the *Hidden Champions* (Simon, 1996). It is privately owned, does not need dozens of MBAs to handle investor relations as Intel does, and makes a single product—orange juice—that it sells to a few private-label customers who handle the complexities of marketing and distribution. Lykes Brothers can have a simple organization because it is a simple business—invisible, selling a single product made in a single state in a single country to a few large customers. To suggest that Airbus and Boeing could use the same simple organization is absurd; the design of millions of parts and their assembly into a commercial aircraft are enormously complex undertakings, and the organizations that these companies must create to execute such tasks are equally complex (Galbraith, 1994, chap. 4).

If one wants a simple, clear organization, one should stay in a simple, clear business. Good advice is available on how to stay simple; staying invisible helps (Simon, 1996). Some suggest that companies should have the discipline to focus on a single-business model and to choose only those customers who fit the model (Treacy and Wiersema, 1995). Others say that synergy is elusive, that multibusiness firms should break up in order to unleash economic value. There are some intelligent ways to "keep it simple" (Sadtler, Campbell, and Koch, 1997), but one can debate the breakup value of a Sony or a General Electric (GE); it is unlikely that Sony, Asea Brown Boveri (ABB), or GE is going to break itself into pieces, and sticking to a single-business model is risky. Today companies compete by changing the business model (Slywotzky, 1996); for these companies, the complexity remains to be managed.

Academics reviewing the research on global organization find that companies must live with "structural indeterminacy"—that is, no single structure is the answer (Doz and Prahalad, 1992, Chapter Six). Instead companies need multiple structures to simultaneously respond to cross-border business opportunities, demands for local citizenship, and cross-border/cross-business purchasing or technology efficiencies (Bartlett and Ghoshal, 1989). Business leaders also support the indeterminacy argument. Percy Barnevik, the former CEO of ABB, says his company has been successful because it has been global *and* local. Akio Morita of Sony, before his retirement, tried to capture this idea by pursuing a policy of "glocalization." However, these statements by leaders and research summaries by academics have not been enough; most people think that *glocalization* is a misprint rather than a clever way to express a complex idea.

Manager reticence in dealing with organizational complexity can stem from direct experience. Usually managers have attempted to create a complex organization without building the required capability. For example, past problems with matrix-type organizations—what will be called multidimensional organizations in this book—have created a belief that matrix does not work. Rather than attribute these failures to a fault in matrix organization itself, the author believes that most managements have failed to apply the concept correctly. In subsequent chapters, this book will provide a fresh look at this type of organization, examining the circumstances under which it could—and should—be employed.

Managing the Multinational

The organizational challenge to a multinational company has always been the integration of activities that take place in different countries. This task has been the mission of managers responsible for product lines (usually called business units) and for functions like research and development (R&D) and finance. The organization of every multinational is therefore a blend of units for product lines, country subsidiaries, and business functions. Different multinational strategies have led to various distributions of power across these three dimensions; changing and balancing this distribution of power remains one of the CEO's principal challenges. This book begins by focusing on mastering the organization of the three standard dimensions.

Additional new complexities are being generated by two changes in the business environment. One is the convergence and realignment of industries. The combinations of new digital technologies, new biotechnologies, and deregulation have blurred the boundaries of many traditional industries. Within companies, these traditional industries have been served by business units with clear differentiation among them; when industry boundaries disappear, so do the clarity and boundaries of business units. I will address this issue of convergence and realignment in an upcoming book coauthored with Ed Lawler. The other change, which this book will concentrate on, is the increase in foreign direct investment (FDI). Indeed, since about 1985 globalization has been driven by FDI, and several new sources of complexity stem from the increase.

Consequences of Foreign Direct Investment

FDI increased some 600 percent after 1985. This is twice the rate of increase of foreign trade, which is itself increasing at twice the rate of the world economy. The result is that FDI is now the driver of globalization, as more companies choose to establish a presence in countries where they serve a market.

Complexity

The first consequence of increased presence is simply the complexity of doing business in many countries. Nestlé and ABB find themselves in over 150 countries; the sheer number of countries, currencies, tax policies, languages, time zones, cultures, and governments contributes to a significant increase in complexity.

Re-creating Competitive Advantages

The second consequence of having a presence in another market is the re-creation of the sources of a firm's competitive advantage. For example, Toyota's competitive advantage is its superior value-to-price ratio, which is made possible by using the Toyota lean-manufacturing system in Toyota City. This lean system depends on a superior supplier network and a loyal Japanese workforce. When Toyota exports product from Japan, these advantages are all embodied in the product. But when Toyota invests and manufactures in the United Kingdom and the United States, it does not have its supplier network and Japanese workforce; it must re-create these resources and assets in the new location. Many other companies also face the complexity of re-creating the sources of their home-country competitive advantage.

The issue of re-creating the sources of competitive advantage is linked to the "resource theory of the firm" (Wernerfelt, 1984), which is the basis of much of today's thinking about strategy. It is also linked to the concept of location-specific advantages (Porter, 1990). To establish a direct presence, a firm must understand the sources of its competitive advantage and whether they can be transferred to other countries. Many firms do not have this understanding or are even mistaken about it. Toyota's belief was that its lean-manufacturing process required a Japanese workforce; it has, however, been able to create a hard-working, team-oriented workforce in the United States and the United Kingdom. Although Toyota has been pleasantly surprised, Benetton has been disappointed. It has been unable to re-create its Italian supply chain anywhere else in the world.

Geopolitical Uncertainty

A third challenge caused by FDI pertains to increasing geopolitical uncertainty. Before 1985, less than 10 percent of FDI went to emerging-market countries; by 1996, this percentage had risen to over 40 percent. To use Turkey as an example, concerns such as these are triggered by this uncertainty: How should a business be positioned there? Will Turkey ever be admitted to the European Union? Will the fundamentalists turn it into another Algeria? Will it slide into the Islamic orbit? Other concerns include whether or not to invest in sub-Saharan Africa, and what will happen in a post-Suharto Indonesia or in China. Political issues like these are now a top priority, with companies having assets and employees in many countries. In the past, multinational companies preferred to separate business issues from political issues, but with the end of the Cold War business has become politics; when governments combine business and politics, companies cannot separate them. Instead, they must face the complexity of articulating a political strategy.

Even when governments do not specifically tie business and politics together, nongovernmental organizations (NGOs), such as

Greenpeace and Amnesty International, fuse them with a boycott or publicity. For example, Shell has tried for years to dissociate itself from the human-rights policies of the generals in Nigeria, but continued publicity by NGOs and the press maintains the association. Today, Shell tries to work with these groups; in exploring for oil and gas in Peru, Shell is negotiating with the Rainforest Action Network and the Peruvian government to follow good practices. This process of negotiation among firms, host governments, home governments, and NGOs is the New Diplomacy, with new strategies being developed to deal with these constituencies.

The Customer

The final complexity caused by increased FDI is the globalization of the customer. Previously, either they were local customers or they were global customers who bought locally. Now, however, more and more global customers are decreasing the number of their suppliers, selecting those few who can supply all their subsidiaries and coordinating the negotiations to get a single global-supplier agreement. Companies are struggling to coordinate across businesses and countries to service global customers. The head of Sony Europe, after coordinating a single pan-European agreement for the French retailer Carrefour, was informed that the agreement was good but not quite good enough. Carrefour had recently expanded into Taiwan, Mexico, and Brazil and wanted those subsidiaries included. It had been difficult getting a pan-European agreement; Sony now faced the complexity of getting a global agreement.

Cross-border and cross-business complexities multiply with the globalization of the customer. In order to satisfy customers desiring a single agreement, suppliers must coordinate purchasing across their own business units and subsidiaries. Next comes the implementation of a common supply-chain process for shared suppliers or a common order-fulfillment process for shared customers; then, the addition of a global purchasing executive and global commodity teams to do the coordinated buying, a global process owner for the order-fulfillment process, and another one for the new-product-development process. Each initiative adds a new dimension and a new champion for it. All the initiatives are then put into enterprise-wide software from SAP or Baan; a global project manager and an SAP team are also added.

Global customers have begun ordering solutions, not just stand-alone products. Hewlett-Packard previously took orders for printers and desktop computers; the orders from banks are now for trading rooms for New York, London, and Singapore, and consumer-goods companies order call centers for the Americas, Europe, and Asia. These solutions require teams from dozens of profit centers in different businesses and different countries. Companies grapple with the coordination process to create these teams.

Many companies are like ABB, with four-, five-, and six-dimensional matrix organizations. In addition to the usual business-geography matrix, the new levels of FDI create cross-business and cross-country dimensions for customers (or customer segments), functions, processes, projects, channels, and so on. The challenge is to coordinate these dimensions without becoming internally fixated on meetings, conflicts, and politics.

The challenges arising from this newly powerful customer influence are extensive; the global customer is, in fact, considered a "fourth dimension" of complexity. A full discussion of this complexity can be found in later chapters.

Summary

This overview chapter has highlighted some of the reasons for adopting a global organizational capability as well as some of the inherent challenges in doing so. It has also spotlighted some of the managerial and business-environment mind-sets that can prevent these strategies from being embraced and employed to full advantage. However, with growing awareness saturating the business environment, the reticence to adopt complex organizational structures is dissipating. Consensus is being reached regarding the necessity of these structures in this global age; the next chapter delineates the strategies and factors that shape global organizations.

Chapter Two

Organizing the Global Corporation

This chapter describes the strategies whose employment requires different types of organizations. Other factors, like the policies of local governments, are described. The organization that is chosen at any particular point in time derives from a balance of these factors. An understanding of the factors and their constant fluctuation is the beginning of adopting a global mind-set—the creation of a matrix in people's minds (Bartlett and Ghoshal, 1989).

Models for Multinational Organization: Structures to Network

Systematic knowledge about the multinational organization began with research about its various structural forms (Stopford and Wells, 1972). Subsequent authors expanded the topic to include coordination processes as well as structure (Galbraith and Kazanjian, 1986; Prahalad and Doz, 1987). The focus then shifted to organization, with structure just one element. Today the emphasis is on the organization as a network (Nohria and Ghoshal, 1997), with subsidiaries best conceived as continuously configurable.

The initial research on the multinational firm built on Chandler's (1962) work and focused on organizational structures. Chandler's historical analysis of U.S. firms showed that companies that remained in a single business, regardless of size, used a functional organizational structure. Companies that diversified into multiple businesses restructured themselves into divisions that were product profit centers. Chandler's work showed that organizational structure depended on the firm's diversification strategy.

This strategy-structure framework was used to examine U.S. firms as they expanded into other countries (Stopford and Wells, 1972), with the diversification strategy associated with different international structures. Those companies with diverse international business portfolios organized around worldwide product divisions; those with a single business or highly related businesses organized by country or geographical profit centers. These findings were supported when the experiences of European firms were examined (Franko, 1976; Fouraker and Stopford, 1968); a good summary of this and other structure work can be found in Egelhoff (1988). Thus, the diversity of the international business portfolio is one of the strategic factors to be considered in establishing the balance of organizational dimensions.

The multinational research on structure was extended to include other organizational factors. The interest in mechanisms of coordination arose because companies were finding that there was no single structure through which they could coordinate and control a large number of subsidiaries (Galbraith and Nathanson, 1978; Martinez and Jarillo, 1989). The question was, What holds all these subsidiaries together? The companies and researchers then focused on information systems, planning processes, performance measurements, product-development teams, project teams, and other resource-allocation schemes (Galbraith and Kazanjian, 1986; Prahalad and Doz, 1987; Bartlett and Ghoshal, 1989). In addition to communication and coordination processes across subsidiaries, interest also developed in "normative integration"—that is, in how widely dispersed subsidiaries could be held together through shared norms and values (Baliga and Jaeger, 1984; Jaeger, 1983). This "common culture" could be built and maintained through the human resource practices of selection, development, and, particularly, rotational assignments across subsidiaries (Galbraith and Edstrom, 1976; Edstrom and Galbraith, 1977). With this thinking, the design concept of multinational organization was expanded from structure to organization, with structure being but one of the factors.

The discussion is summarized in Figure 2.1. The Star Model serves as the definition of what is meant by *organization* in this book. The diagram shows that the design of organizations consists of choices of structural form, management processes, reward systems, and human resource practices (people). The other "point" in the diagram (strategy) illustrates that the four other policies of the star must also align with the international strategy. Different strategies require different configurations of structure, processes, rewards, and people practices.

The lines in the Star Model indicate that the choices of policies are related; the most effective organizations are those whose policies are aligned (Ghoshal and Nohria, 1993; Nohria and Ghoshal, 1997). For example, if a company chooses a structure and a set of management processes that require integration across countries, it must also select and develop people who have cross-cultural skills, as well as a reward system that motivates them to cooperate. All the points of the star must "fit" with each other (Nohria and Ghoshal, 1997).

The most recent extension of the concept of organization conceives of the multinational as a network of national subsidiaries and partners or of organizational units within the subsidiaries (Ghoshal and Bartlett, 1990; Nohria and Ghoshal, 1997). When structures were simple, the multinational organization appeared as in Figure 2.2. The network representation was one-dimensional and hierarchical or like a hub-and-spokes model; all power was concentrated at headquarters in the home country. But with increasing improvements

Figure 2.1. The Star Model.

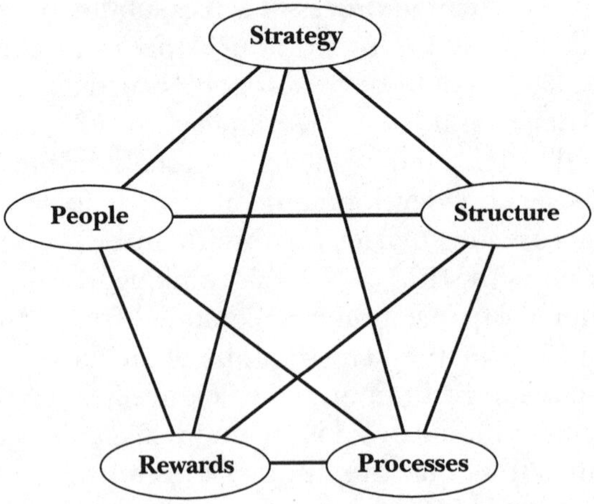

Source: Galbraith, 1977, chap. 2.

in and decreasing costs of communication and transportation, the links between subsidiaries have vastly increased. The links have also changed: today there are many more partnerships than in the past; one estimate is that there are four times as many partnerships as there are wholly owned subsidiaries (Contractor and Lorange, 1988, p. 4). Also, the home-country headquarters does not have all the power and control that are often attributed to it; ask the headquarters people of a company in a small country like Sweden how much control they have over their German subsidiary. In addition, the leadership in some activities is being taken by advanced subsidiaries. A network representation of the multinational that has distributed its leadership would resemble Figure 2.3. As companies increasingly link their subsidiaries and partners through internal trade networks—international trade is increasingly intracompany trade (Encarnation, 1993)—and intranet telecommunications systems (O'Hara-Devereaux and Johanson, 1994), a network is the best representation of these companies' organization.

The one-dimensional hierarchical model shown in Figure 2.2 is inadequate to handle even the multidimensional capabilities of today's wholly owned multinational. The organizational units of a modern multinational must be configurable into a business-unit dimension to create new products or into a geographical unit able to speak with one voice to the European Union or the Chinese government. Some of them must be integrated into a single research unit, with others configured to serve a global customer across countries and across businesses. Organizational units that are distributed

Figure 2.2. Simple Headquarters-Subsidiary Model as Hub and Spokes.

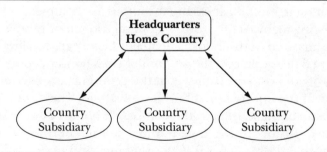

**Figure 2.3. Distributed-Headquarters
Model of the Multinational.**

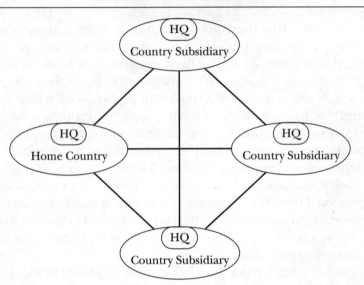

around the world must be capable of integration along a number of dimensions, the priority of which is determined by the firm's strategy. A network representation of the organization appears to be the one that is most effective; it is the best basis on which to conceive of the constant balancing of the strategic forces and organizational dimensions.

Factors Shaping the Organization

Multinational, multibusiness organizations are complex as a result of balancing many factors; four major and two minor groups of factors are analyzed in this book. The major factors are the level of international development, the amount of cross-border coordination, the activity of host governments in the economic process, and the diversity of the international business portfolio. The minor factors are the size of the market in the company's home country and the company's history or heritage in international business (Bartlett and Ghoshal, 1989, chap. 3). Choosing the right organization is a constant balancing of these factors.

Level of International Development

One of the factors influencing the choice of organization is the level of international development that a company has attained, which is itself a combination of factors. The first is the mode of participation in a country's economy—whether the firm participates with exports, joint ventures, or wholly owned subsidiaries. Another factor is the role assigned to subsidiaries. A third is the percentage of assets and management located outside the home country.

The proportion of a company's activities conducted in other countries is regarded as the best measure of how internationally developed, or global, the company is. Often companies claim to be global based on the percentage of sales outside the home country, but it is quite possible to be a national company with a high level of exports. The real management and organizational challenges arise when fully functional subsidiaries are created in other countries. Thus, a better measure of the level of international development includes the percentage of assets, employees, and, particularly, management that are located outside the home country, along with highly valued activities like R&D.

Once a company creates fully functional subsidiaries and develops into a multidimensional network, the other factors come into play to influence the type of organization.

Cross-Border Coordination

A key strategic factor influencing organizational type is the amount of cross-border coordination—what has been called "global integration" (Prahalad and Doz, 1987; Bartlett and Ghoshal, 1989). The amount of cross-border coordination directly affects which dimension will become the primary axis of the network. When there is little coordination, as implied in Figure 2.2, the countries or geographies are the basic profit centers and the axes for the network. As companies trade across subsidiaries and service customers with multiple locations, the organizations resemble those portrayed in Figure 2.3; in these companies, the business units and functions coordinate the cross-border activities. If the company has a multibusiness strategy, the business units become the axis and profit centers; a single-business company uses the functions as the main axis. In between are various distributions of power among the dimensions. A power balance between two dimensions results in a matrix organization.

The amount of cross-border coordination necessary is based on several factors that vary in importance depending on the industry, the structure of the industry, and the company's strategy. These factors are the level of fixed costs; the homogeneity of products and markets; the nature of customers, competitors, and suppliers; and the transportability of the product or service.

Fixed Costs

When a firm invests heavily in R&D, manufacturing plants, telecom infrastructures, and marketing promotions, it cannot generate enough volume in its home country to pay for the investments; it must generate revenues in other countries, using cross-border strategies, product-development processes, distribution, and so on.

Some of the most global companies are those that invest 10 percent or more of their sales in R&D; the pharmaceutical, computer, and semiconductor industries are good examples. To bring a new compound to market, pharmaceutical companies must invest several hundred million dollars. These companies cannot rely on domestic volume alone to earn back this fixed investment; they must plan products to be cross-border from the beginning of their development. For firms with large R&D investments, cross-border product-development processes are essential. Similarly, large investments in manufacturing plants or telecom infrastructures for service industries require multicountry volumes to cover costs.

However, every country in which an organization operates cannot justify an investment in a certain type of chemical plant, for example, so the company's one European plant might supply the plants in other countries with cross-border trade. The next semiconductor factories are estimated to cost several billion dollars, and so firms will supply the world from only a few locations. Cross-border coordination—in the form of cross-border logistics systems—is essential for these companies.

A common brand, with large investments in advertising and promotion, also requires cross-border coordination to spread packaging costs. Procter & Gamble spent $3.5 billion on advertising in 1996; it would like one ad from one agency to be transferred and translated around the world for a global brand and the creation of a common package for it that is printed, for example, in fourteen languages in eastern Europe.

In each of these cases there is a need for a cross-border strategy to coordinate investments and eliminate duplication. Investments are made in one or a few countries; then management processes coordinate the transfer of technology, products, services, and ads across borders. This coordination usually takes place within a business unit or a function.

Products and Markets

In order for products and services to cross borders, they must be relatively standard and markets must be relatively homogeneous. When standard products can be designed for homogeneous markets, the volumes can meet the scale requirements for high-fixed-cost investments. In many businesses the markets became increasingly homogeneous in the 1980s; consumer buying habits were influenced more by disposable income, education, and exposure to global media than by nationality. The Japanese were quite skillful at providing universal products for these emerging, homogeneous markets—products like Sharp calculators, Seiko watches, and the Sony Walkman were nearly the same all over the world.

Other industries, such as major appliances, still have a great deal of market diversity. The size and function of refrigerators vary considerably across markets; consumers in different countries have different food preferences, shopping habits, home size, and electrical costs. Locally differentiated products are supplied to these diverse markets.

Most markets are neither 100 percent homogeneous nor completely divergent, so firms learn how to create partially standardized products and services that can be easily modified to account for local differences. Advances in modular product design allow the creation of a common platform to which various additions and modifications can easily be made (Sanchez, 1995; Garud and Kumaraswamy, 1995). On other occasions, a standard hardware platform can be created on which a variety of local software applications can be run. These product-design capabilities exemplify how firms can be global (standard, scale) and local (variety) simultaneously. This product-development skill (detailed in the Appendix) is one of the organizational capabilities that need to be built by the global firm.

Customers, Competitors, and Suppliers

Cross-border coordination is required too when a global company's customers, competitors, and suppliers are also global companies who themselves must coordinate their actions across borders. Or these stakeholder companies may be present globally but act locally; in this case, there is less need for the global company to coordinate its own actions across borders.

In all probability, service is provided to local, regional, and global customers, necessitating responses across borders and within them. Most situations require a capability to respond to a mixture of all three types and an ability to rebalance when the proportion changes. Some companies may choose strategies to focus on one type or another: some global commercial banks, like Citibank (a cross-border bank), focus only on the global customer; other banks are local, serving the local customers whom Citibank does not serve.

Most companies have or are developing a global-accounts capability to service the global customer; if a firm does not have the capability, it will be dropped from the customer's supplier list. Also, if a company wants to shop the world for the best suppliers, it must have the capability to coordinate the purchasing function across borders and, often, across business units.

When facing a global competitor, a company's subsidiaries should, at the very least, share information on competitor moves and effective countermoves. In addition, coordinated action may often be needed. Assume that a company and its competitor face each other in three markets, with the market shares shown in Table 2.1. If the competitor cuts price in Market 1 to increase its market share, the company will reduce its cash flow significantly if it meets the competitor's price. The competitor, with its smaller share, can afford a price war in Market 1, but it cannot afford a war in Market 3, where the situation is reversed; if the company has cross-border coordination capability, it can retaliate with a price cut in Market 3. The company hopes the competitor will see the connection between markets and call off the price reduction. Here, both the company and the competitor need cross-border coordination capabilities to act and react effectively. Often, the existence of a cross-border capability deters a competitor at the outset, so many companies seek a significant presence in their competitors' main markets as a security factor.

Table 2.1. Market Shares of a Company and of Its Competitor.

	Market 1	Market 2	Market 3
Company	85	50	15
Competitor	15	50	85

Transportability

Cross-border coordination takes place when a product or service can be created in one place and sold to a customer in another; transportability occurs when the product has a high value relative to its transport cost. Semiconductors are an example of high-value products with low transport costs; cement and concrete products, in contrast, have low value and high transport costs. Today, more and more services are becoming transportable because of advances in telecommunications.

The distance over which manufactured products are moved is a function of the minimum efficient scale of the factory and the value-to-transport-cost ratio. When the minimum efficient scale is high and the value-to-transport-cost ratio is high, there is substantial cross-border trade. With high fixed costs, one large factory builds the product for all the neighboring countries, with business units and distribution functions coordinating the product flows. But when scale is low and the value-to-transport-cost ratio is low, the business is a local one. Examples are building products such as cement, bricks, tiles, and glass—materials that are bulky, heavy, and costly to transport. In a large country, these are not even national businesses; the country is supplied by several regional profit centers.

Service businesses have traditionally been local businesses, with the service produced and consumed at the same site. Some services—like hotels, restaurants, and construction—are likely to remain local; others are becoming more transportable because of telecommunications advances and will become still more transportable with the Internet. Until now, retailing, banking, education, and health care all required the customer to go to the store, branch, hospital, or school; these businesses were structured around regional profit centers. But with home shopping, home banking, distance learning, and remote medicine, these industries and their organization are changing. With transportable services, business units, which are focused on market segments or product lines, will become the basic profit center and principal axis of the network. The more transportable a product or service, the more the customer will be supplied across borders; the more cross-border supply that takes place, the more strategies must be formulated—and distribution coordinated—on a cross-border basis.

As mentioned above, most companies are going to be organized to respond to a mix of global and local pressures; they must have capabilities to be locally responsive and globally integrated. The pharmaceutical industry is an example. It invests enormous sums in R&D and has moderate-sized factories with stringent quality requirements, local customers, and products with different approval requirements in different countries. The result is that sales and marketing are local and organized by country, manufacturing is regional, and R&D is global. Most companies are a mixture, with the balance guided by the amount of cross-border coordination needed for particular activities.

Active Host Governments and Institutions

A third strategic factor, which operates independently of the first two, is the degree to which the government participates in a country's economic process (Doz, 1988). The government may be a customer, a partner, a regulator, or some combination of the three. When it is active and demanding, the company needs a strong country manager to maintain a relationship and negotiate with the appropriate governmental units. When a company needs a strong country manager *and* cross-border coordination requires a strong business-unit manager, the matrix organization is appropriate.

Royal Dutch Shell is a good example. Shell has moved away from its matrix organization by increasing the decision-making power of the business units. However, a strong country manager—and the matrix—is still maintained in places like Malaysia, where oil is a strategic industry managed by a state-owned oil company that is simultaneously the regulator of the industry, a partner, and a competitor. It competes in the upstream exploration and production business as well as in the downstream refining and marketing business. A strong local Malay is the chairman and country manager of Shell Malaysia; his task is to balance the multifaceted relationship between the businesses, the state-owned oil company, and the Malaysian government in the best interests of Shell. Similar situations arise in other Asian countries, most of them following the Japanese model of government-guided economies. In many of these countries, connections *(guanxi)* are more important than a company's quality program in gaining market access; having a country manager with connections and power is requisite.

There will always be some form of country managers as long as there are country governments, unions, and other institutions. The more active and demanding these local institutions, the stronger the country manager must be to represent the company and negotiate on its behalf.

Host governments can limit cross-border strategies in numerous ways. They can require exports, local value-added, local suppliers, partners, or product certification, as well as limiting imports, profit repatriation, access to foreign exchange, and so on. They can also provide incentives like subsidies, tax forgiveness, and privileged access to markets or resources. All these limits and incentives are usually negotiable. The country is looking for jobs, industrial activity in depressed areas, promotion of some ethnic groups, and, most of all, modern technology; the company is looking for market access. Countries with large, attractive markets—like China, India, and Indonesia—use their bargaining power to extract technology in return for market access. This bargaining between countries and companies is the New Diplomacy (Stopford and Strange, 1991).

The trend has been to weaken national governments' role in the economic process; free-trade agreements, global capital markets, deregulation, and privatization are shifting the power from national governments to markets. This trend results in increased cross-border trade, with strong business-unit managers to coordinate it. It also results in increased activity from regional governments; national governments are losing power, and the players are changing. Very local governments—like Saxony, Lombardy, and Catalonia—are becoming active to attract and hold companies; governmental regulatory units such as the European Union are now regional. Because of these shifts, some companies are seeing a decline in the power of the country manager and an increase in the power of the regional manager and the local plant or sales managers.

In parts of the world where governments and institutions are strong, demanding, and active in the economic process, the company needs decision-making power in the geographical dimension of the network. This power can be vested in a country manager, a regional manager, or a local one; it is another example of a company's needing to have global and local capabilities simultaneously.

Diversity of the International Business Portfolio

Diversity is measured by the number of different businesses in the portfolio, especially the differences in business logic (Galbraith, 1984; Galbraith, 1993, chap. 2). For example, ethical and over-the-counter (OTC) drugs are both pharmaceutical businesses, but they differ in their fundamental logics. The OTC business is marketing-driven, with heavy expenses in advertising and promotion; the ethical-pharmaceuticals firm is an R&D business, with expenses going mostly to discovering and developing new compounds. When portfolios have several different business logics in them, it is difficult to coordinate across the business units; in general, the greater the diversity of the international portfolio, the stronger the business-unit manager and weaker the geographical manager. With a diverse portfolio, it is easier for a business manager to coordinate across borders within a business than for a geographical manager to coordinate diverse businesses within a border.

The strategic factor of interest is the *international* portfolio diversity; a company's international organization is influenced by its international portfolio diversity, not its domestic portfolio. Often a company is diverse in its home country but takes businesses international only when it has an advantage. Toyota, for example, is more diverse in Japan, where it is involved in the construction and mobile-phone businesses, than it is abroad, where it is superior only in cars and trucks.

The range of portfolio diversity can be represented as a continuum, as in Figure 2.4. Starting with the least diverse, the diagram shows increasing amounts of portfolio diversity: multiple but related businesses; mixtures of related and unrelated features; and—the most diverse—a portfolio of unrelated businesses, as in a conglomerate.

Figure 2.4. Business-Portfolio Diversity.

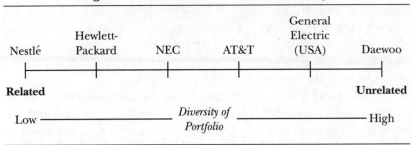

Nestlé is an example of a company following a related-diversification strategy: it has multiple products in multiple businesses but operates with a single business logic. Nestlé has thousands of products and brands in the food and beverage businesses, all consumer packaged goods. They are marketing and distribution businesses that have a customer—the mass merchandiser—and are driven by a system of brand management. When Nestlé diversified into bottled waters, it had to learn a new business but not a new way of doing business. Not surprisingly, Nestlé builds its profit centers around country managers; the marketing-oriented country manager can comprehend the business range and coordinate businesses by going through shared distribution channels to a common customer.

The other extreme is the conglomerate. This multibusiness entity has a portfolio of highly unrelated businesses and makes no attempt to coordinate them. In the West, this type of company is disappearing; companies like Hanson Trust, ITT, and Daimler-Benz are breaking up and focusing on fewer and more related business portfolios. In other parts of the world, however, the conglomerate form is in flux. In Asia and Latin America, companies are short of management talent, do not have access to liquid capital markets, and receive the support of their governments. Many are run by families who diversify their wealth by diversifying their companies' business portfolios; the Korean conglomerates, or *chaebol*, were a good example, with business portfolios that reflected the industry portfolios of their countries. The Korean government is attempting to break these companies apart, but in many emerging-market countries—and China—these conglomerates still exist. There is little cross-business synergy; each business is a global, cross-border unit run by a worldwide business manager. Conglomerates, whether Western or not, are run business by business, and each business has its own country manager. The largest business in a country may serve as the company country manager, but the country or geography is not the profit center; worldwide businesses are the profit centers—and the main axis—of the network.

GE (United States) has moved from the conglomerate type to a mixed model. This hybrid has aspects of both the related and the unrelated business models. GE's businesses in power generation, motors, locomotives, jet engines, and medical electronics are related and have a common business logic. They are all electrical businesses, with commercial customers and a significant after-sale service component; all share technology and an R&D unit, and they are all long-cycle businesses that require significant investment over a number of years. But GE also has GE Capital, a financial-services company with twenty-five business units like Aircraft Leasing. GE also has plastics, the National Broadcasting Corporation (NBC), and information-systems businesses that are not related to the others. So GE has aspects of an unrelated and a related portfolio, positioning it somewhere in the middle of the continuum shown in Figure 2.4. Other factors notwithstanding, the farther to the right on the continuum—in other words, the more unrelated the portfolio—the stronger the business dimension of the network. Of course, the other factors never are notwithstanding, and the design of the organization results from a balance of all four factors.

Table 2.2 summarizes the factors to be balanced. When all the factors in Table 2.2 support a strong geographical dimension, the network of subsidiaries is configured as country or regional profit centers. This type of company is usually referred to as multinational or multidomestic (Bartlett and Ghoshal, 1989; Porter, 1986); the company's international strategy is the sum of the country strategies. When all the factors support a strong business dimension, the subsidiaries are configured into worldwide businesses. This type of company is usually called global (Bartlett and Ghoshal, 1989); each business formulates its own cross-border strategy. In most cases, some factors favor a strong geography and some a strong business. The subsidiaries configure into geographical units and business units as applicable. For example, many Western companies with businesses requiring cross-border coordination are organized by business units in Europe and North America but by country in Latin America and Asia. These Western companies are less developed in Asia and Latin America; they deal with local governments that are more active in the economic process, so the organization structure must be varied to address differing requirements.

Table 2.2. Factors Influencing the Balance of Power in the Network of Subsidiaries.

	Strong Geographical Dimension	Strong Business Dimension
Level of International Development	Strange, new geography	Known geography
	Few assets and resources in the geography	High proportion of assets and people
	Geography plays contributor or leading role	Geography is an implementer
Amount of Cross-Border Coordination	Low fixed costs (R&D capital, promotions)	High fixed costs
	Heterogeneous markets and unique products	Homogeneous markets and standard products
	Local customers, competitors, suppliers	Global customers, competitors, suppliers
	Low transportability	High transportability
Activity of Local Institutions	Government active and demanding	Government passive
	Strong unions, local partners	Weak unions, wholly owned subsidiaries
Diversity of International Business Portfolio	Multiple businesses but single business logic	Multiple businesses and many business logics

Minor Factors

The four factors just discussed are the major shapers of organizational form, but two additional factors are significant.

Size of the Home Country

Another factor influencing the choice of organization is the size of the market in the home country. Managers and companies from small countries are usually more internationally minded than those from large countries; they know that most people are not going to speak their language, that their economies and businesses are affected by events in other countries, and that they have to address foreign markets to get any reasonable volume for whatever scale economies they have. This international mind-set is an advantage in most circumstances.

Alternately, companies with big home markets are usually less adaptable. They expand domestically first, perfecting their success formula, and then enter international markets. Their domestic success usually makes them arrogant, less internationally minded, and less willing to learn and to adapt to foreign markets than companies in small countries—until a crisis forces them to respond effectively to international markets.

Also, if a company from a large country creates a worldwide manager for a business, it is usually the person who is also running that business in the home country. This situation creates a potential conflict of interest between what is best for the global part of the business and what is best for the domestic portion; when the domestic portion is 50–60 percent of the total, the manager can become preoccupied with domestic issues at the expense of international ones. These managers are often seen by subsidiary managers as being biased toward the home country, likely to give priority to domestic investments and managers, and unwilling to develop new products for international markets if they differ from domestic products. In one study, U.S. companies that organized around worldwide product divisions, giving worldwide responsibility to the manager also running the U.S. product division, achieved lower international performance than companies that kept an international division or used a product-geography matrix (Davidson and Haspeslagh, 1982).

The situation is quite different in companies from small countries. Nestlé is a Swiss company, but Switzerland provides only 2 percent of Nestlé's sales. A worldwide business manager is located in Switzerland, although he is British; his decisions are seen as being driven by global business needs, not by those of the Swiss or U.K. subsidiaries. Over time, the large-country companies can match the neutrality of the small-country companies, but they usually begin with a bias to the home-country market.

History or Heritage

A final factor that moderates how a company responds to the strategic factors is its history or heritage (Bartlett and Ghoshal, 1989, chap. 3); a company's past creates capabilities and constituencies that can provide either inertia or momentum for change. For example, European firms that began expanding internationally early in the twentieth century established country subsidiaries during a time of two world wars, protectionism, and virtually no cross-border trade. Each subsidiary was self-sufficient and autonomous, so when free trade and the European Economic Community were created, these companies were not free to immediately integrate across borders; their country subsidiaries and country managers were a source of considerable inertia. However, their long experience in international markets and working across cultures was an advantage.

Japanese and German companies expanded internationally in the 1970s and 1980s. This was a time of free trade and free-trade institutions like the General Agreement on Tariffs and Trade (GATT). When integration was needed across borders, they were free to create integrated businesses rather than autonomous country subsidiaries. However, these companies had to build international experience and know-how.

Today many companies start as international companies. They immediately open sales companies in Europe, North America, and Japan. They put manufacturing in Taiwan and software in India. These companies literally start as Level V transnationals (the highest level of international development; see Chapter Three). A firm's history—or lack thereof—often moderates the effects of the previous factors on the choice of organization.

Summary

The global organization is a complex, multidimensional network. Some businesses, such as the Norwegian firm that has 70 percent of the world market for fish hooks, can remain relatively simple. But for the IBMs and Deutsche Banks of this world, complexity is the name of the game to be mastered. These companies consist of multiple businesses that are operating and competing in dozens of countries. Each business consists of functions, such as operations, sales, and marketing, and of processes, such as order-to-cash and new-product development. The search for a simple, single organizational structure has proven to be unfruitful for these companies. Instead, the organization is an aligned complex of structures, management processes, reward systems, and human resource practices, which must be aligned with each other and with the international strategy. This strategy consists of four factors; Table 2.2 shows their impact on the distribution of power, with the subsidiaries best conceived as a network that can be configured into businesses and geographies. (Later, we will discuss how they are also configured around customers, projects, competencies, processes, and issues.) The next chapter expands on the concept of levels of international development.

Chapter Three

Levels of International Development

The level of international development—one of the strategic factors that influence how a company organizes its international operations—consists of three dimensions: the role of the subsidiaries, the mode of participation in the local economy, and the proportion of assets and employees located outside the home country. In this chapter these three dimensions will be more fully developed. The role of the subsidiary features the transfer of competitive advantages among geographies. The first section of the chapter defines the different types of competitive advantages; some transfer easily, some transfer only with adaptations and modifications, and some do not transfer at all. It is important for a firm to know the bases of its success formula and their transferability to new geographies. Advantages can be transferred through different modes of participation, such as exports, joint ventures, or foreign direct investment (FDI), leading to majority-owned or wholly owned subsidiaries. Different types of organizational structures and processes are used for different modes of transferability.

The second section of the chapter focuses on the different levels of international development and how a firm changes from one level to another. Changing to higher levels of development has been called *internationalization* (Johanson and Valne, 1977)—the process by which a firm creates assets and employees outside its home country and changes the role of the subsidiaries. It is the process by which a firm converts itself from a national company to a global one.

The Transfer of Competitive Advantages

A firm has a competitive advantage when it can profitably create value in the eyes of the customer in ways that competitors have difficulty copying. A firm's strategy is defined by its search for advantages, and transfer of those advantages into new geography is requisite for international expansion. This section will first delineate why advantage transfer is central to internationalization, and then describe the different types of advantages. Different types of advantages are differently transferable, and different modes of participation transfer advantages differently; the better a firm understands the sources of its own advantages, the better prepared it is for organizing internationally.

The Centrality of Advantage Transfer

Advantages are central to international expansion because a foreign firm is automatically at a disadvantage when it enters a new country. Compared with local firms, the foreign company has no local know-how, no reputation, and no local relationships. Simply being foreign can disadvantage a firm. The foreign company must bring advantages from its home country to overcome these local disadvantages (Yu, 1995).

Evidence shows that a country's exports and FDI come from industries in which that country is superior. Japanese autos, U.S. software, and German chemicals are good examples. For developed countries, these industries are also R&D–intensive; technological advantages are typically used to overcome the inherent advantages of local firms. When foreign companies enter industries in new countries in which they have no home-country advantages, they do not perform very well or last very long. When companies from Korea, Taiwan, and Singapore—without a transferable home-country advantage—enter the U.S. market by acquiring a firm with an advantage, these companies quickly lose the advantage and a lot of money (Yu, 1995); Japanese companies in Hollywood are simply the latest chapter. Thus, international expansion is all about transferring advantages from the home or existing geography to a new geography where those advantages are not available to local firms.

Types of Advantages

For many products and services, advantages are quickly matched by competitors and are not sustainable. Yet some companies in these dynamic industries are able to maintain superior performance, an observation that led to identifying different types of advantages. The first type is at the level of the product or service—advantages directly experienced by the customer. The product or service can have superior features, price-to-value ratio, servicing, or financing terms (advantages not sustainable in some industries).

The second type of advantage is based on having superior resources, assets, competencies, skills, or capabilities (Wernerfelt, 1984). This resource advantage is the basis on which product and service advantages are built; superiority in these assets and resources allows companies either to sustain their product advantages or to continually re-create them. Hewlett-Packard (HP) is an example: with product life cycles and development cycles of less than a year, the company maintains its dominance in the printer business with continued superiority in inkjet and other printing technologies, cross-unit product-development processes, and relationships with distributors. HP combines superiorities by designing products for ease of distribution; printers can be assembled in local markets, with local-language software, service manuals, and features added at the last moment. Other companies maintain their advantages because of superior supply networks; Toyota, McDonald's, and Wal-Mart all achieve consistent quality and value prices (product-service advantages) because of their superior networks of suppliers (a resource advantage).

Resource advantages can be specific to a firm or specific to a location or country in which a firm operates. Superior inkjet technology and superior capability in the product-development process are HP-specific resource advantages. The obvious country-specific advantages are low wages and favorable exchange rates, and there are also natural-resource advantages. Norway and Canada produce low-cost energy because of hydroelectric resources; energy-intensive businesses like aluminum are at a disadvantage if they are not located near these low-cost energy sources. Locations can have other advantages resulting from a unique combination of advanced and demanding customers, leading-edge competitors, and supporting infrastructure (Porter, 1990). Often these combinations are accidents of history; California became a multimedia center because of the combination of Silicon Valley's electronic hardware and software competencies and Southern California's entertainment competence. Locations sometimes try to build a local competence, like Singapore or Rochester, New York. Rochester is trying to become an optics or imaging capital; building on the presence of Kodak and Xerox, it is growing a consortium that includes other local firms, local governments, universities, trade associations, technical schools, and chambers of commerce, focusing resources to make Rochester attractive to optics businesses.

Location-specific advantages are usually available to all firms in that location. All firms in Bangalore, India, have access to the hardworking, educated, English-speaking, low-cost software talent that is unique to the area, but firms not located in Bangalore may be at a disadvantage if their location does not possess equally low priced and equally talented people. Location resource advantages can sometimes be unavailable to all firms at that location: Japanese semiconductor manufacturers all had access to low-cost capital, government support, and captive Keiretsu customers, but U.S. and European companies did not have equal access and were disadvantaged as a result.

Transferability

Today, the focus is on the sources of sustainable advantage—those advantages that result from superior resources, assets, or skills. These resource-based advantages are harder to copy, more difficult to observe, and take longer to build than product or service advantages. Advantages are also analyzed to see whether they are transferable by using a firm's superior resources from existing geography in order to give its operations a competitive edge in a new geography. The firm can make the transfer either through an export mode, a joint-venture mode, or a foreign-operations mode resulting from FDI.

Export

When using an export mode, the firm can draw on all its resource advantages, whether firm-specific or location-specific. The issue for the exporting firm is whether the product-service advantages experienced by the customer are transferable. As discussed in Chapter Two, some products, like Levis, Swiss watches, and French skis, are directly transferable; for these products, the different national markets are sufficiently homogeneous. However, most other products and services are not directly transferable; they require some modifications to match the varying requirements of different geographical markets. Thus, in order to make the exporting firm's advantages transferable, a product-development process must be designed to get both scale for the expensive components and variety by using other inexpensive components. A cross-border, cross-function product-development process is the international organizational capability needed by the exporting firm.

Joint Venture

Exports, however, are not always feasible; the firm may have to invest directly in the country in order to serve its market, or it may encounter circumstances where resource advantages are not directly transferable—location-specific advantages, by definition, are never transferable. When some advantages are transferable and others not, a joint-venture mode of international business can be employed. Take the case of Benetton, the Italian fashion merchandiser. Benetton's advantages include its supply chain of low-cost Italian manufacturers and a distribution system of independently owned, Benetton-exclusive stores run by Italian agents. The resource advantage of agent-run distribution has been transferred easily throughout Europe, and the manufacturing advantage—part firm-specific and part location-specific—has been transferred through exports to its own stores. However, Benetton has been unable to re-create its distribution system in Japan, and its exports are too expensive in Brazil; it has concluded that it cannot re-create its resource advantages in these countries. Instead it has formed partnerships with local firms that have the supply-chain resource advantages Benetton lacks by transferring its firm-specific and country-specific design competencies to local partners for manufacture and distribution. Resource advantages are transferred by exporting the semiannual collections of Italian fashion designs and by licensing the Benetton brand.

This joint-venture, or partnership, mode of entry is used when exports are not feasible, and some resource advantages are transferable and others are not; the firm transfers those that it can and chooses partners to provide those that it can't. A typical example is the transfer of product and process technologies to a local partner who manufactures and distributes the product or service. The joint-venture mode is also chosen when a firm enters a strange new geography and is uncertain which advantages can be transferred; in this case, the joint venture is a learning vehicle. Firms using joint ventures need an international product-development capability, like exporters, plus an international partnering capability. This partnering capability will be further described in Chapter Four.

McDonald's provides insight into transferable resource advantages. Like Benetton, McDonald's has a superior supply chain in its home country; it also has superior market-research skills for locating profitable retail sites. However, it had neither of these when entering Japan. Instead McDonald's brought its brand, its "Americanness," and its knowledge of how the fast-food business system works. A joint-venture partner was chosen to provide the retail-site expertise and other complementary business skills that McDonald's lacked. The partner knew the local franchising laws, how to hire and manage a Japanese workforce, how to secure local financing, who were the best franchisees, and how to get permits from the government for building and serving food. However, there was no supply chain for U.S. hamburgers and French fries, and McDonald's could not find a partner to operate it. Instead, McDonald's had to build a supply chain from scratch.

When resource advantages—like supply chains—are not directly transferable, they must be re-created in the new geography. Indeed, McDonald's new competitive advantage may be its organizational capability to build superior supply networks anywhere in the world; it has rebuilt its supply chain in Japan and Europe and is re-creating it in China and Russia. Compare McDonald's to Benetton: Benetton has been unable to re-create its network anywhere else in the world, and while McDonald's global revenue and profits grow, Benetton's have plateaued. Today, Benetton is an Italian company with exports, licenses, and joint ventures in fashion; to get revenue growth, it is diversifying into sports equipment and other businesses. McDonald's has developed three international organizational capabilities in order to generate growth: it has learned to adapt its products to local markets through an international product-development process (like exporters); it has developed an international partnering capability; and it can transfer resource advantages by re-creating them in new geographies.

Foreign Operations

The third mode of participating in the global economy is with majority-owned or wholly owned subsidiaries; through FDI, the firm can grow or acquire its own foreign operations. These firms face the challenges of transferring their resource advantages to new geographies. Sometimes this transfer occurs easily, as in Benetton's European distribution system; other times, the advantages can be re-created only after trial-and-error experimentation and modification. On still other occasions, advantages are not transferable but substitutes can be found, or advantages may not transfer and the firm has to compete without them. In some pleasant cases, which will be examined first, location-specific advantages can be re-created in new geographies.

Sometimes the transfer is easily accomplished. Both Benetton and IKEA, the Swedish furniture retailer, re-created their superior distribution systems in Europe; their resource advantages transferred as easily as using exports. Other direct operations, such as Sony and Sharp, were easily established because they did not involve the transfer of resource advantages like superior supply chains or manufacturing workforces. The Japanese competitors of these companies had exclusive and extensive distribution systems in Japan, which Sony and Sharp lacked. Both companies circumvented this advantage by producing innovative, superior products that people wanted; they created resource advantages in the form of electronic technologies and product-development processes. These superior products received home-market distribution, but it was not a source of advantage. When they expanded into other countries, they used existing distribution systems and locally manufactured the easily produced merchandise. The resource advantages—product and process technologies—transferred easily and combined well with the local distribution and manufacturing advantages, allowing these firms to re-create their success formulas relatively easily in other countries.

On other occasions, resource advantages are transferable only with considerable effort. The Toyota Production System (TPS) was initially a firm-specific advantage that was copied by many Japanese manufacturers. It came to be considered a country-specific advantage of the Japanese because TPS required supplier relationships that were common in the uniquely Japanese Keiretsu system, and it was also believed to require a Japanese workforce that was hardworking, loyal, educated, and team-oriented. However, Japanese and Western companies have discovered that a workforce with the same qualities can be created in the West if some intense selection and training are used; one Japanese factory interviewed and tested twenty thousand people for fifteen hundred U.S. jobs. Supply networks are being re-created, with a combination of invited Keiretsu partners and specially trained local suppliers forming the networks. These networks are not as efficient as Toyota City in Japan, but they are improving. It is even suggested that Chrysler's revival is due to the creation of its own Keiretsu. Thus, with some work and adaptation, advantages believed to be location-specific and firm-specific can be transferred to new geographies and serve as advantages there as well.

On other occasions, substitutes for location advantages may have to be created. Up until the 1990s, German companies were reluctant to move manufacturing out of Germany; they believed a "Made in Germany" label was an advantage. They also believed that their manufacturing processes depended on the "German Way," uniquely German apprenticeship programs for a skilled, disciplined German workforce. Today, that workforce is the world's most expensive, and German companies are searching for a new model in eastern Europe. Many are trying a combination of lean manufacturing and well-educated, low-wage eastern European workforces to substitute for the high-wage German Way.

In other situations, the firm may simply have to compete without a resource advantage. A good example is a European company that dominates the power-tools business for the construction industry by providing a steady stream of new and improved products. The company believes that one of its advantages is its direct sales force—technically trained salespeople who work with leading-edge customers to generate and try new products and product improvements. They provide rapid feedback from the field, while their slower competitors lack direct customer contact because they go through distributors. The company has re-created this sales force in every country that it enters but is encountering problems in Asia. In several Asian countries the construction companies are run by owner entrepreneurs who make all the decisions; there is no purchasing department. The owners are constantly at job sites and not available for sales calls; when they want some tools they simply call the distributor, with whom they have a relationship. After years of trying to call on the customer, the company has decided to use distributors where that is the local—and apparently only—practice; in these countries, the firm must compete solely on its product advantages and brand name.

In order to be best prepared for international expansion, a firm should first understand its own sources of competitive advantage—which is not always the case. To facilitate this understanding, the firm should analyze whether its product- or service-type advantages are transferable. It should also analyze its resource advantages, which create the product or service superiority: Are these firm-specific or location-specific? Are they easily transferable and re-created? Must modifications be made or substitutes be found? These are important issues for organizing the start-up phase following the FDIs.

Levels of Internationalization

Internationalization is the process of changing levels of international development, usually (but not always) to higher levels of development. Through this process a national company is converted into an international company, enters new markets, and creates value-adding activities in geographies outside the home country. A firm will be more internationally developed when a higher proportion of its assets are outside the home country and more of its employees, managers, and officers are non-nationals. For example, if the United States constitutes 20 percent of the world economy, then a U.S. company that is truly global has 80 percent of its sales, 80 percent of its assets, 80 percent of its R&D, and 80 percent of its employees outside the United States. Additionally, such a firm has changed its international mode from exports to foreign operation and has changed the role of subsidiaries from implementers to generators of advantages for the global network. The different levels of development are shown in Table 3.1.

Table 3.1. Outline of Levels of International Development.

Level	Role of Subsidiary	Mode	Organization	Percentage of Value Added (assets, employees)
0	None	None	National company	Zero
I	Seller	Exports	National company plus sales companies	Low
II	Local partner	Partnerships	National company plus partnerships	
III	Start-up	Foreign operations	Geographic division	
IV	Implementer	Foreign operations	Multidimensional network	
V	Contributor/leader	Foreign operations	Transnational	High

Level I

The first level of development, the export mode, uses subsidiaries as sales companies. This level involves transferring product or service advantages that embody the firm's home-country resource advantages, exploiting product superiority, and building a global brand. The subsidiary initially consists of sales and administrative employees; it is also the primary link with distributors for product companies. A service firm could also have a small sales office for consulting, advertising, or banking services. For any projects or deals landed by the subsidiaries, bankers or consultants from the home office conduct the studies and analyses and are flown in for delivery. Besides sales, the subsidiary's responsibility is to provide input to the product- or service-development process by suggesting improvements that would make the company's offerings more saleable in the new market.

This is the simplest level of international involvement; this book will focus on the other levels of development, those that involve FDI and the transfer of resource advantages.

Level II

The second level of international development occurs when a firm invests in another country and begins to conduct foreign operations but chooses a partner—usually a local company—to join in the investment. There are many reasons for choosing a joint venture, but partnering is used here to get market access in a foreign country. The firm—usually inexperienced in or unfamiliar with the country or international markets in general—uses a partner to learn how to do business in the new country. The firm can learn which advantages are transferable, which can be learned from the partner, which must be modified, and which must be discarded for substitutes. After a period of learning, the firm may expand the venture, start a wholly owned subsidiary next to the joint venture, buy out the partner, or sell out and retreat. The joint venture is usually a stepping-stone or learning platform. On other occasions the joint-venture mode may be required by the host government as a price of entry. In these cases, the options of the firm may be limited.

The joint-venture mode is a higher level of development than the export mode because it creates more assets and employees outside the home country. It may also require the transfer of home-country resource advantages. The joint-venture mode also requires international partnering skill because it requires various amounts of interaction and cooperation with the foreign partner. Plus, the firm still needs the organizational capabilities required of a Level I exporter.

If the firm expands the venture or buys out the partner, it moves to Level III, the start-up of a wholly owned business in a new subsidiary.

Level III

The third level of international development occurs when the firm engages in FDI and creates multiple functions within the subsidiary. Product companies may use a direct sales force rather than distributors, invest in warehouses and distribution, and create customer-service units. When volume permits, the subsidiary may manufacture and manage its own supply chain. Service businesses also add functions; advertising agencies, for example, may add creative functions and lease a television studio.

The subsidiary changes from having a simple sales role to being a start-up and eventually a multifunction business. Start-up issues vary with how many functions are created in the subsidiary and whether resource advantages must be transferred. If supply-chain advantages are transferred and must be modified, substantial effort and subsidiary autonomy are needed; if the transfer is routine, the subsidiary may still be controlled from headquarters. (Chapter Five contains a further discussion about managing the issues of start-up.)

The major organizational challenges begin at the start-up phase; the company must now coordinate and manage employees from different cultures, speaking different languages and in different time zones. Why does the company take on these additional challenges in lieu of the simpler export mode? There are several reasons, some economic. When volume in a geography hits minimum efficient scale, it is simply cheaper to manufacture locally than to transport the product from the home country; for a service firm with sufficient volume, it is cheaper and faster to meet customer needs locally than to fly in consultants and pay for their lodging. The other economic reason is rising wage and exchange rates in the home country. Many German, Japanese, Korean, and Taiwanese manufacturers would prefer to continue exporting, but their home-country costs are simply too high; they are forced to move labor-intensive operations to lower-wage countries in order to stay competitive.

In other cases, companies are forced to invest locally by host governments and customers. Some governments use or threaten tariffs or barriers unless a firm produces locally; often a country negotiates an arrangement with a company to provide jobs in exchange for market access or other concessions. In any case, there is pressure from the host government to add value in its country in exchange for access to its market—the bigger and more attractive the market, the more demanding the government can be.

Customers may also demand that suppliers be local because they expect rapid support or just-in-time delivery from them. Automobile assemblers—both Western and Asian—are insisting that their suppliers follow them into new geographical markets. Fiat wants its key suppliers to supply just-in-time to its plants in southern Italy, Turkey, Poland, and Brazil; suppliers are chosen for their willingness and ability to invest in these countries.

When a company shifts to FDI, it must still manage the international product-development process and support an international brand, while now also managing the transfer and modification of resource advantages to a new geography. The start-up phase requires the firm to develop this transfer capability, make the transfer, and build a local business around its advantages. When these activities are reasonably complete, the next level of development is possible: integrating the subsidiaries into a network.

Level IV

The fourth level of international development brings further complexity to the foreign-operations mode. While the typical Level III firm is a national company with an international, or geographical, division, the Level IV firm, having acquired some international capability, gives more responsibility to the subsidiaries and organizes them into a multidimensional network. The role of the subsidiaries in this multidimensional network is implementation; although they may be multifunctional, large, and effective, their role is still one of implementing advantages and strategies generated in the home country.

Companies operating at Level IV continue to generate and transfer advantages, enter new geographies, and develop themselves internationally. Their primary challenge, however, is to develop cross-unit coordination capabilities—that is, the managerial skills to forge and maintain strong links across borders, functions, and businesses. This capability is the key to making the organization at Level IV function effectively. The company establishes coordination links among the subsidiaries and between the subsidiaries and the business units of the national company; the strength of these links varies considerably, depending on the amount of cross-border coordination.

At one extreme is a company comprising a portfolio of foreign subsidiaries with little cross-border coordination; the subsidiaries have weak links, sharing financial resources, ideas, and people in a geographical structure with subsidiary profit-and-loss centers. If the company has few subsidiaries, the geographical division may remain in place; if there are many subsidiaries and a larger per-centage of assets and employees outside the home country, a geo-graphical structure known as multinational or multidomestic will emerge, with the home country as one of the geographies. This structure emerges earlier for companies from small countries. An example is Holderbank, the Swiss cement and aggregates company.

At the other extreme is a company with strong links among subsidiaries and a substantial amount of cross-border coordination. In this case, the subsidiaries and the geographical division are bro-ken apart and assigned to their respective business units; if the business portfolio is diverse, the geographical division may disap-pear altogether. At Hoffman–La Roche, only worldwide business units and functional staffs—no corporate geographical units—report to the CEO. The business units have country managers, with the largest business unit usually acting for the whole company within its country. Figure 3.1 illustrates these extreme links, as well as those occupying middle ranges. At the left of the figure, the Holderbank building-products company, with weak links, repre-

Figure 3.1. Strength of Subsidiary Links and Business-Unit Power.

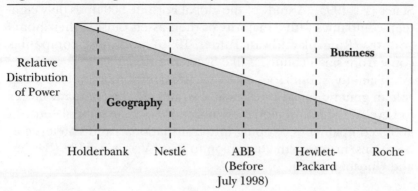

sents the multidomestic model, where the power and the profit and loss (P&L) are in the geographical subsidiaries; moving to the right, the links between subsidiaries get stronger, there is more cross-border coordination, and the business units receive more decision-making power. The next company, Nestlé, retains the power and P&L in the geographies but moves some decision-making power to the businesses, which coordinate the global brands and product R&D. The next company, ABB, operated a matrix organization, with a balance of power between the geographical and business dimensions; there was a shared P&L responsibility, but a division of other responsibilities for which either the business or the country was accountable. HP and the new ABB are the converse of Nestlé, with considerable new-product development within a business unit; the activities in the subsidiaries report to the businesses, which are the P&L centers; the geographies still report to the CEO, but the extent of their responsibility is as coordinators for local-customer and government relations. Finally, representing the strongest subsidiary links, is Hoffman–La Roche, where the corporate-level geographical dimension disappears; units within subsidiaries report to their respective worldwide business managers. (Subsequent chapters will treat each of these types in detail.)

Most companies operate at Level IV or lower; despite the rhetoric about being global, most still have a national bias. Although the United States constitutes 20 percent of the global economy, the average U.S. firm has 60 percent of its assets within the United States (Yu, 1995). A study of the global Fortune 500 finds only eighteen companies with a majority of their assets outside their home country (Ruigrok and van Tulder, 1996), and these companies come from small countries like Switzerland.

When the subsidiaries take an active contributory or leadership role in generating advantages and strategies, the company moves to Level V, the transnational organization. Despite some skepticism about companies developing into transnationals and stateless corporations, many see the transition to Level V as inevitable (Bartlett and Ghoshal, 1989).

Level V

The highest level of international development is the transnational form, which occurs when subsidiaries assume a leadership or contributory role in developing strategies and advantages for a business. These strategies and advantages are transferred to and implemented in other subsidiaries as well as in the home country.

A subsidiary that plays this role is usually in a geography with location-specific advantages. The company builds the competencies of the subsidiary and uses it as a source of advantage for the network of subsidiaries. Ford's global reorganization is an example. Europe is more advanced in the manufacture of small front-wheel-drive cars and standard transmissions; North America is more advanced in the manufacture of large cars and automatic transmissions. The European subsidiaries export the small-car designs for assembly in North America and provide standard transmissions for all assembly plants; in this way, Ford gets scale and excellence through specialization, and each geography does what it does best for the global network.

Banking is another industry in which countries and cities have location-specific advantages. Switzerland and Luxembourg are centers for private banking; London has the largest volume of foreign exchange; and New York is the center of innovation for new products and financial instruments. A global bank must, at the least, have subsidiaries in these centers. Over time, the subsidiaries develop and play a contributory role in generating advantages; some banks then locate their business headquarters in these centers and delegate global strategic leadership for that business to the subsidiary. For example, Citibank's Private Banking business stems from Switzerland, its foreign-exchange product line comes out of London, and its derivative and option products are centered in New York.

Complexity is the main drawback to the transnational form; it has all the complexity of the multidimensional network plus the complexity of managing a distributed headquarters. Indeed, the superior management of complexity may become the prime source of competitive advantage. If all the major players in an industry create subsidiaries in countries having location-specific advantages, those centers of excellence cease to be sources of advantages; they become part of the price of entry into the business. Advantages then become firm-specific, and foremost of the firm-specific resource advantages is the management skill to operate a transnational organization.

The transnational form has all the international challenges of the preceding levels plus the task of coordinating the intensive communications shown in Figure 2.3. In other words, the transnational requires an international product-development process like that of a Level I firm, the international partnering skill of a Level II firm, a resource-advantage-transfer process like that of a Level III firm, the multidimensional-coordination processes of a Level IV firm, plus the coordination of multiple strategy centers and the transfer of advantages from multiple advantage centers. This greater level of coordination and communication must take place in the face of greater obstacles: the transnational has more subsidiaries in more countries managed by more different nationalities. It requires a greater amount of integration, part of which is made possible through modern telecommunications. The other part is achieved through normative integration, created through the company's human resource systems. Normative integration is the reduction of barriers through the sharing of norms and values. (The transnational will be discussed in detail in Chapter Ten.)

If the transnational is more complex to manage than the multidimensional network, why would a company want to be a transnational? There are two motivators: significant location-specific advantages outside the home country and competitive intensity. In a business with significant location-specific advantages abroad, a firm will be at a disadvantage compared with competitors who have networked subsidiaries at that location. The greater the competitive intensity of the business, the less a firm can allow competitors that kind of advantage. The firm must have a subsidiary in the location and use it as a contributor or leader in the creation of advantages.

The five different levels of international development represent increasing proportions of assets and employees located outside the home country. The different levels also represent different modes of participating in the international economy and different roles played by subsidiaries in the global network. Other features vary with the levels, as summarized in Table 3.2. Note the variance in the transfer of advantages at the different levels. All advantages from the home country are transferred in export mode; in Levels III and IV, location-specific advantages are not transferable; at Level V, the firm-specific resource advantages are transferred from any subsidiary creating them. The last column of the table shows the international organizational capabilities required; Level V requires the mastery of all of them, hence it is the most internationally developed level.

This discussion of internationalization seems to imply that a firm starts as a national company, Level 0, and proceeds to internationalize by moving sequentially through the levels, eventually ending up as a Level IV or a transnational. That is a possible sequence—and for internal growers it may even be probable—but not all firms follow that sequence. This process of internationalizing has been studied extensively; the next section reviews the results of these studies.

The Process of Internationalization

International expansion happens in incremental stages, in an experiential learning and development process. The company must learn how to transfer its competitive advantages to other countries, modify those advantages, and build a local business around them. The studies of the process by which national companies expand into new geographies have focused on two topics: stages and paths. Does a company pass through identifiable stages in a sequence when becoming global? If so, then a model of these stages could be a useful planning tool. What path does a firm follow in expanding internationally? Is there an optimal or predictable path of countries in the sequence?

Stages Models

Stages models appeared early in the study of multinationals and became very popular (for a review see Galbraith and Nathanson, 1978, chap. 8; Galbraith and Kazanjian, 1986, chap. 8). A number of empirical studies reported that the internationalization process they observed took place in stages. Stages models were used to describe U.S. firms (Stopford and Wells, 1972), Swedish firms (Johanson and Weidersheim-Paul, 1975), European companies (Franko, 1976), and Japanese companies (Tsurumi, 1976). Like any idea that achieves widespread popularity, however, stages models then became the object of criticism (Melin, 1992).

The stages model appears to be flawed in two basic ways. First, although all the studies reported finding stages, they were never the same stages, and it was never clear what was a stage and what was a substage. Second, when put to the test, the models did not stand up well. For example, if a company was at stage one, could it go directly to stage three and skip stage two? The answer was usually yes. Thus, if stages could not be consistently identified—and if one did not have to follow them—what good were stages models? It seems a bit foolish to discard the stages models altogether; it is unrealistic to expect that different companies in different industries from different countries expanding internationally at different times in history would all follow the same stages. Indeed, it is unrealistic to expect the same firm to follow the same stages when expanding into different countries at different times. But it is realistic to expect that there will be stages—the one consistent finding in all the studies. There may be many or there may be few, but there will be stages. Why?

The internationalization process requires a firm to learn and develop the organizational capabilities listed in Table 3.2, a trial-and-error process that inevitably unfolds in stages. For example, the firm must learn to transfer resource advantages; often, which advantages require modification cannot be predicted in advance.

Table 3.2. Features of Levels of International Development.

Level	Role of Subsidiary	Mode	Advantages Transferred	Organizational Capabilities
I	Seller	Export	All types from home country	1. International product development 2. International brand management
II	Local partner	Partnerships	Some product/service and other resources from home country Most resource advantages from partner	1. International product development 2. International brand management 3. International partnering
III	Start-up	Foreign operations	Some product/service Some firm-specific (from home country)	1. International product development 2. International brand management 3. International partnering 4. Transfer and modification of resource advantages from home country

| IV | Implementer | Foreign operations | Some product/service
Some firm-specific (from home country) | 1. International product development
2. International brand management
3. International partnering
4. Transfer and modification resource advantages from home country
5. Cross-unit integration |
| V | Contributor/leader | Foreign operations | Some product/service
Some firm-specific (from any country) | 1. International product development
2. International brand management
3. International partnering
4. Transfer and modification resource advantages from any country
5. Cross-unit integration
6. Management of distributed headquarters |

IKEA's business model transferred easily to Europe, but not to North America, sending the company into a new stage of trial-and-error learning, from which it emerged several years later with U.S.-specific modifications to its products and store layouts. As IKEA expands to Asia, it can expect more experimentation and learning—a new stage of development.

It is sometimes believed that the internationalization process can be accelerated by using acquisition as the entry strategy. Indeed, acquisitions accelerate the creation of assets and employees abroad. If home-country advantages are easily transferable to the acquired company, the process will accelerate; if they are not, then the learning process will occur, with the learning taking place *after* the assets are created. This learn-by-doing process does not accelerate easily, inspiring some authors to search for a faster or easier path for international expansion. Is there an optimal sequence through which the firm can accumulate experience?

Learning Paths

A number of authors who consider internationalization a learning process have tried to discover optimal learning paths; because firms do not have the resources to enter all countries simultaneously, they must choose which ones to enter first, second, and so on. The researchers asked whether there is a path of least resistance, an optimal learning path by which a firm can most easily and rapidly expand from a national company to a global one.

The initial research found that the firms studied had not done a financial analysis to choose the most profitable country to enter first; they did not evaluate countries and enter the one with the highest net present value. Instead they appeared to minimize risk. Similar expansion policies were found for Swedish (Johanson and Valne, 1977) and U.S. firms (Davidson, 1982). These companies expanded first into countries that were familiar and nearby, then to the less familiar, and finally to the unfamiliar and distant; Swedish firms expanded first into Norway and Denmark, then northern Europe; and U.S. companies went to Canada first, then the United Kingdom.

This pattern of expansion purportedly minimized the "psychic distance" or "cultural distance" between the home or existing geography and the new geography. Cultural distance is greater for countries with different languages, religions, political systems, economic systems, legal systems, levels of development, and education; an index has even been created to measure this distance (Kogut and Singh, 1988). The greater the cultural distance, the less likely that advantages will transfer easily, and the greater the learning needed to successfully establish a subsidiary. Ultimately, the uncertainty and risk of doing business in a country becomes too great; there is simply too much to learn or too much culture shock if the cultural distance is too wide. Some evidence also indicates that cultural distance influences the mode of entry into a new geography; joint ventures appear to be preferred over start-ups or acquisitions in countries with large cultural distances from the home country (Kogut and Singh, 1988). It has been hypothesized that companies start with those countries that have the smallest cultural distance and the lowest learning curve; as companies accumulate experience, they expand by stages into more unfamiliar and distant countries. Subsequent studies of this hypothesis have been mixed in their support (Melin, 1992).

The cultural-distance theory does not account for the opportunistic nature of some business decisions, an example of which involves a U.S. electronics company planning its international expansion into Europe and Asia. The company specifically rejected a proposal to open an office in South Africa but received an unsolicited order from there the very next week. The order fit into the production schedule, and the company filled it. The first order was followed by a second and a third, and by the end of the year the company was expanding throughout South Africa. There are hundreds of comparable examples: the CEO has relatives in India, a businessman from Dubai shows up at your booth at the Hanover Fair, and so on. Therefore, internationalization should probably be considered a mixture of planned entries and opportunistic expansions.

It is suggested that some cultures are more focused than others on learning and planning—the Japanese, for example. They planned their entry into the United States in just such a manner. Their path was via Australia and Canada—countries, presumably, with small cultural distances from the United States. The Japanese developed and perfected their business model in markets similar to the U.S. market but lower in risk. Then they opened a small factory in California. When their business met with success on the West Coast, they expanded across the rest of the United States. This sequence allowed the Japanese to learn in a market similar to the U.S. market, with a similar workforce demographic. They also stayed off the radar screens of large U.S. competitors who may have been able to prevent or anticipate their entry. Another learning path of the Japanese involved entering the U.S. market in a small way, through the low and unprofitable end of a business, then moving up as they learned to do business in the United States. Learning paths such as these—with their slow growth and manageability—can be valuable when transferring and modifying resource advantages; they are a means of managing the risks until a company gets "street smart" about doing business in a new country.

The principle underlying both the planned learning paths and opportunistic examples is that they minimize risk and maximize learning. The orders from South Africa gave the electronics company, which had underestimated the market potential, information and experience, which minimized risk.

From Stages to Levels

This book uses levels rather than stages to characterize international development. The concept implies nothing about the sequence of moving between levels; a firm may not progress stagewise from Level 0 to I to II, and so on. Although it will probably start at Level 0, a company could start anywhere; it can move forward and backward and skip levels when doing so. It is entirely possible for a Level 0 firm to buy a Level V company and begin operating at Level V, but the acquiring firm will have to learn all the organizational capabilities of the Level V transnational. Although any movement is possible, the company must adopt the organization and organizational capabilities associated with the level.

Take the case of the Swiss computer-mouse manufacturer Logitech, which started as virtually a Level V company. Logitech was founded in the United States by a Swiss and two Italians attending Stanford University. They formed a software company but became aware of a computer mouse invented by a professor at the polytechnic university in Lausanne, Switzerland. They contracted for the technology, the professor, and the funding, and set up product development, finance, and manufacturing in Switzerland. Software and marketing remained in the United States, where their most likely customers were located. After receiving orders from HP and Apple, they realized that Switzerland was too expensive for volume manufacturing, so they created a manufacturing subsidiary in Taiwan.

From start-up, the company located its activities in different places around the world, exploiting location-specific advantages. Hardware R&D is located in Switzerland, where the manufacture of miniature and precision hardware has been a local skill since the time of the watchmakers; software is located in California, along with sales and marketing; manufacturing is in Taiwan, now moving to China; and sales is located in every country with a market for personal computers. Logitec began as an international company and within a couple of years was a transnational, a progression typical of new companies from small countries.

Westinghouse provides a different example. A Level IV multidimensional organization in the early 1980s, it encountered some financial problems and sold many of its international businesses. By 1995, Westinghouse was a national company with exports, operating at Level I; it is thus possible to move backward as well as forward.

It is also possible not to move at all; there is no imperative to become a Level V transnational. A firm could stay a national company with exports. A company could have all its assets and people in Bangalore, remaining a totally Indian company and exporting its software over satellites. A firm must respond to some forces—increasing wage and exchange rates, demanding customers, and protectionist countries. But if these factors remain below threshold levels, the Indian company need not internationalize beyond Level I.

Finally, it is probable that firms will be at different levels in different parts of the world. This is especially the case for Western companies that have vast experience in Europe and North America yet are relative newcomers to Asia. For example, Ford has moved to a Level V transnational in the West, but uses a geographical organization associated with Levels II and III in Latin America and Asia. To be effective, companies must utilize different structures in different parts of the world when they are differentially developed there.

Summary

This chapter focused on the different levels of international development that influence a company's choice of organization. It also focused on the process of internationalization by which a firm changes its levels of development. Internationalization was described as a process of transferring competitive advantages from a firm's home or existing geographical base to new geographies. These transferred advantages are necessary to overcome the natural advantages of local firms. Whether these advantages are transferable—and how easily—depends on the type of advantage: product/service or resource. Resource advantages may be specific to the firm or location-specific and available to all firms at the location. True location advantages are not transferable, and a firm using them at home must either export or find substitutes. The other advantages are more or less transferable depending on the mode of participation: with exports, all types of advantages can be transferred; joint ventures permit a firm to transfer some resource advantages and choose a partner who will provide local advantages that cannot be transferred; a wholly owned subsidiary requires that all advantages be transferred, modified, or replaced. The more complex foreign operations require stagewise learning in order to re-create the firm's success formula in other geographies.

Each level of international development was associated with a mode of organization and with various types and amounts of organizational capabilities. These two categories will be the focus of the remainder of the book. The next chapter describes the partnership mode, followed by the role of the geographical division in Chapter Five.

Chapter Four

Partnering

One way to limit risk when entering a new country is by taking a partner in the subsidiary; when a firm moves beyond exports and licenses and begins direct investments in other countries, a joint venture or alliance may be the preferred route of entry. These partnerships are halfway tactics—between exporting from the home country and establishing a wholly owned subsidiary. This level of development may end up being the permanent mode of participation, or it may be a stepping-stone to a higher or lower mode.

A variety of cooperative arrangements may be undertaken, for a variety of reasons. Contractor and Lorange (1988, p. 6) have identified a continuum of arrangements, from a simple technical-assistance agreement to an equity joint venture. The focus here will be on equity joint ventures and alliances, which require FDI by the firm and a close working relationship with the local partner.

Entire books have been written on partnering. Others have focused on joint ventures (Killing, 1983), alliances (Yoshino and Rangan, 1995; Doz and Hamel, 1999), and international cooperative arrangements (Contractor and Lorange, 1988). This book addresses the organizational issues and partnering as a level of accomplishment in the internationalization process. After briefly discussing the reasons a firm might choose partnering as the entry mode, this chapter focuses on the partnering process itself and the organizational skills—particularly the organizational design—that a company must build to master this level of international development.

Choosing the Partnership Mode

A firm often has a choice of entry mode into a new market: a joint venture, an acquisition, or a green-field start-up. The choice has been the subject of numerous studies, and many factors influence the decision (Kogut and Singh, 1988).

One influencing factor is the maturity of the industry. In an industry suffering from overcapacity, an entering firm should choose a joint venture or acquisition rather than a start-up (which adds capacity). Making use of existing capacity is also preferred to a start-up when speed of entry is a priority. In emerging industries, however, an entering firm may prefer a start-up because of the lack of local candidates for partnership or acquisitions.

Firms from industries characterized by high R&D and advertising expenditures have been less likely to form joint ventures than those with little R&D and advertising. It is suggested that these firms have proprietary knowledge and are concerned about leakage to a partner, who often becomes a competitor. R&D-intensive firms also have more cross-border coordination than firms with less R&D, with a subsidiary's role being to serve the network; the local partner's interests and the firm's interests conflict when the subsidiary is not autonomous.

It has been observed that small companies are more likely than large ones to use joint ventures because they cannot afford the investment required for a wholly owned subsidiary. Large companies, however, can afford to make small acquisitions for entry.

This book proposes that firms with low levels of international development are more likely than experienced multinationals to choose a joint venture for market entry, particularly when there is a large cultural distance between the home country and new countries (Kogut and Singh, 1988). When a firm enters a strange, new market with little experience outside the home country, it will prefer to enter with a joint venture in order to learn the new market and how to transfer its advantages to a different business situation. Once the firm has learned the lessons, it may buy out the partner or invest in its own wholly owned subsidiary.

Kogut and Singh (1988) found that companies coming from risk-averse cultures—as measured by Hofstede's (1980) "uncertainty avoidance" variable—were also likely to enter by joint venture. Eliciting the help of a partner is a cautious entry mode.

Many factors influence the choice of entry mode; those most likely to lead to partnering are the inexperience of the firm and the cultural distance between the home country and new countries; uncertainty about doing business and transferring advantages encourages firms to spread risks and learn from partners. As the firm learns and develops international organizational capabilities, it can move to a higher level of international development. However, the partnering process is sometimes voluntary and sometimes not; when entering some countries in some industries, even internationally sophisticated companies may be required by the government to take a local partner. The next section describes the partnering process and the capabilities that are needed for it.

The Partnering Process

The partnering process can be conceived as a series of steps, as shown in Figure 4.1. The process is, of course, never as clear and sequential as in the figure, but the steps are useful for explaining and identifying the capabilities that need to be built.

Courtship

Courtship is the term used to describe the process of finding a partner. The desired result is to build a relationship, and courtship is the beginning phase. The first issue in a courtship is to

Figure 4.1. The Partnering Process.

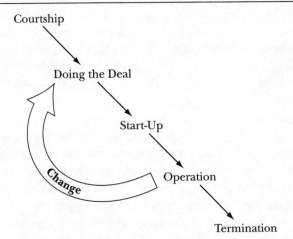

understand the strategic intentions of the local candidate, a key piece of intelligence. Some overseas-Chinese conglomerates are basically traders and distributors; they may be happy to supervise local manufacturing and distribution of the foreign firm's products. Other Asian firms are interested in partnering, with an eye to learning the technology and then entering other countries as a competitor; these companies are not content to be just a local supplier or to export only with the partnering firm's approval.

By choosing as a partner a strong local firm in the same industry, the entering firm can get its products into rapid distribution to the right customers at minimum cost. However, this partner is the one most likely to learn the technology and become a competitor. Another option is to choose a local partner who is not in the same industry and is thus unlikely to become a competitor. This partner can provide capital and local expertise but not a ready-made factory and channel of distribution. If speed of entry is not a high priority, this kind of partner may prove a better long-run choice.

When Xerox entered Japan, it was forced to take a local partner. From a list of candidates, Xerox chose the only one that was not an electronics company: Fuji Film. Fuji-Xerox has become one of the best success stories of Japanese-U.S. joint ventures. As a matter of fact, the thirty-five-year-old company is so successful that it now threatens to become a competitor of Xerox itself.

McKinsey's studies (Bleeke and Ernst, 1993) show that, of the thirty still-existing Japanese-U.S. joint ventures formed before 1950, twenty-seven were created with partners from outside the industry of the entering U.S. partner. The partners were individuals, small companies, trading companies, and banks—firms not likely to learn the technology and become competitors, yet able to provide local expertise and capital.

The choice is often a trade-off between short-run and long-run advantages. The best short-run partner may be a strong company in the foreign firm's industry, even though it is most likely to learn and absorb proprietary features and, if it has global aspirations, perhaps even become a competitor in other markets. A local firm from outside the industry may provide a better long-run partner, even if more time and investment are initially needed. In major appliances, GE has chosen to maximize short-run returns, while Whirlpool is investing for the long run. Not surprisingly, GE reported the best results during the first three years.

Information about a potential partner's strategic intentions may be neither offered nor obvious. Some local intelligence can be obtained through consulting firms, banks, accounting firms, or the local embassy of the home country. An inexperienced firm may use a third party, who then becomes a third partner. When Japanese companies first expanded in Asia, the trading company from their Keiretsu found them a partner and taught them how to do business in the new country. (The trading companies have had offices in all Asian countries for decades, staffed with longtime-resident Japanese who went to local universities and who speak the local language.) U.S. firms entering China often bring a Hong Kong company with them to play a similar role by becoming the third partner.

Choosing a partner can range from being simple to being complex. It is simple if the government assigns a partner for you; when AT&T (now Lucent Technologies) and NEC split a contract to provide telecom equipment in Indonesia, they were asked to partner with companies controlled by the Suharto family. The decision becomes complex if a company is free to choose its own partner. In Indonesia, for example, a business can choose a partner company that is state-owned, overseas-Chinese-owned, publicly traded, controlled by the military, or affiliated with one of various ethnic groups. The pros and cons of each alternative vary in every country, so acquiring good local intelligence should be a decisive factor.

The next courtship issue concerns the alignment of goals and objectives. Even if strategic interests coincide, differences may arise, especially about money. How quickly must a subsidiary become profitable? What losses can be sustained? How much is the company willing to invest? Another major difference may concern organizational decision processes. Asian firms may put all decisions in the hands of the managing director; Western firms have discovered empowerment. The list of differences may include cultural factors—both company and country—and business philosophy. Eventually the firm must decide which key factors must be aligned; there will never be alignment of all factors. What mutual interests must obtain in order to transfer advantages and operate a successful local business? Having a mutual interest to maximize profits quickly can be an effective alignment factor.

An example of a courtship process is the one used by Corning, which sees itself as a "network of companies" and has extensive partnering experience. Corning continuously surfaces partner candidates for investigation. Having found that one can learn much about a company—particularly about a company's values—from how it reacts to adversity, Corning investigates the company's behavior during something like a plant closure or a hazardous-waste spill. The next step is becoming acquainted with the candidate's managers by inviting them to speak at meetings and to attend the annual Corning officers' meeting. They are asked to bring their spouses so that Corning can get to know them informally. A small joint project may be next. Each test is a screen; if a candidate passes all of them, Corning may try an alliance. If that is successful, a larger alliance may be next, evolving toward an equity relationship and, eventually, a joint venture. This selection process requires a lot of time and effort from management. This degree of up-front effort, though, is a characteristic of successful partnering. It's like the old saying, "You pay me now or you pay me later"; issues not discovered in the courtship will arise later in the partnership. They are then more difficult to solve, and the relationship is more difficult to dissolve.

Today, the evaluation of partner candidates is becoming easier; more companies now have a partnering history that can be examined. Indeed, being seen as an attractive partner will be a requirement for competitiveness in the future. Maintaining a reputation as a good partner also controls certain temptations to behave opportunistically in alliances.

Doing the Deal

Although partnership is largely an amorphous process of negotiation, eventually the partners must do a deal or reach an agreement. For Japanese companies the agreement is a 10-page document stating the venture's philosophy; for U.S. companies it is a 450-page legal document. In any event, the discussions that lead to the agreement are crucial.

International agreements are a negotiator's nirvana. Independent of the important cultural factors, countless issues need to be resolved: Will the subsidiary be able to repatriate profits? In what form? What will the transfer prices, import duties, taxes, and access to foreign exchange be? Will the government provide loans, exclude competitors, build infrastructure, provide work permits? Will the firm have to hire certain ethnic groups, transfer technology, export, or provide training? Building a negotiating skill becomes a priority for international partnering. The skill involves managing the myriad issues and also understanding the trade-offs among them. The skillful negotiator knows the key factors necessary to transfer the firm's advantages and build a successful local business.

The negotiator must also be able to understand the partner's perspective. Seeing issues as the partner sees them is critical to a successful agreement, as is the mind-set to achieve a mutually satisfying negotiation rather than "winning" it. One company celebrated a victory in its negotiations with its Japanese partner, then was back a year later renegotiating; the deal was so favorable to the company that the Japanese partner had no incentive to use the technology.

The other component of a successful agreement is eliciting organization-wide involvement. Negotiations usually begin between a few top people, with specialists brought in as needed. Eventually, though, many people need to support the partnership. At Corning, small projects on the working level introduce operating-level employees. Corning's is a lengthy process, however, and not all negotiations can take place over an extended period. In time-intensive situations some firms use a large meeting, convening seventy-five or eighty key people for two days. They are given the proposed venture plan, discuss it, and are then broken up into subgroups to suggest changes, ask questions, and attain a thorough understanding of the proposal. This meeting informs a large percentage of the organization, while the company benefits from their timely participation.

Start-up

The venture begins after the agreement is signed and the employees are informed. The next decisions revolve around the structure and staffing of the venture. The structural models will be described first, with a discussion of staffing to follow.

Structure

Firms can choose among three basic models of governancę structures for a joint venture: operator, shared, and autonomous (Killing, 1983). A firm with low levels of international development may start with the operator model until it learns the area. It may then migrate to either of the other two models or to a wholly owned subsidiary. Each of the three basic models provides a different orientation to the general partnership structure, which is shown in Figure 4.2. The two partner structures are probably business units of their respective companies, or one is the international division of the foreign, entering firm. Both partners contribute members to the board of directors, which supervises the activities.

The Operator Model. Under the operator model, one of the partners assumes management responsibility for the venture. This role is independent of the ownership split; the operator may or may not have the majority share. The operator manages the venture, providing leadership, day-to-day coordination, and use of its management systems and processes. The operator model is shown in Figure 4.3. The shading shows the decision-making orientation.

**Figure 4.2. Partnership Structure
for Sourcing, Alliances, or Joint Ventures.**

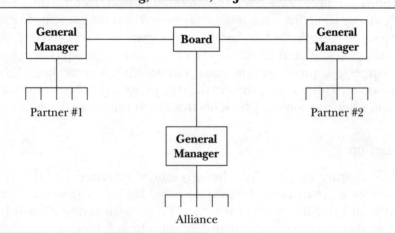

The operator usually supplies the managing director and the directors of the functions. Most decision making takes place within the joint venture and between the venture and operator partner. There is usually a small board, with two or three members from each partner plus the managing director. The role of the joint-venture board is similar to external boards: reviewing operations and approving large investments and key management appointments.

The operator model is usually chosen when a firm has little experience in a particular geography; the entering firm relies on the local firm to run the joint venture once the advantages have been transferred to it. The entering firm contributes technical people to transfer advantages and help with start-up activities; if the entering firm has expansion plans, it will probably leave several key people to learn the local business environment. Many Western firms entered Japan using the operator model, with the Japanese partner as the operator.

At times the entering firm is the operator. At NUMMI—the General Motors and Toyota joint venture in California—Toyota is the operator. The management responsibility was desired by Toyota, who wanted to try operating the Toyota Production System

Figure 4.3. The Operator Model.

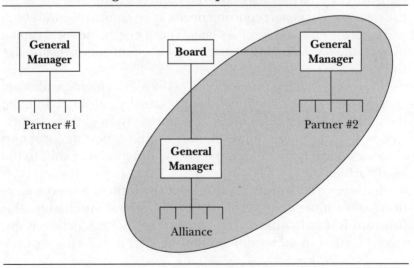

(TPS) in the United States using United Auto Workers members. General Motors wanted to learn TPS, so, even though the joint venture was 50–50, General Motors was perfectly happy to have Toyota become the operator.

The data show that the operator model is the one most likely to be successful (Killing, 1983). It is the simplest to execute, makes one company responsible, leads to quick decisions, and minimizes conflicts, as long as one partner is willing to be more passive. When one company has all the operating skills, this model can be successfully implemented. When a company is entering developing countries, however, the operator model is less successful than shared models.

The Shared Model. The shared model is what people usually think of when they describe a joint venture: each partner contributes complementary skills (which the other usually lacks), and both partners share in the management. The shared model is frequently chosen when a company is entering a new, unknown country. The entering firm contributes technology, product development, and manufacturing; the local firm contributes human resources, sales, marketing, and distribution. Each partner does what it does best, and some functions may be shared.

The choice of which partner should manage finance is not automatic. One partner may take the controllership and the other the treasury. Financial reporting needs to be compatible with both partners' systems and local tax laws. There may be no local capital market; the local banking contact may be a multinational bank like Citibank.

Choosing which partner should manage purchasing is also not an automatic choice; the function may actually transition. Initially, the foreign partner may import materials from its global network. The host government, however, may begin requesting local purchases. As local firms qualify, the buying function may shift to the local partner.

In the current corporate structure, the human resource function plays a more central role than finance and purchasing; this function is usually shared. The human resource function is discussed further in the section on staffing later in this chapter.

The shared model, as shown in Figure 4.4, allows each partner to contribute its skill and provide guidance. Although it offers the advantage of combining complementary skills, a high level of conflict is likely. This conflict should be anticipated, with a mechanism to resolve it designed ahead of time. A distinctive characteristic of this model is the small active board of directors; the shading in the figure shows the shift in decision making. The board is usually four or five people; if it must be larger, then a committee of the board—such as a compensation committee—may become the center of decision making. In any event, a conflict-resolving capability must be accessible and commensurate with the high level of potential conflict.

The selection of the managing director or general manager is a key decision. Firms often rotate the position, with the local partner providing the first, and the foreign partner—after having learned the local environment—providing the second. The venture may eventually develop its own leadership. Another practice is to balance the leadership: one partner provides the managing director while a manager from the other partner chairs the board.

Figure 4.4. The Shared Model.

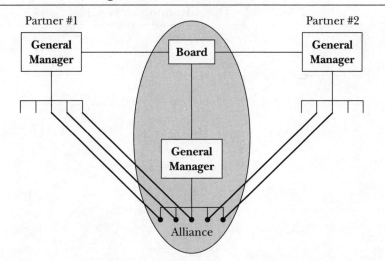

The shared model is less often successful than the operator model. The potential for dysfunctional conflict and indecision is great; responsibilities can be ill-defined; and managers from the partner company (not on the board) can interfere with operations. All the problems companies have with matrix organizations are also possible in shared ventures. However, if the participants are skilled at partnering and the board is active, the joint venture can capitalize on the combination of complementary skills.

The Autonomous Model. The third model is the autonomous joint venture. As shown in Figure 4.5, the decision making moves to the joint venture itself, which becomes like a normal local company with a board of directors. It is likely that a venture may start as one of the other two models and eventually become autonomous as it becomes successful, grows its own talent, and becomes less dependent on the parents. This autonomy is more likely in companies with low rather than high amounts of cross-border coordination. For companies with tightly integrated global networks, such autonomy is not likely; their ventures are most likely to be operator models, eventually purchased to become wholly or majority owned.

Figure 4.5. The Autonomous Model.

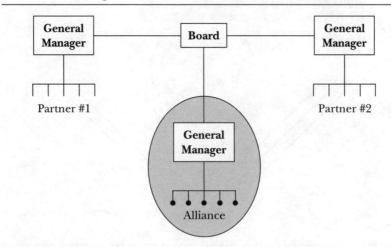

Staffing

Staffing decisions for the venture are crucial because they influence who learns what in the venture (Pucik, 1988, 1992). If the entering partner cedes control of the human resource function to the local partner, it may lose control of the venture altogether.

When a firm forms a partnership in an unfamiliar geography, it may have the local partner do the staffing and training for the venture. If the local partner intends to learn the entering partner's technology, it is quite willing to do the staffing. The technical activities will be partially staffed with engineers from the local partner, some of whom will subsequently return to the local partner and begin duplicating the technology in their own labs. The engineers in the local partner will confer with those in the venture until the duplication is complete, at which point the rest of the engineers will return to the parent. The venture has thus been staffed for the benefit of the local partner, not the venture, with the entering firm losing its advantages over local firms.

The local nationals in the joint venture become well aware of this process. In countries like Japan, much of the training is socialization rather than skill acquisition, with local nationals having been trained in the local partner's culture. As they see the local partner learning the technology and the foreign partner not learning local distribution, the employee population views its long-term future with the local partner. No matter how much equity the foreign partner has, it has lost effective control of the venture. Voicing the prevalent Japanese sentiment regarding joint-venture staffing, Pucik (1988, p. 496) has said, "From the typical Japanese perspective, control over human resource strategies should over time push the joint venture firmly into the orbit of the Japanese parent firm."

The typical entering firm does not usually staff the venture with its own learning in mind; the venture is more cost-effective using the local partner for staffing and training. The foreign partner sends in technical people to transfer the firm's technology but does not send marketing and distribution people; these functions are staffed and provided by the local partner. If the foreign firm places no one in the distribution activity, how will it learn about local distribution? For the foreign firm to be a long-term player, it must learn the ways and means of doing business in the new country; it should learn distribution as fast as the local partner learns technology. Otherwise, the firm will always be dependent on its local partner.

Pucik (1988) suggests that the entering firm build its own local management team, even before concluding the joint-venture agreement; this team can make the final adjustments to the agreement, which it will then implement. A key member of the team should be a competent human resource specialist; once the agreement is concluded, this specialist hires locally and independently for the key roles. The new hires are aware that this joint venture is independent of the local partner and are trained by the joint venture. If people from the local partner are used, they should be approved by the joint venture's human resource department. Staff should be obliged to remain in the joint venture for a period of time, such as five years; such a policy minimizes the number of people rotating in and out on a short-term basis. This approach is longer-term, more costly, and much slower than most companies prefer, but it results in less leakage of proprietary advantages and creates local management capability for the continued expansion of the venture.

Operation

The next phase, after start-up, is the operation of the venture. Conflicts are inevitable; they arise either as normal frictions or as major problems. In order to manage them, the challenge is to maintain sufficient contact among the parents and between the parents and the venture.

Frictions can easily develop in a joint venture. To some degree, they can be minimized by good courtship work to align interests and objectives; any misalignment not found during courtship will cause friction during operations. Frictions can be brought to the surface and resolved by skilled partners; if the partners *expect* differences and *respect* differences, frictions can be seen as natural and can be managed smoothly. The significance of frictions should not be minimized. Joint ventures are more fragile than ongoing businesses, and rumors—a key source of frictions—can easily lead to a degradation of trust. Management from the partners needs to be available when rumors start in order to prevent them from becoming problems.

A second, more serious category of conflicts is major problems. The McKinsey study (Bleeke and Ernst, 1993) of cross-border alliances showed that 67 percent encountered a major strategic or financial problem in the first two years. One such problem pertains to the contributions balance. Although both sides expect a balance between the partners' contributions when the joint venture begins, the contributions of one partner may decay over time. As illustrated in the staffing example with the Japanese firms, one partner may no longer be as dependent as the other, and the reason for the venture is likely to disappear; basically, the ability to learn and acquire capabilities keeps firms contributing to partnerships. Maintaining the balance over time is key to continuing the venture; the contributions balance should be an agenda item for the board.

When a problem arises, the venture management team will certainly be the first group to act on the issue, but the board also needs to be active at this time to remove obstacles or provide resources from the parent. The venture may have to be redefined or relaunched after a crisis; if board members have been meeting regularly, they should know the background and can begin problem solving. If the board has not stayed involved or has new members, they must start from scratch.

The idea is for all levels of the organization to keep in contact and stay informed. This challenge is met by establishing a minimum of four levels of contact. The first is the leadership level. It may be between the CEOs (for large and complex joint ventures), between the heads of business units, or among the heads of a region. Delays and disagreement are likely if the leaders must build a relationship and become informed during a crisis.

The second level of contact is among the members of the small, active board. Some companies have two-day board meetings—the first for the formal proceedings and the second for informal personal contact. The informal portion may involve playing golf, going deep-sea fishing, visiting Disneyland, or other events considered fun and interactive. Many companies believe it is valuable for the relationship to have people meet outside their formal roles.

The third level of contact is between partners, originally from the parent companies, who now work within the venture. This level is the day-to-day management of the venture.

The fourth level is the contact between the partners and the venture. This contact is usually easier for the local partner, who may be very aware of the venture's status, than for the entering partner. Communication with the foreign partner is critical. The foreign partner may be producing the next-generation product; the venture needs to be apprised and then the development team provided with the changes necessary to fit the venture's local market. Too often information comes *from* the foreign partner and not *to* the foreign partner. If the foreign partner is to develop its international capabilities, it must learn through dialoguing with the local ventures.

Change in the Venture

Some joint ventures return to the doing-the-deal phase, as illustrated in Figure 4.1. Successful partnerships are often expanded, with the partnership agreement renegotiated. An example is CFM, the partnership between the GE aircraft-engine business unit and France's SNECMA. The 1974 agreement was formed to develop an engine to qualify for Airbus's aircraft. The partnership allowed GE to enter the market in Europe by taking on a partner inside the Common Market, but it has since taken on loftier goals. The partnership has proven to be successful, with several engines co-designed, manufactured, and sold; by 1991, it had sold ten thousand engines, with $39 billion in revenues.

Yokogawa–Hewlett-Packard (HP) is another example of a partnership that has greatly expanded its product lines and volumes. In this case the contributions balance has tilted in favor of HP; as a result, more of the equity and control of the venture is passing to HP.

Termination

Some ventures are not changed and expanded, but instead are terminated. In the early history of partnerships, termination was regarded as tantamount to failure. Today, a terminated venture may be a failure, or it may be the successful conclusion of an alliance that met its goals. The Korean joint venture of General Motors and Daewoo ended in acrimony; the strategic interests of the partners deviated and the venture had many problems. In contrast, the R&D alliance between IBM and Siemens ended amicably when the project was complete.

In another example, Sandoz and Sankyo terminated their Japanese joint venture after meeting the partners' goals. Sankyo was able to acquire some products developed by Sandoz (now Novartis), which filled holes in its product line; Sandoz got access to distribution and contacts at the Japanese ministry that approves pharmaceuticals and learned how to distribute its own products and get approval for them. The two partners are phasing out the agreement over four years.

The McKinsey study (Bleeke and Ernst, 1993) of cross-border alliances showed that, of those ventures that were terminated, 78 percent were purchased by one of the partners. The rest were dissolved (17 percent) or bought by a third party (5 percent). Typically, the partner that is no longer dependent will buy out the weaker partner when the contributions balance shifts in its favor. If the entering firm learns the local market and business environment, it no longer needs the local partner; if the local partner builds up its technical skills, it no longer needs foreign technology. Acquisition of the venture by the less-dependent partner results.

A feature of joint ventures is that one of the partners is often surprised at the attempt to terminate; it is ill-prepared despite the evidence that most joint ventures terminate. The usual recommendation is to discuss the termination at the outset, when the relationship is at its healthiest. Corning has been a dissenting voice on this issue, believing that such discussions will poison the relationship and that ways should be found to make a joint venture work. But Corning's strategic intentions are to create permanent, autonomous joint ventures; other entering firms envision a buyout as an option from the beginning. An initial discussion about termination is probably a useful investment of time; because most joint ventures are sold—and most to one of the partners—it is best to discuss the process.

Discussing the end of the venture is necessary in countries where closing down a venture may be difficult or forbidden. In Japan, a venture cannot just be closed; the partners are expected to take care of the employees, as well as stakeholders such as suppliers. A Western firm that walks away will have great difficulty finding another partner; closing a venture may be tantamount to exit.

Summary

After exporting, the next level of international development is investment in foreign countries with a partner. This option is sometimes required by a host government and is sometimes chosen by the firm. It is chosen most often when the firm has little international experience and the new market is very different from the market in the home country. The firm uses a joint venture to learn about the unfamiliar business environment and determine whether and how its advantages can be transferred.

The use of joint ventures requires a set of partnering skills: selecting a partner, negotiating the deals, maintaining multilevel contacts, seeing the venture through the partner's eyes, achieving mutually satisfying outcomes, and managing changes and termination. Acquiring a reputation as a good partner is advantageous. A venture can be continually expanded, like Fuji-Xerox. Or it can be slowly acquired by the dominant partner, like HP's Japanese venture. Or it may be terminated, like Sandoz-Sankyo, with one of the partner's starting a wholly owned subsidiary. The next chapter discusses the management of these new subsidiaries.

Chapter Five

The Geographical Division

The first international organization that most companies adopt is the geographical division. For a company with large domestic markets and no international experience, adopting this organization typically means adding a geographical division to its national company structures. When an internationally experienced company enters a new geography, however, it usually adds a new division for that geography to its existing structure; today, a company expanding into Asia typically adds divisions for the Southeast Asia region and for large countries like India and China. This chapter describes the task of this geographical division and the organizational design decisions involved in performing that task.

The first section explains why a geographical division is the initial organizational choice. The second section describes the tasks of the geographical division in the transfer of advantages to the new geography, with an extended discussion of organizational capabilities. The following section describes the key issue in managing the new geographical division—autonomy. The last section provides examples of the geographical division.

Why a Geographical Division?

Firms use geographical and international divisions when they have a low proportion of assets and few subsidiaries in other countries (Egelhoff, 1988, chap. 5). For a firm just entering the international arena, a geographical division is a good structure for several reasons. First, the customary start-up activities of an expansion—sales, distribution, service, and local marketing—are best organized on a geographical basis; the geographical structure minimizes travel and transportation costs, while giving local customer support.

The second reason to create a separate, dedicated division is to provide emphasis and focus. If international activities are scattered in different organizational units, they do not usually receive the attention they need; in a business unit, international sales may constitute 10 percent of the total; in the geographical division, they constitute 100 percent. For companies with large domestic markets, the geographical division provides a separation from domestic priorities and a focus on international concerns. The need for a special focus is particularly understandable when one views the foreign entry as a start-up and a diversification. Start-ups require separation and special attention, along with trial-and-error learning to transfer advantages and modify them in a new geography. The management of this new entity usually wants to do things differently from the way they are done in the home market. International activities generate a low proportion of revenues and a high proportion of problems at start-up; an international venture always seems to request changes—to product designs, to business processes, and so on. Everything appears to be an exception. It is thus good practice to create a separate, dedicated unit to do the start-up; this separate unit will minimize the priority conflicts with the existing businesses and focus on the unique task of starting up a business. Just how separate the start-up should be will be discussed later in the chapter.

A third reason for the geographical division is to signal a strategic change. Unifying all international or geographical activities gives them critical mass, which attracts talented people. A high-profile executive assigned to this position can report directly to top management. Thus, the division is placed so that it has visibility and a voice in competing for resources and talent.

Fourth, the geographical division also conserves a scarce resource. A company entering a new geography usually has few managers with experience in that locale. By placing all activities serving the market in a single division, those activities can be managed by the few people with experience in that geography. The division can then grow experienced managers. Although, at start-up, the new division requires dedicated resources and separation from the firm's ongoing activities, the division should not remain too separate for too long lest it result in separate and divided companies. Instead, the division should be separate long enough to make the necessary changes in the success formula; once a strong local business is built, it can be integrated into the network from strength. The subsidiary is to be integrated into the network, not dominated by it.

The Tasks of the Geographical Division

The geographical division has six tasks, as shown in Figure 5.1.

Transfer Advantages from Existing Geography

The first task, as detailed in previous chapters, is to transfer the firm's advantages to the new geography and overcome the natural advantages of local firms. The transfer is usually accomplished by expatriates familiar with the business formula, who work with the local nationals to start up the business in the new country.

Localize the Success Formula

Sometimes the task of localizing the success formula is straight-forward, and the firm's advantages are implemented in the new country with minimal changes. Usually, however, adaptation and

Figure 5.1. Roles of the International or Geographical Division.

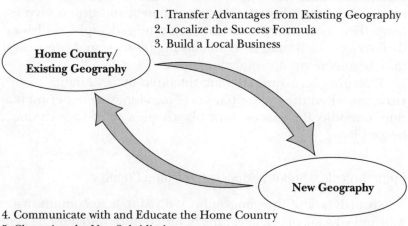

1. Transfer Advantages from Existing Geography
2. Localize the Success Formula
3. Build a Local Business

Home Country/
Existing Geography

New Geography

4. Communicate with and Educate the Home Country
5. Champion the New Subsidiaries
6. Build International Organizational Capabilities

modification are necessary, and sometimes trial-and-error experimentation is needed to find substitutes for advantages that do not transfer. Expatriates work with local nationals to accomplish this task, with input from headquarters in the home country.

The Mandarin Hotel chain provides a good example. In order to capitalize on its reputation for good service, as well as the Mandarin-Oriental brand, it expanded throughout Southeast Asia. The transfer of its service advantage was relatively easy; it was implemented with a large ratio of staff to rooms. When the chain expanded into North America and London, however, this ratio proved to be economically inefficient, and the firm attempted to attain the same level of service by experimenting with various human resource policies to motivate a service orientation: hiring younger and more enthusiastic people, training employees extensively, implementing various incentive schemes. Ultimately, the service advantage could be maintained in the West but only by modifying the staffing and human resource policies.

Build a Local Business

Once the advantages are transferred and modified, a business needs to be built around them. All the complementary tasks—the hiring, the training, and the building of supplier networks, distribution networks, and customer and government relationships—need to be accomplished. Of course, if an acquisition is used for entry, then the business is already built; the geographical division then transfers advantages to an existing business and prepares it for integration into the global network.

If all goes according to plan, the build-up is straightforward. However, when the build-up takes place alongside experimentation to modify the success formula, the new subsidiary can be a hectic place.

Communicate with and Educate the Home Country

The fourth task of the geographical division is to communicate with and educate managers in the home country, who must be kept constantly informed during periods of adaptation. Communication is difficult under the best of circumstances, and start-ups in new countries rarely offer the best of circumstances. There is usually a large cultural distance, along with inexperience in the home country; communication can be anxious and tense, particularly if the issues are unexpected. Most companies anticipate difficulties in communication because of different cultures, languages, and time zones, but other factors further hinder the process.

One hindrance is the attitude of home-country managers, who are usually prepared to teach but not to learn. Management from the home country has already perfected a success formula, which it is prepared to transfer to a less advanced country in which it is inexperienced. A combination of arrogance and ignorance can result in problems. For example, many Western firms expanding in Asia bring a superior technology to gain market access and are not usually interested in learning from their Asian colleagues; for the Asians, the situation can result in a loss of face. It is easy to create complications to the communication process over and above the language and cultural factors.

Communication in the early phases of a start-up is about problems, often combined with a request for changes. Communicating problems from the field to headquarters is always difficult, but it is particularly so when the problems and changes concern a factor at the heart of the firm's competitive advantages. The European power-tools company mentioned in Chapter Three is a good example. Its direct sales force—a source of great advantage at home and in every country previously entered—was proving to be a failure in certain Asian countries. These facts were the last thing that management in Europe wanted to hear; the response was to send a new group of expatriates from the home country to show the locals how to do it. When the second group of expatriates also failed and losses continued, management finally capitulated and listened to the local feedback.

Champion the New Subsidiaries

The geographical division is a listening post for the new subsidiaries and a champion for their causes. The geographical division of a Japanese television-manufacturing company executed this task on entering the U.S. market. The company originally designed its product for the Japanese market, where it was quite successful, but initial sales in the United States were disappointing. The U.S. subsidiary convinced the geographical division in Japan that the product needed to be changed: Americans preferred a larger, somewhat different television with additional features. The product engineers in Japan were skeptical about the request.

The geographical division then chose a few influential Japanese engineers and traveled with them to the United States, returning with a couple of U.S. customers to dialogue with the other product engineers. Meanwhile, the geographical-division managers were convincing the top managers about the size of the market opportunity, and they secured the necessary funding for a redesign. A larger product with different features is now selling in the U.S. market.

Home-country managers in the geographical division can play a useful role, listening to feedback from new subsidiaries and championing their requests for change. Local nationals often need this support from trusted home-country managers when presenting new ideas and requesting changes.

Build International Organizational Capabilities

The geographical division is often a focal point for the creation of international organizational capabilities. The request to change a product design, for example, may be the first step toward an international product-development capability and process. Similarly, sending an expatriate to staff a position in a new subsidiary may be viewed as simply finding someone to do the job, but it also develops internationally experienced management, which is a key to developing the cross-unit coordination and integration processes needed to manage the multidimensional network. It is easy to see the decision to modify a product, change an advertisement, or send an expatriate as solving a unique problem at the new subsidiary. But the same problem will arise again at the next new subsidiary, and the next after that. Instead of creating time-consuming custom solutions for every subsidiary, the geographical division can—and should—invest some of that time in developing cross-border organizational capabilities.

It is important to build capabilities in advance of their use, when the first requests occur. Too often the immediacy of the task prevents the recognition that learning is necessary and the accumulation of knowledge: people with experience are lost in the system and are not available to new start-ups; the same problems are solved again and again. However, the firm that is building capability develops its second- and third-generation organizations along with its second- and third-generation talent. Then, when it is time to implement third-generation strategies, the firm is ready but only because it took the time and effort to build capabilities in advance.

At this point some stepwise thinking from the internationalization studies may be useful. If a firm has set a strategy of international expansion, it will probably need four of the international organizational capabilities shown in Table 3.2: cross-border product development, brand management, transfer and modification of competitive advantages, and cross-border coordination and integration. Using stepwise thinking, the geographical division can begin creating these capabilities as it solves the issues surrounding the subsidiary requests.

One of the first capabilities needed is an international product-development process, which usually germinates when a country manager requests a change to the product or service to fit the country's market. At this point the firm building the capability will not design a process to handle these current change requests; it will see that they are expensive or impossible because the products or services have already been designed. Instead the firm will implement a process to gather country inputs before new designs are started, creating a cross-functional, cross-border task force for the development of future products. This task force will study best practices, design a process, create a course to teach the process to others, and then execute the first few products using the process. Over time, a product-creation strategy will evolve that determines what is standard and common, as well as what is changeable for different markets. The capability to design products that are easily changeable is essential; this type of product-development process provides platforms for global scale but allows easy modification to satisfy the variety of local markets.

A stepwise process such as that detailed above is necessary to build the second capability, that of creating and managing global brands (Yip, 1992, p. 147). By employing such a process, the firm not only develops products and brands but develops the capability to do so across borders.

The third useful capability is the ability to transfer and modify the firm's advantages. To create a successful local subsidiary, the firm needs a local network of suppliers, a network of distributors, a direct sales force, a motivated workforce, relationships with customers, and so on. In order to build this capability, the geographical division must capture learning from each previous start-up. The division should create an experienced group at headquarters and the subsidiaries who can be called on to help new subsidiaries. This group captures the knowledge, teaches it in company seminars, and prepares a database that can be accessed by new start-ups.

The fourth capability is the cross-border integration of subsidiaries. The geographical division begins building this capability by creating an internationally experienced network of managers and by implementing the formal management systems. The building of international experience—a continuing responsibility of top management—starts with the staffing of the first subsidiary. International assignments create experiences for the individual and relationships with others; they create "know-who" as well as "know-how." Although it is easy for the geographical division to ignore the long-run network building—the pressure is to find someone who can do the job, and the short-run urgency always gets top priority—some time and staffing decisions should be dedicated to it, for this network of interpersonal relationships is the foundation of cross-border coordination processes. Building good relationships and mutual understanding at key interfaces involves strategic hiring on both sides of the interface; the geographical division needs to take the initiative in growing these networks.

The other aspect of cross-border coordination concerns the formal management systems used by the company. The geographical division must build and implement the financial systems, human resource practices, and other information and decision processes that coordinate across borders and with the home country. Because a fledgling subsidiary may be overwhelmed by the home company's full-blown systems, the geographical division must develop an incremental evolution of systems that match the size and maturity of the subsidiary. The geographical division must also adapt the systems to local culture and legal requirements.

The adaptation of systems is never easy, and a balance must be found. Companies requiring a great deal of cross-border coordination and rotating managers need common systems and processes across subsidiaries; companies with relatively independent country subsidiaries can tolerate less commonality. Systems may need to expand and change as customers grow across borders; many prefer one contract, one price, and one bill instead of a different invoice from each subsidiary. In such cases, systems may need to be compatible yet different; the use of intranets can allow common processes using different subsidiary systems.

In executing its six tasks, a geographical division needs to search constantly for the right balance of subsidiary autonomy and headquarters control. The next section explores this issue further.

Subsidiary Autonomy

Probably the most studied aspect of multinational organizations is the level of autonomy and decentralization in the headquarters-subsidiary relationship (for a review see Egelhoff, 1988; Nohria and Ghoshal, 1997). On the one hand, the geographical division argues for freedom and autonomy to learn how to do business in the unfamiliar new geography; on the other hand, the home country wants control in order to transfer its advantages and integrate the subsidiary into its network. It is not difficult to find companies that have erred in giving too little or too much autonomy to their new subsidiaries; finding the balance is key.

The headquarters-subsidiary relationship is like every headquarters-field unit relationship. The subsidiary sees its situation as different from those of other subsidiaries and feels it should be an exception to common policy, with the freedom to act differently. Headquarters tends to see field units as being similar, therefore subject to common policy and systems; it believes that, if given autonomy, each subsidiary will duplicate overheads and reinvent the wheel.

In addition a new subsidiary has the added requirements of a start-up: it needs the freedom to experiment with the success formula, adapting it to local conditions. Even if the subsidiary is going to be part of a tightly coordinated, cross-border network, it requires some autonomy during the start-up period.

IKEA was mentioned previously as expecting full compliance from new subsidiaries. When the company was expanding from

Sweden into Europe, this approach worked fine; IKEA was able to re-create its success formula virtually unchanged. When it expanded to the United States, subsidiary managers requested product changes that were rejected by the Swedish headquarters. After three years of losses in its U.S. expansion—with all subsidiary requests for change rejected by headquarters—a Swedish manager was finally sent to work with the local managers; they tried different products and store layouts to match the needs of U.S. customers. The U.S. subsidiary is now profitable.

Dell Computer gave full autonomy to its European subsidiary, with no better results. Dell's competitive advantage rests in its direct telephone and Internet sales process; it does not assemble a personal computer (PC) until it gets an order. It can customize yet minimize inventory and respond quickly to price changes for semiconductors. When the company entered Europe, local managers said that the French and Germans would not buy PCs over the telephone or use credit cards, so Dell modified its success formula and sold through computer dealers, in the process becoming just another PC manufacturer in Europe. When demand and semiconductor prices changed, the inexperienced Dell was stuck with inventory. A new manager has since replaced the dealers with direct sales and is now succeeding; customers in the United Kingdom and elsewhere are becoming willing to use the phone. By granting too much autonomy to its subsidiary, Dell had apparently adapted its success formula when it did not need to.

There are some guidelines for managing the subsidiary relationship, with three factors influencing the level of autonomy. The first is the amount of cross-border coordination required by the international strategy. If the subsidiary will eventually be integrated into a tightly coordinated multidimensional network, it is delegated less autonomy than one that will stand alone. More autonomy will be given to a subsidiary with little cross-border coordination, an active host government, and a business portfolio with little diversity.

The second influencing factor is the cultural distance between home country and new country. The greater the cultural distance, the less likely that advantages will transfer easily or management systems will transfer directly—and the more likely that some experimentation will be needed. The more experimentation necessary, the greater the autonomy that should be provided.

The third factor concerns the types and amount of advantages being transferred. If the firm has to create supply-chain advantages, workforce advantages, customer-relationship advantages, or other resource advantages, there is usually a need for adaptation. The more adaptation, the more autonomy the subsidiary needs; it may require quick turnarounds and thus need to avoid time-consuming approvals from headquarters. In addition, most information and knowledge is located locally. The balance of control and autonomy is achieved between a team of expatriates (who know the firm's advantages) and local nationals (who know the local business environment).

The problem is that the transferability of advantages cannot always be determined in advance. IKEA thought its advantages would transfer to the United States and was surprised; Dell thought it had to adapt its advantages in Europe and was also surprised—it *had* no advantage in Europe without its direct sales and custom assembly. International expansion is a costly process without advantages, and the skill is to predict their likelihood of transfer. Dell could have kept its direct-selling model and focused only on the United Kingdom initially. Then it could have searched for modifications, as it has subsequently done in Germany. IKEA was slow to respond when advantages did not transfer; it took three years. The dialogue between headquarters and the new subsidiary must be constant. The firm can prepare by knowing its advantages and their likelihood of easy transfer, but surprises should always be expected. It is easier to be thankful afterward that the surprises were few than to be caught unaware by—or to remain oblivious to—major issues.

The correct amount of autonomy for the new subsidiary is partially planned and partially emerges as the start-up unfolds. Knowledge of cultural distance, the possibility of future integration into the network, and the transferability of advantages can prepare the division for the launch of a new subsidiary, but the division needs to be equally prepared for issues that require adaptation. The resolution of these issues is best when a local team comprises expatriates and local nationals and when a constant dialogue is carried on with a prepared home-country headquarters.

Examples of the Geographical Division

The international or geographical division may become a long-term component of the company's structure, or it may be a stepping-stone to a different, longer-term structure. If the firm maintains most of its assets and employees in the home country, it may retain the geographical division and develop coordination processes to link it with the domestically based organization. Many Japanese companies have used this structure; Sharp maintains most manufacturing and R&D in Japan and uses its geographical division for sales and distribution.

Other companies may use the geographical division as a stepping-stone. Danone (formerly BSN) of France currently has about 45 percent of its sales in France, 45 percent in the rest of Europe, and 10 percent outside Europe. It has formed a geographical division to promote growth outside Europe. If the strategy is successful, the geographical division will probably be broken down into regions—Europe, North America, and Asia—with each region becoming a profit center when large enough.

Another example is the U.S. firm of Bausch & Lomb (Laidler and Quelch, 1993). In 1984 it formed a geographical division to signal and implement an international-growth strategy. The structure is shown in Figure 5.2(a). International sales varied across the business units, accounting for 20–35 percent of total sales. Bausch & Lomb had all its R&D and most of its factories (twenty-one of thirty-one) in the United States. By the mid-1990s, international sales had risen to approximately 50 percent of all business, with thirty-seven factories outside the United States and only twenty-five within. With this increase in assets and employees outside the home country, Bausch & Lomb eliminated the geographical division and moved to the regional structure shown in Figure 5.2(b). The regions perform sales, marketing, distribution, and manufacturing, with R&D remaining in the United States. The regional structure became justified for several reasons. First, decision making was decentralized because of considerable product and market differences across the regions. Second, the firm had sufficient internationally experienced general managers. Finally, it had enough regional volume to justify factories and regional administrative overheads.

Figure 5.2. Bausch & Lomb International Structures.

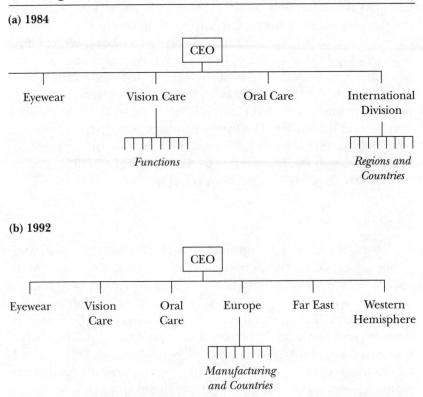

(a) 1984

CEO

Eyewear   Vision Care   Oral Care   International Division

Functions   *Regions and Countries*

(b) 1992

CEO

Eyewear   Vision Care   Oral Care   Europe   Far East   Western Hemisphere

Manufacturing and Countries

This regional structure itself may be a stepping-stone to a worldwide business-unit structure for Bausch & Lomb. The market differences between Europe and North America are becoming smaller; the business units in North America are gaining significantly in international experience; and the percentage of assets and people outside North America continues to grow. In addition, R&D is moving to the best place in the world for a particular activity. At some point the regional activities will become organized by business units, then migrate to a business-unit structure; the regions will probably remain, providing infrastructure and shared services. In this way the company could migrate from a geographical division to regional profit centers to worldwide businesses. (3M is used as an example of this evolution in Chapter Nine.)

There are many variations of the geographical division. For a company that takes only one or a few of its businesses international, the geographical division may report to the business and not the corporation. Toyota was mentioned earlier as having several businesses in Japan that have not been expanded internationally; the geographical division is part of the (expanded) automotive business. When the division is part of a business, it is often reluctant to help other businesses that expand later; none of those in the division have experience with other businesses. The corporation usually needs to fund the new businesses but can build on the presence of the previously established one by having it share facilities and infrastructure. A sizable effort, however, is usually required.

Summary

An international or geographical division is usually the first international organization adopted by internationalizing firms. With few assets in the new geography, the division gives these resources a focus, priority, and critical mass. The geographical division has six basic tasks of implementation, from transferring the firm's advantages and management systems to creating international organizational capabilities. A key managerial decision is how much autonomy to grant the subsidiary; this decision results partly from planning—based on the transferability of advantages, cultural distance, and the level of cross-border coordination—and partly from a great deal of communication and adjustment.

When substantial numbers of assets and employees are located outside the home country, the company moves to another level of development—from the geographical division to the multidimensional network. These multidimensional structures are the subject of the next chapter.

| **Multidimensional Structures**

The multidimensional network—Level IV in the sequence shown in Table 3.1—emerges as the firm increasingly engages in foreign direct investment and executes a large percentage of its operations outside the home country. The international division structure is disbanded, and multidimensional structures are implemented; these structures become the axes around which the networking processes take place. This chapter describes these structures, with subsequent chapters describing the coordination and communication processes that constitute the networking.

The Single Business

Companies following the strategy for a single business, which may have multiple product lines, adopt geographical and functional structures, with one the principal axis and the other the secondary. The determinants of which axis is primary are strategic factors such as the amount of cross-border coordination, as shown in Table 2.2. Recall that companies choose geography as the primary axis when fixed costs are low; products, markets, and brands are heterogeneous; and competitors, suppliers, and customers are local. The axis will be functional under the opposite conditions.

Geographical Organization

The factors for choosing geography are well illustrated by the situation of a British tobacco company. Initially serving only the U.K.

market, it set up an international department to handle exports to Commonwealth countries and the United States and subsequently to Europe. The company was structured as a functional organization in the United Kingdom, with the international department handling all sales abroad. The department was expanded to handle sales in duty-free shops and was organized as a stand-alone duty-free sales unit with individual sales offices for each country.

In the late 1970s and throughout the 1980s and 1990s, the company reinvested its U.K. profits in acquisitions in North America and Europe and then in joint ventures in Asia. Today the United Kingdom constitutes 35 percent of sales and about 40 percent of assets and employees. The current organizational structure, shown in Figure 6.1, evolved by adding geographical profit centers alongside the U.K. profit-center structure.

The structure consists of regions and countries with some global, functional staff units. It is appropriate for this company because there is little cross-border coordination; the tobacco industry is regulated and heavily taxed in most countries, and country borders make a difference. There is little R&D (less than 1 percent of sales), and minimum-efficient-scale factories can supply medium-sized countries like Spain. Because the company grew by acquisition, it has different brands, products, and blends of tobacco to match tastes in different countries. Except for a few global competitors such as Philip Morris, competition, customers (often the government), and suppliers are usually local. For this company the business is local, organized on a country-by-country basis.

The functions are the secondary axis of the structure. The sales and marketing function is the least important cross-border activity; it is handled locally by experienced country managers. The manufacturing function coordinates across borders, sharing expertise and spearheading process R&D. Not all countries have manufacturing plants, so the central unit decides which plants will supply which markets. The tobacco-buying function, which is important because all countries are not self-sufficient in supply, tries to use the company's entire buying power to negotiate prices and quality. In most decisions, however, country managers take the leadership.

Figure 6.1. Geographical Profit Centers Plus Central Functions.

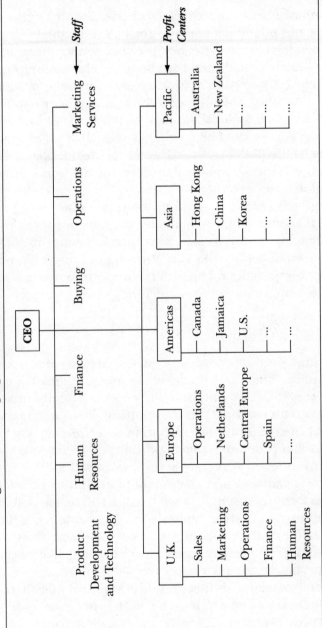

Functional Organization

The opposite set of strategic factors prevails for Logitech, which designs and manufactures mice for PCs. Like the PC industry itself, Logitech is a fast-cycle, new-product-development business. It invests heavily in R&D and has about a twelve-month product life cycle in which to recoup its investment. It must also produce at the lowest cost, which means high-volume manufacture in Asia. Customers are the few global PC manufacturers who adopt Logitech's mouse as their own. The product is standardized except for different electric power sources around the world. Logitech designs and manufactures a universal product for the world market, with a few global competitors.

Logitech's organizational structure does not need to be illustrated. It is a functional organization with functional vice presidents for human resources, finance, sales and marketing, manufacturing, software engineering, and hardware engineering; all report to an office of the president. Logitech is a single business that treats the world as a single market with different global customers.

Combination Organization

Most single-business companies are a mixture of functions and geographies. The two examples above illustrate the extremes; most companies will fall somewhere in between. The pharmaceuticals business is an example. Pharmaceuticals is an R&D business; it invests 12 percent or more of sales in that function. Once a compound looks promising, the new-drug application (NDA) process takes up to seven years and several hundred million dollars of investment; current manufacture of biotechnological substances requires factories costing approximately a half billion dollars. These expenditures cannot be duplicated in every country. A functional organization, with the addition of a sales and marketing function, would appear to satisfy all requirements of this global business. But, like most businesses, pharmaceuticals is complex.

A pharmaceuticals business, like a multidomestic company, may function differently in each country: preferences of patients and physicians vary in different countries; every country must grant its own approval; the active ingredient in a pharmaceutical may be identical in each country, but the strength of the dosage may vary; a drug taken as a powder dissolved in water in one country may be taken as a capsule, tablet, liquid, or injection, or be a skin patch in another country; and if the dosage and form vary from the original certification of the NDA, more clinical trials may be needed in that country. Further clinical trials can be advantageous in countries where the recommendations of opinion-leader physicians may be needed; they will conduct the trials in order to understand the product. Thus, some country-by-country product development is needed, and if the product is different in dosage and form, some local product mixing and packaging are necessary as well. Because the customer is often the government health service or a government-influenced buyer, having local investments in clinical trials and manufacturing helps influence the government buyer.

In many cases, it can be clearly determined which strategic factors in a combined organization are geographical and which are functional. Research is a global function; its activities may be located in different countries, but they should be coordinated to eliminate duplication. Sales activities are local and are managed country by country. The volume manufacturing of the active ingredient is performed in a single global function, and the global manufacturing unit decides which countries obtain ingredients from which plants. The other activities are managed jointly, to varying degrees, by functional and country managers. The structure is shown in Figure 6.2.

The marketing function has both a local and a global component. Promotion and positioning of products may vary by country, and the sales force will need local marketing support; marketing, however, must also participate in the new-product-development process, which is a global company endeavor. The packaging function, also a joint strategy, puts the active ingredient into the proper dosage and form for the local markets but also coordinates across borders to share best practices, use common manufacturing processes, and pool purchases of packaging materials. Most decisions for sales, marketing, and packaging, though, will be made by the country manager, who has the P&L responsibility.

Location of the development function is probably the most contended. Geographical units may want to control local clinical trials to approve modifications of existing products, while the development

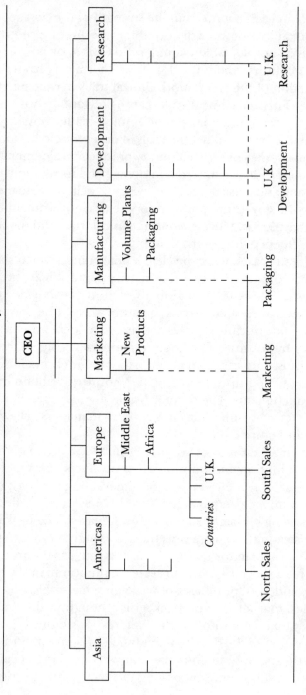

Figure 6.2. Combination of Country and Functional Structure.

function may want to use those resources to perform trials for the launch of a new global product. Today most companies put the decisions in the development function (which funds the local trials) and not the country managers. With the funds becoming a revenue source for the country, the country manager wins even though losing control of the decision. Because of the increasing cost of new drugs and the need for speed in the development process, the company priority is development; the firm installs common processes and systems for trials in the best global location and then collects the results in a central database. These data from several countries can then be combined to support the NDA process in any country. This common process also allows development to be linked with research, manufacturing, and marketing in the process for new-product development; this interfunctional connection may become the most important link in the company. The development function, not the country manager, needs the greater voice in allocating development resources.

Although R&D is managed as a global function, country management may have some limited responsibility for research sites; a pilot plant at a laboratory may employ members of the same union as the manufacturing plant, or some cross-function coordination within a country may be needed. Most decisions concerning research resources and priorities, however, are made within the global research function.

Single-business pharmaceutical companies are thus a combination of geographical (local) and functional (global) structures. Functions such as sales are clearly local, while research is clearly global; other functions may be a combination. In each case, the firm's strategic factors must be weighed to determine the balance, which will certainly change over time. In many industries, investment in new products is shifting the balance toward the global functions. In every case, though, the company must define which decisions are geographical, which are functional, and which, if any, are joint.

Multibusiness Company

Unlike the single-business structure, whose two axes are geography and functions, the multibusiness structure is largely a balance of geography and business, with functions a possible third axis. In this structure, cross-border coordination is more likely to take place within a business unit than within a function; the operating functions are usually placed within the businesses, with the P&L responsibility balanced between business units and geographical units. This balance can be adjusted on the basis of strategic factors: one company may require a dominant geographical function, another may balance the two functions in a matrix organization, and a third may shift power to the business managers for a dominant business function. All these possibilities are examined in this section.

Geographical Profit Centers

In the 1950s, almost all companies, whether single-business or multibusiness, were organized around country profit centers. Country managers are still strong in single-business companies and within business units of multibusiness companies, but with the emergence of freer trade, deregulation, and privatization the power in diversified companies has swung away from country managers to the managers of the business units. In certain multibusiness situations, however, the strong geographical dimension must be maintained.

It is difficult today to find a multibusiness company with a pure geographical structure; most are a balance of business and geography. The cement and building-products industry may be the last example. Holderbank is a Swiss building-products group organized by country and regional profit centers. Inside each profit center are several businesses. The principal one manufactures ready-to-mix cement powder, which is sold in bags and bulk. Another business sells aggregates—rocks and crushed rocks—to other cement makers and construction companies. Holderbank combines its cement and crushed rocks in a third business, which makes concrete; the product is delivered wet by truck to construction sites. The fourth business fabricates concrete products that can be assembled rather than poured at construction sites. One could argue that these four businesses are actually one vertically integrated cement business, but each stage of the value chain can sell outside and is a profit-center business with some autonomy; the structure is almost identical to that of the tobacco company shown in Figure 6.1.

The profit centers are geographical units, with some cross-border functional coordination.

The cement business is a classic multidomestic business: it has low fixed costs, little R&D expenditure, no global brands or advertising, and minimum-efficient-scale plants that supply areas smaller than countries. Customers are local construction companies often involved in public-works projects; the government is influential in giving them contracts for buildings and highways. It is to their advantage to be seen as a local member of the community and to have connections. Although the industry is consolidating with the appearance of global players like Lafarge and Cemex, the competitors are still mostly local. The product is not transportable, so there is little cross-border coordination, and a premium is put on being locally well connected. Virtually every strategic factor is aligned with a local business focus and a geographical profit-center structure.

Before 1992, Nestlé was organized like Holderbank, with country profit centers and strong central functions. Most of the strategic factors still favored a geographical axis for the businesses: moderate-scale plants, most countries supplying themselves, only about 1 percent of sales spent on R&D, and food products and consumer tastes varying from country to country.

Nestlé was doing business in a multitude of countries, many of them African, Middle Eastern, and Asian nations that insisted on using local ingredients in Nestlé products. There was a minimum of cross-border product development to serve heterogeneous markets, and Nestlé historically put decision making in the hands of the local, self-sufficient country managers.

The constraints on country managers were primarily functional, with Nestlé dealing extensively in commodity markets for coffee, cocoa, and other ingredients; its strong purchasing function often reported trading profits. When not forced to buy locally, the purchasing function was strong. The manufacturing function was also strong; many Nestlé products—like instant coffee, freeze-dried coffee, powdered milk, and other soluble products—are the result of manufacturing innovations. Country managers, who usually came up through marketing, needed some manufacturing backup, which was provided by the functional staff.

The two-dimensional structure of country profit centers and central functions served Nestlé well until the mid-1980s. At that time, several factors began to arise that eventually resulted in Nestlé's reorganization in the early 1990s. Nestlé began a series of acquisitions of food and beverage companies, increasing the diversity of the product lines. Many differences arose across the lines, challenging the universal standards of the functions and countries: frozen foods require different supply chains than dry foods; mineral waters are managed differently than instant coffee, although both are classified as beverages; pet foods are sold through different channels than groceries.

There was also the need for new products. The rise of private-label products in the grocery trade required packaged-goods producers to refresh their brands with new value through new products. New products are inherently cross-functional, requiring cross-functional processes. The strategic demands of diverse products and new products tipped the balance of the network, requiring that lines of business rather than functions serve as the second axis.

Another influence was the importance of brands, especially global brands; Nestlé's focus had been on its thousands of mostly local brands. With the cost of brand support rising, Nestlé had the potential to exploit its global presence; products required restructuring, and assets had to be managed and monitored across borders. (Today Nestlé has ten worldwide corporate brands such as Nestlé, Nescafé, and Buitoni; forty-five worldwide product brands such as Kit Kat, Crunch, and Coffeemate; twenty-five regional brands; and some seven hundred local brands with cross-border potential.)

Another factor, joint ventures across borders—such as a joint venture to manufacture and sell cereal with General Mills in Europe—affected the country-based P&L structure. Previously, when Nestlé made an acquisition like Rowntree, it was broken up and its pieces allocated to each of Nestlé's country managers; this type of breakup was not possible with a joint venture, which is a stand-alone unit that operates across a region and coordinates with the country managers only when necessary.

Yet another factor was the customer. The retail grocery trade and distributors have always been local businesses, but Carrefour and other mass merchants began expanding across borders. These expanding merchants do not like price or policy differences across countries or getting invoices from each country subsidiary of their suppliers. The trend is toward a single contract across borders.

The last influence resulted from global competitors, who began shifting from country profit centers to business-unit or business-unit-within-region profit centers. Danone in Europe, Unilever in Europe, and Mars around the world have given businesses (usually product lines) increasing autonomy; this change reflects the diversity of the product portfolios, the attainment of scale (less need to pool assets within a country), and the need for speed as a priority across functions within a business.

All these factors caused Nestlé to shift power away from central functions to central business units and from countries to regions (Lorenz, 1992). The reorganized Nestlé structure is shown in Figure 6.3. The usual central functions of finance and R&D were retained. The important purchasing function, which deals in commodity markets, also remained a central function. However, marketing and manufacturing were disbanded and assigned to business units. The number of zones was decreased and their strength increased. This increase is a result of the opportunities for cross-border purchasing of materials like packaging and for cross-border distribution. The emergence of the European Economic Community and Mercosur in South America also provides opportunities. The cross-border customer became a regional concern; the customer—the mass merchandiser—also expanded across borders in these regions and began requesting a single, cross-border purchasing agreement.

Each business unit is a functional organization focused on products, brands, and global competitors. The business structure is further elaborated in Figure 6.4.

Each large country is also organized around business units. In large countries such as Germany, the business-unit structure mirrors the corporate-business-unit structure; this one-to-one correspondence minimizes interfaces and simplifies communication. The core structure can be simplified to the one shown in Figure 6.5, which shows a business-geography matrix dominated by the geographical axis.

Changes in Nestlé's structure have been driven by changes in the strategic factors, with diversity of the product lines and the need for new products the primary reasons. Nestlé retains its geographical and country profit centers, but the power base of the country managers has been diminished; more decision making has been decentralized to the country business units. Some power has gone to

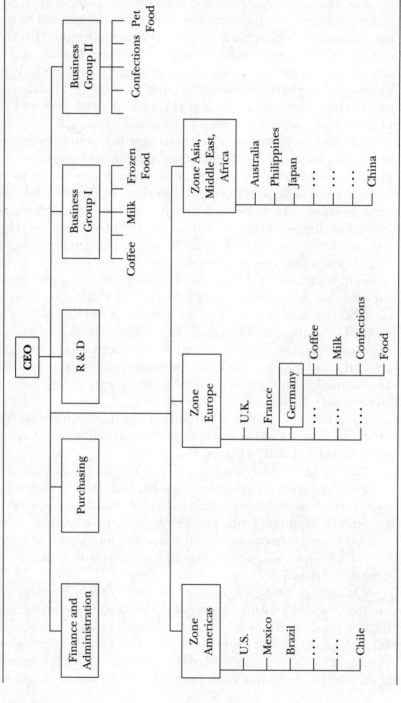

Figure 6.3. Nestlé's Geographical Profit Centers with Central-Business-Unit Coordination.

Figure 6.4.   Nestlé's Central-Business-Unit Structure.

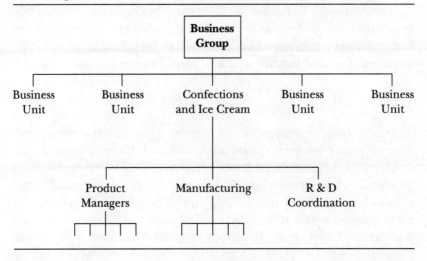

Figure 6.5.   Geographically Dominated Matrix.

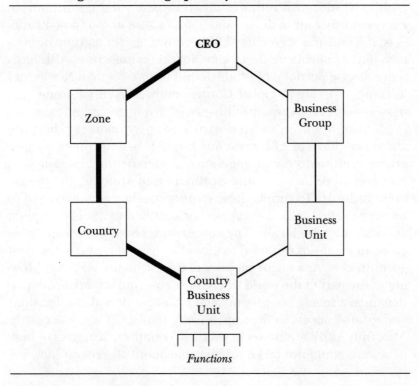

the regions to coordinate cross-border product and material flows, and some power has gone to the central business units to coordinate cross-border brands and focus on global competitors. Other functions were eliminated or combined to form business units. The traditional central functions of R&D and finance remain as before.

Matrix

The multibusiness international matrix organization creates a balance of power between the business axis and the geographical axis (with the functional axis a lesser priority). Matrix is required when strategic factors demand simultaneously strong business units and countries. Up until July 1998, ABB, the Swedish-Swiss electrical-equipment manufacturer, was the classic case. ABB spends around 8 percent of sales on R&D; new-product development is expensive because power-generation equipment requires several years of investment. Products like motors, generators, and robots are fairly universal, and these large products require large-scale factories. Unlike Nestlé, ABB requires much cross-border coordination. Every country cannot design and manufacture its own power products; the business segments (ABB terminology for a group of business units) coordinate development and manufacture. ABB has a more diverse portfolio of products and businesses than Nestlé, and its competitors are all global. Consequently, ABB chose strong businesses—with P&L responsibility—over strong geographies.

It also, however, needed strong country managers because about two-thirds of ABB's revenue came from government or government-influenced customers such as electric utilities, railroads, state-owned refineries, waste-treatment departments, and the cement industry. To supply these customers, the vendor needed to be perceived as a local company, be certified as a local supplier, and manufacture locally. The country was also a profit center because of local—as opposed to global—customers and active host governments. As a major supplier of infrastructure, ABB was growing in the part of the world where host governments are active participants; a strong country manager capable of making decisions and getting access to the appropriate ministries was a necessity. Also, with ABB's businesses in over 140 countries, managers of business units could not be knowledgeable about all geographies.

The former ABB structure is shown in Figure 6.6. Four business segments, such as power generation, were broken into forty business areas like steam turbines, gas turbines, hydro power, and nuclear power; three regions comprised the 140 countries. The key unit, the one at the intersection of the two axes, was the business area in a country. The manager of this country business unit had two bosses in the balanced matrix. The unit could be a functional organization, or it could be further subdivided into product-line profit centers; there were approximately five thousand profit centers worldwide.

The management systems and the definition of roles were key to the ABB structure. One management tool was a common accounting system that permitted the computation of joint P&L statements; this system would, for example, provide the profit of the steam-turbine business across and within all countries or the profit of Brazil across all the businesses. The system allowed management to plan the profit level of a business within a country; the country manager and the global business manager then had the same goal for that business in that country.

The second feature of the ABB matrix was the definition of responsibilities. Although decision-making power was balanced overall, either the business or the country took the lead on particular decisions. Businesses led in product development, acquisitions, purchasing, internal sourcing, and pricing; country managers in human resource development, customer strategies, the day-to-day running of the business, local relationships, and so on. No matter how well defined the responsibilities were, however, overlaps and conflicts always occurred. These conflicts were meant to be rapidly resolved by the country manager, business manager, and country business manager triumvirates. (A more complete description of the matrix will be presented in Chapter Seven.)

The third leg of the structure was functions. Finance and R&D were, again, the key central functions. Also, given the behavioral skills needed for resolving conflicts and communicating in a matrix, human resources was an increasingly strong activity.

ABB had attained a balance of power between its geographical and business axes. It needed both strong country managers and strong business managers—strong country managers because of the government customer and government-led infrastructure

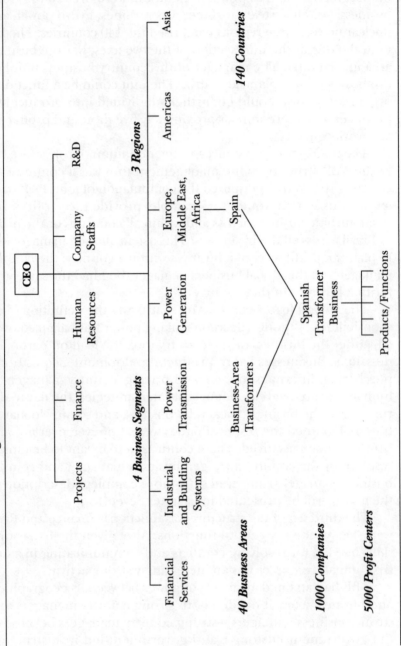

Figure 6.6. ABB's Business-Geography Matrix.

projects, and strong business managers to coordinate large-scale activities across borders without duplication.

From Matrix to Business: What Happened at ABB

In July 1998, Goran Lindahl, who replaced Percy Barnevik as CEO of ABB, announced a new organizational structure. Instead of the balanced matrix, the new structure would feature businesses and downgrade the geographies. The countries in the developed world would no longer be profit centers except to report taxes. The four business segments would be split into eight—still comprised of global business areas—which would become the primary global profit centers.

What caused the change? One reason was the changing customer. Continued deregulation and privatization of utilities, railroads, and so on reduced the government role as customer. The new private buyers were less interested in local value-added and more interested in quality and price. In developing countries, for example, governments turned to independent power producers (IPPs) to build, finance, and operate infrastructure projects. These IPPs were often the international arms of Western utilities that were expanding outside their home countries. In addition, some U.S. electric utilities began acquiring the privatized utilities in Europe and Latin America. ABB was encountering a global private customer in place of the local government customer. Being local and providing local content became less important; the customer wanted a global standard and possibly cross-border supply agreements.

The customers were also interested in speed. Like all manufacturers, ABB had shrinking product-development and life cycles. The business-area and segment managers were made predominantly responsible for product speed and cross-border coordination; country managers were an increasing source of inefficiency. They still participated—or wanted to participate—in decisions that affected their profit centers, but this input was becoming less valuable, not to mention being a source of delay. Hence the move to stronger businesses. As with all industries in the 1990s, globalization shifted the power to the businesses.

Fewer and fewer companies are adopting the balanced business-geography matrix; even Dow Corning has moved to stronger business units. The balanced matrix remains difficult to manage well;

many companies are moving to a front-back structure, which also permits a global-local orientation. (This structure carries its own challenges, which are described in Chapter Thirteen.)

Business Profit Centers

A number of companies have moved to a worldwide-business-unit structure, following the trend toward more cross-border trade and coordination. Some companies retain the geographical dimension, but in a diminished role; others have subordinated the geographical dimension altogether, with the business manager with the largest responsibility in a country also acting as the country manager.

Hewlett-Packard (HP) is an example of a company retaining a limited geographical dimension. In the 1970s HP was organized like Nestlé, but step by step it has transferred activities from the countries into the businesses. In 1999, HP used worldwide businesses built around product lines as the profit centers; the geographical dimension, however, remained.

Many of HP's strategic factors favor a business-unit organization that can coordinate across borders: the business portfolio is reasonably diverse, with the bulk of business in computer products and computer systems; product lines serve the defense, health care, analytical chemistry, telecommunications, and automotive markets, among others; most competitors are global players; and customers are mixed, with some local (defense), some regional, and an increasing number global. But the key factor is product development. Today around 70 percent of HP's revenues come from products less than two years old; it is a product-development dynamo, managed and focused around worldwide product lines. HP spends over 10 percent of sales on R&D. A new computer line can cost hundreds of millions of dollars to launch, and the life cycle during which HP can recoup its investment is shrinking to less than a year. HP must have global volume and have it quickly. It needs inherently cross-border products, with product-design and launch strategies coordinated across the countries in which it does business. This coordination takes place within a business unit by using a highly sophisticated product-development process that works across borders and across functions.

As mentioned, though, the geographical dimension remains. Regions and some large countries have full-time managers who focus primarily on relationships with governments and customers. Some customers are shared across businesses, requiring some cross-business coordination; some services, like financial reporting and human resources, are also shared (human resource issues like salaries and pensions still vary by country).

Except for the strong central functions of R&D and finance, HP has collected its functions into a product-processes organization. With an emphasis on speed, this organization continually works to perfect the product-development process, handling development and life cycles of less than a year. HP works on common software for CAD, computer-aided engineering, and computer-aided manufacturing, as well as experimenting with different types of product teams, team incentives, and training programs.

As its profit-center structure, HP has adopted worldwide businesses fashioned around product lines. Its businesses are dominated by technological investment and rapid customer supply; getting quickly to market is accomplished through cross-border product-development processes and order-fulfillment processes within product businesses. Geographical managers deal with local relationships, provide cross-business services, and handle human resource activities.

ABB has adopted a structure similar to HP's, as shown in Figure 6.7. Up until 1998, ABB had the balanced matrix shown in Figure 6.7(a); the changing strategic factors for customers and product cycles now favor the business-dominated structure shown in Figure 6.7(b).

An example of a company without full-time geographical managers is DuPont, which is organized around eighteen worldwide business units and two joint-venture businesses. It also has the customary central functions of R&D, finance, and human resources, plus an engineering-operations function. The structure is shown in Figure 6.8.

The driver of the DuPont structure is the diversity of the businesses, which range from joint-venture (50–50) businesses in pharmaceuticals and coal to upstream oil and gas, agricultural chemicals, polymers, fibers, electronics chemicals, and packaging materials. Many of DuPont's businesses have their own logic; each

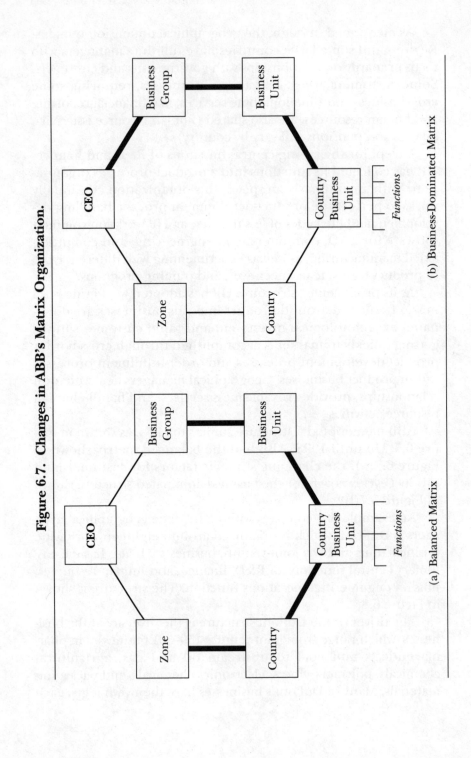

Figure 6.7. Changes in ABB's Matrix Organization.

(a) Balanced Matrix

(b) Business-Dominated Matrix

Figure 6.8. DuPont's Worldwide-Business-Unit Structure.

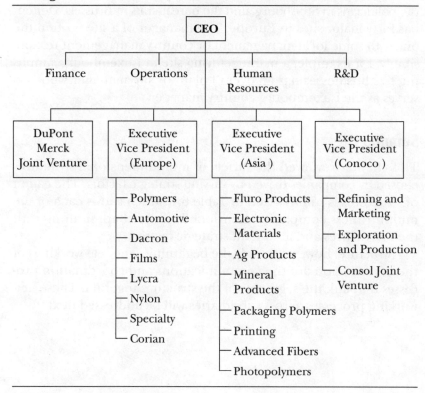

is structured to be competitive in its own industry. Some are global, others are regional, and some—like downstream oil and gas—are local. The majority are global, have high fixed costs, require R&D, and are capital intensive; their competitors are mostly global. The strategic factors all line up to make business units the primary axis of the structure, a choice driven by the capital intensity of the businesses and the large amount of variety across them. The functions are the secondary axis, and geography is tertiary.

The geographical dimension is usually a second responsibility for managers. For example, two of the executive vice presidents (EVPs) who manage some of the business units are located in Europe and Asia and represent their parts of the world; the European

EVP develops relationships with the European business community, the politicians in Strasbourg, and the bureaucrats in Brussels. DuPont has forty major sites in Europe. The manager of a site is often the one with some local-management or country-management responsibility; for example, a manufacturing site in Luxembourg supplying five businesses has an overall plant or site manager who also serves as the Luxembourg country manager.

Summary

This chapter reviewed the variety of multidimensional structures chosen by companies driven by varying strategic factors. The gamut of structures is summarized in Table 6.1, which shows each of the multibusiness companies mentioned in the chapter along with their structures and attendant strategic factors.

Structure, however, is only the beginning. The real workings of the organization are the communications and coordination processes that link the segments of the structure together. These networking processes across subsidiaries will be addressed next.

Table 6.1. International Strategy and Structure.

Company	Holderbank	Nestlé	ABB	HP	DuPont
Structure	*Geographical only*	*Geography dominant*	*Matrix—geography and business*	*Business dominant*	*Business only*
Strategic Factors					
Fixed Costs	Low	Low	High	High	High
Markets	Heterogeneous	Heterogeneous	Heterogeneous	Mixed	Mixed
Products	Standard	Varied	Standard	Standard	Standard
Customers	Local	Local	Local	Global and local	Global and local
Competitors	Local	Global	Global	Global	Global
Transportability	Very low	Moderate	High	High	High
Portfolio Diversity	Very low	Low	Moderate	Moderate	High

Chapter Seven

Coordination Across Networks

A single-business company and the business unit of a multibusiness company need the capability to coordinate across functions and across countries; in addition, a multibusiness company has to be able to coordinate across businesses. Cross-unit coordination is the capability central to the success of companies using the multidimensional organization. Different strategies will create different needs for cross-unit coordination; these needs translate into different types and amounts of lateral organization. The various patterns of coordination across units in different countries give an organization its network-like quality.

This chapter describes these different types and amounts of lateral network coordination, which will be related to the strategic factors described previously. As will be demonstrated, these coordination mechanisms are the means by which power is shifted among the various dimensions of an organization; they are key tools for managers in the continuous balancing of organizational dimensions and changing strategic factors.

The Lateral Organization

The lateral organization is an informational and decision-making process that coordinates activities whose components are located in different organizational units. Each organizational unit with information about—and a stake in—an activity contributes a representative to communicate about and coordinate that activity. The lateral organization is a mechanism for decentralizing general management decisions. As shown in Figure 7.1, managers working on the same business issue but in different subsidiaries coordinate their work on the issue as if they were the regional manager; through such processes companies coordinate businesses and functions across countries. The types of processes and the amount of effort invested in them will vary with the strategic factors described in previous chapters.

The lateral organization gives the multinational its multidimensional and network qualities. If the company is organized with countries as profit centers, then the business dimension is coordinated laterally across the countries as shown in Figure 7.1. The managers of businesses within the countries form a network to communicate about and coordinate the business issues across borders; the managers of a function would do likewise. These lateral networks decentralize decisions about businesses and functions and increase the organization's capacity to make more decisions more often and about more issues. The organization can then respond to more dimensions in its environment. The lateral organization usually results in faster and, often, better decisions by placing decision making in the hands of people with direct customer and product contact.

The task of the organizational designer is to create the type and amount of lateral coordination that are commensurate with the cross-unit requirements of the strategy. Figure 7.2 illustrates the five basic types of lateral organization. Each involves different amounts of lateral coordination, power and control over resources, and management time and energy.

Figure 7.1. A Lateral Organization Across Subsidiaries.

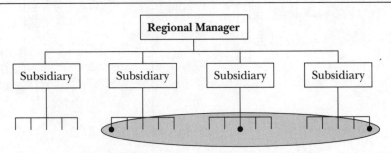

Figure 7.2. Types and Amounts of Lateral Coordination.

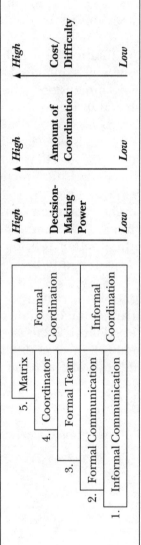

Figure 7.3. Interpersonal Network Foundation.

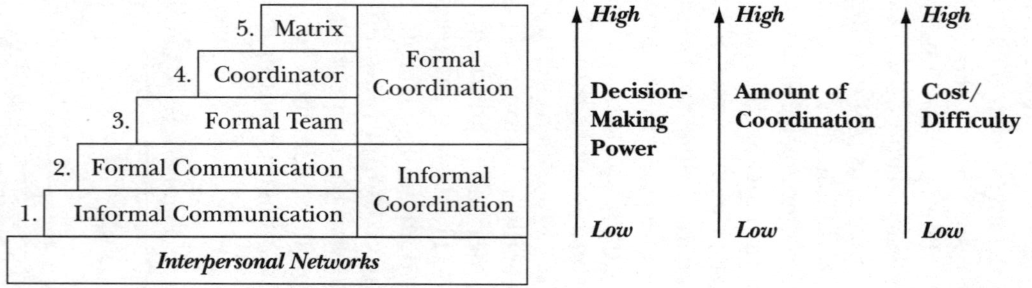

The further up the steps the company proceeds, the more difficult and expensive the forms of lateral organization become. Therefore, the organizational designer should proceed only to the point where the costs of organization match the benefits of coordination—a point that will be determined by the strategic factors.

Informal Communication, Informal Coordination

The simplest lateral organization is the purely voluntary organization. Communication is on an informal and voluntary basis, after which participants can choose whether to act on the information. It is a voluntary organization because it is formed on the initiative of those constituting it; the managers perceive a situation and spontaneously communicate among themselves to respond or to resolve the issue. The response is improvised by those with direct contact with the customer or issue at hand; top management may be informed, but is otherwise not directly involved.

The advantages of this natural form of organization are speed and responsiveness; those directly involved and informed about an issue can resolve it quickly. Informal communication, however, requires that people know one another. In a small research laboratory, this "hallway" communication can take place; in large organizations, spread across countries and time zones, it is limited. Software companies are developing "improvisational software" to foster this communication from common interests. Companies can also encourage this process by adding a formal component to ensure communication, the next step up in lateral coordination.

Formal Communication, Informal Coordination

The company itself can create a communication network among people sharing a common interest. A chemical company created a network among all the technical people working on the polymerization process; another one for all technical people working on catalysts; and others for managers in the maintenance function, marketing people responsible for the textile market, and sales personnel serving common customers. These networks typically meet once a year to cover a common agenda, reinforce the network, and improve the communication process. Throughout the year there are newsletters, e-mail, computer conferences, chat rooms on a Website, intranets, and other, more formal forms of communication. In addition, the usual informal contacts supplement the formal communication.

Although the communication may be formal, the coordination along the network is still informal. The participants choose to act on the information in ways that benefit their line organizations; coordination is voluntary. This informal coordination may be perfectly adequate for certain purposes, such as sharing best practices: a country learns of a practice, modifies it to fit local circumstances, and implements it; another practice may not apply to the country and can be ignored.

If the cross-country coordination requirements of a strategy for the business or functional dimension can be met using only the voluntary organization, the organizational designer should not employ any of the more complicated forms; additional lateral mechanisms would unnecessarily complicate decision making and raise costs. Voluntary coordination, however, is limited, and formal groups or teams may be required in order to obtain the needed coordination. For example, a large enough number of countries may not agree on a common product to cover its fixed costs, or a group of countries may want a product but don't have enough resources to create it; formal groups can manage conflict and acquire resources.

Formal Teams

Informal organizations may not arise spontaneously for every company need or may require access to additional resources to fulfill their purpose. In order to guarantee coordination and increase accountability, top management may create a group to act in a specific capacity, such as a cross-border product team.

These formal teams are more expensive and more difficult than the previous types. Because they do not form spontaneously or naturally, they may require more time and effort to function effectively. Additionally, because companies strive to get a balance of nationalities on cross-border teams, these groups require extra cross-cultural training and team building to become effective decision-making bodies.

Formal teams are also more costly because they augment voluntary groups rather than replace them. The use of lateral organization shown in Figure 7.2 is a cumulative process. As more complicated forms are added, the simpler forms are not abandoned; they are still needed, but are insufficient by themselves to achieve outcomes like the time-to-market goals for new products. In order to achieve these goals, the company needs additional coordination across borders and across functions. The organizational designer adds complex forms until the desired coordination is attained. Adding fewer would fall short of accomplishing the strategy; adding too many would incur unnecessary costs.

These formal teams can be simple or complex. Many companies form simple cross-border product teams to speed products to market. Some companies, however, are also under pressure to reduce prices and costs. They create commodity or component teams to coordinate across their product teams; if all product teams adopt the same component from the same supplier, the larger volume can lead to volume discounts, decreased inventory, and decreased administration. These product and component teams are multidimensional and hierarchical; they require increased coordination to simultaneously meet lower cost and faster time-to-market goals. But such coordination across product groups is fraught with potential conflicts, and steering committees are created to resolve disputes rapidly. When still more cross-unit coordination is required, a full-time leader is introduced.

Coordinators

The coordinating role is the next level of complexity in lateral organization (see Galbraith, 1994, chap. 5). At some point, the groups may require some full-time leadership; in order to achieve time-to-market, product teams probably require a full-time new-product manager to convene the groups and resolve cross-unit conflicts. These leaders are referred to as coordinators or integrators (Lawrence and Lorsch, 1967; Galbraith, 1973). They often have titles such as project manager, program manager, product manager, worldwide business manager, global account manager, process owner, or brand manager. Regardless of title, they all have two characteristics in common. First, they are all "little general managers";

they have a portion of the general-manager decision capacity and guide the lateral groups in their activities as well. Second, they execute their role without any formal authority, which resides in the line organization.

Implementing the coordinator role is more expensive than implementing the previous lateral forms of organization because it involves hiring a group of people whose sole task is to integrate the work of other people; when extensive information is needed, coordinating departments may be created. The cost is incurred in addition to the cost of voluntary and formal groups of various types. This investment is intended to achieve time-to-market, global integration, or leveraged buying—strategic goals that cannot be achieved by the country hierarchy acting alone–and give the organization the multidimensional capability.

The coordinator role is also difficult to execute because of the conflicts it generates. In an international company, people represent businesses, functions, or geographies; each sees situations differently, and conflicts result. Top management must adopt a resolution process to handle these inevitable conflicts on a timely basis and in the interests of the company; this type of cross-border decision process is difficult for most companies to create.

When creating coordinating roles, the organizational designer must select and develop candidates who can influence without authority and who can exercise this influence across national boundaries. The designer should also create additional power bases—other than authority—to augment the personal skills of the coordinator. These issues must be addressed to successfully implement the coordinator role; they are discussed later.

Matrix

The highest level of lateral organization is the matrix; adoption of the matrix shifts the company to a two-line organization by increasing the power base of the coordinator, who becomes a line manager. Some in the organization have a country-manager boss as well as a business-unit or functional boss because strategic factors require a balance of strong countries and strong businesses (as described in Chapter Six for ABB).

The matrix organization may be required for the most demanding strategic tasks, such as compressed time cycles and cross-border integration. This form of organization is difficult for most companies to manage. One way to prepare for the matrix is to move progressively up the steps in Figure 7.2, accumulating the necessary lateral competencies. As will be described later, for its successful execution the matrix requires an integrated set of policies for reward systems, selection, planning processes, and so forth.

In this chapter and the next, each of these lateral forms of network coordination is examined more fully. An example or case is also provided for each.

Building Networks

Fundamental to the use of all lateral forms is the quality and extensiveness of the company's interpersonal networks; a key leadership role is valuing and building these networks. They are usually by-products of other activities that a company undertakes, like training, rotational assignments, and audits. Here we view these activities from the perspective of network building.

Management development and training is a good example: one result of convening twenty-five managers for two weeks to learn a company's total quality program is that twenty-five people know a great deal about each other. Soon, the training department is justifying its budget as much for networking as for training. The only commonality among these attendees is availability when the course is offered. What would happen, however, if a course were planned for twenty-five cross-functional employees who shared active participation in, say, the development of global products? These people could subsequently use the "unplanned" relationships for communication and coordination during product-development projects. In this manner, a company can design an informal organization for developing global products.

Creating informal organizations and networks by design occurs when management and human resources gather the optimal collection of employees. Management's knowledge of the strategy and its key interfaces can ensure that the pivotal workers at those interfaces become the participants in an activity.

The next step advances the group from training to action learning. If the group members' common interest is product development, they are given the task of redesigning the company's process for the development of global products. In order to do so, they first learn about product development and become exposed to global best practices; they still receive the training input as before but now immediately put it to good use. The group then redesigns the process and reviews it with top management; some of the group then implement the process by participating in the next new-product launch. At the completion of the new-product introduction, they review the experience and make further improvements to the process. They then teach the process to the next new-product-development team.

Through this process, normal training and development activities are converted into vehicles for organizational changes, capability building, and continuous improvements. People still get trained, but they also develop useful relationships and use both the training and the relationships in solving the company's problems. Action learning gets the right people trained in the right subject at the right time; they learn the latest practices while learning about each other. They get exposure to top management, and management gets to see who is good at cross-border activities. The knowledge and network acquired are immediately used to develop a product and, then, to improve the process. When this cycle is repeated several times a year for five years, a network for developing global products is built, and it evolves into a competitive organizational capability.

Another activity that builds informal organizations is the rotational assignment (Galbraith, 1973, chap. 5; Galbraith and Edstrom, 1976; Edstrom and Galbraith, 1977). While providing international experience and development for future leaders, these assignments have as a by-product the creation of a personal network for the individual. Today, a company's network is recognized to be the sum of its individuals' networks. If individual networks are not specifically being developed along the company's important strategic dimensions, the company could benefit by making rotational assignments at the key positions.

Some companies also have policies about staffing subsidiary management boards, creating enormous opportunities for network building across subsidiaries. For example, managers may not join the board in their home country until they have had at least five years' experience abroad, and all management boards must have one non-national as a member. These policies facilitate networking across key interfaces and shared issues. As a case in point, Latin American companies view Spain economically as their developmental precursor and are eager to learn about Spain's experience and their company's experience in Spain. Placing Spanish managers on Latin American management boards—and vice versa—is a natural conclusion, with the bonus of the language commonality. The participating individuals learn and contribute, but they also build networks; they learn who should be talking to whom in the subsidiaries. In this way, the company builds and develops its cross-border organization as it develops its managers.

Exchanging pairs of people across key interfaces is a particularly effective practice; both sites are simultaneously receivers and senders, and they can agree to send a top person because they will get one in return. Plus, at the completion of the assignment, the person exchanged has a place waiting at the subsidiary. A packaging company offers an example of using exchanges to create a business network and to pursue business goals. The company's subsidiary in Argentina has been successful in getting the wine industry to use its packaging, and the company sees the wine industry as a new source of growth. Subsidiaries in Australia and South Africa are interested in learning about the application from Argentina. The company and the subsidiaries have sent Argentines to South Africa and Australia in exchange for marketing managers from those countries.

Several purposes are served by these exchanges. First, four managers receive international experience; the company can add them to its international talent pool. Second, Australia and South Africa learn a new application and find a source of growth. Third, a network is built across the subsidiaries; the four expatriates make links as they learn who should talk to whom, and they may discover other mutually advantageous applications. Finally, Argentina may get more subsidiaries into the wine application (where they exercise leadership), which would mean a stronger voice with which to speak to R&D regarding the wine industry.

Another useful activity is the audit function with its role expanded beyond financial audits to broader management versions. Audits are opportunities to learn and develop, both for the unit being audited and for the auditors themselves. When correctly positioned the function can spread best practices and provide the opportunity to develop talent and build networks across borders. About 20 percent of the function should be staffed with long-term audit professionals, who know the function and its history and practices; the other 80 percent should be promising young people from across the company on two-year rotating assignments.

The audit function has enormous potential to create networks. An individual participating on a cross-national audit team in Malaysia for three months will get to know the other team members, while also meeting people in the Malaysian subsidiary. After ten or so such experiences, each individual in the audit function will have an extensive network. They will be most inclined to build a network if the long-term auditors give them encouragement and motivation to do so.

The audit experiences also shape the values and mind-sets of the participants. These assignments, occurring early in an employee's career, are powerful socialization experiences; they build common values across the management group in the company. Top management can observe the people assigned to audits in action and impart company values. The audits are also early tests to see who is adept at cross-border experiences and working across cultures.

Management development, international assignments, and auditing still maintain their originally intended purposes. The offshoot function of building interpersonal networks, however, has evolved from a useful by-product to an additional intended purpose. The role of human resources is quite important in this evolution; by working with management, human resources can adopt design thinking to use these networks as a means of coordination along important strategic dimensions.

Role of Human Resources

The policies for management development, international assignments, and staffing are all responsibilities of the human resources function, which is therefore central to the building of personal networks and their use as informal organizations. This responsibility is quite consistent with the evolving role of human resources as a "business partner" or "change champion" (Ulrich, 1996), particularly as the traditional "personnel" activities are automated and outsourced.

Human resources and the management team need to see their role as one of building and valuing these personal networks. The more connected these networks are within an organization, the more flexible and multidimensional the organization's capability. When networks are richly connected, almost every possible organization is latent in that network (Eccles and Crane, 1988). Some have referred to these networks as social capital (Nohria and Eccles, 1992); the management of complex multinationals should be cultivating this capital. Human resources is the natural leader for building and investing in these cross-subsidiary networks.

In order to execute this role, human resources needs to understand the business strategy and organization by finding answers to the following questions:

1. What are the strategic dimensions—countries, products, customers—and their priority?
2. What are the management processes associated with these dimensions?
3. What are the key interfaces in the organizational units or subsidiaries?
4. Who are the people at the key interfaces?
5. How can we build relationships between these people?
6. How do we grow and develop people who will perform well at these interfaces?

Human resources should bring a design view to any activities that create networks as a by-product; all kinds of meetings, reviews, social events, and gatherings have the potential to create and maintain networks. An example is a manager who serves as a mentor to eight people; she now has a network of eight people throughout the company and invites them all for a dinner once a year to maintain her network and build theirs. The greatest danger to cultivating networks is "bean-counter" thinking; if companies cancel travel, social events, or review meetings as cost savings, they are cutting investments in network building, ultimately depreciating the company's social capital.

The long-term human resources role is to build social capital by creating richly connected interpersonal networks across the organization. These networks support all the types of lateral relations shown in Figure 7.2 and indeed are the foundation on which lateral decision processes are built. In the short term, human resources connects segments of the network to activate the informal organization; the wine-industry network of Argentina, South Africa, and Australia is a good example. The foundation role of interpersonal networks is shown in Figure 7.3.

Case Study: Australian Multidomestics

A group of Australian multinationals provides a good example of the competitive use of informal lateral networks. These multinationals have perfected the geographical form of organization, which is tied together by networks that transfer technologies and share best practices (Yetton, Davis, and Craig, 1995).

Many of the firms are cement and building-products companies with low transportability of products, which favors geographical profit-center structures. Australian geography is another influencing factor: Australia is the size of the United States but with one-tenth the population, which is concentrated in six coastal centers separated by long distances; the distance between Sydney and Perth is equal to that between New York and Los Angeles. Also, highways and railroads connecting the population centers are notoriously poor. Thus, firms that manufacture bricks and roofing tiles must use six small plants to serve these six separate markets. Significantly, these firms have perfected the ability to manage as a network multiple small plants separated by long distances and the ability to generate and implement new practices in all plants in the network.

The winning firms in Australia have taken this skill across borders; managing a firm on the other side of the ocean is not so different from managing one on the other side of Australia. Historically, these firms were family businesses that bought out family businesses in the other five population centers. Their international expansion has been a continuation of this acquisition strategy; they first bought small family businesses in New Zealand and the United States and then in other countries. In unfamiliar countries or emerging markets, they formed a green-field joint venture with a local firm and then expanded. In mature markets, they used friendly acquisitions to expand, buying the firm and keeping the management and family or brand name in the local market; this approach kept them from paying acquisition premiums. From their due-diligence work and intimate knowledge of cement or brick plants, they also knew how much performance improvement they could implement. Alternatively, if the plant was superior in some technology, they knew how much improvement they could capture by transferring the superior practice to their existing network. This transfer skill was at the heart of their competitive advantage.

Initially learned in Australia, this transfer of best practices was the advantage they brought to the new geographies. The winners in Australia were those firms that initially developed superior process technologies and also continuously generated improvements to maintain that superiority; they continually transferred superior technology and practices from the best- to the worst-performing plants.

One of the central practices is a system of controlled competition. All plants are compared with each other using a common and detailed set of process measurements. In addition to the usual financial measures, the brick plants are all measured on raw-material usage, energy efficiency, kiln temperatures and yields, speeds, and so on, with the common measures collected and published monthly. This system is powerful; everyone knows who is doing what and who the low and high performers are. The implicit message, which management will eventually deliver, is for the low performers to contact and learn from the high performers.

Competition is controlled by a set of company values that promote information sharing; plant managers who continuously generate new ideas and share them are acknowledged by their peers as well as by the company. However, a high-performing plant manager who covertly or overtly does not share best practices is ostracized and removed. With frequent transfers and multiple contacts among plants—one firm rotates its managers every several years, measuring the improvement they generate over the plant's previous performance—it would be difficult to keep best practices secret.

Another central feature is the interpersonal network comprised of managers and engineers from the plants and R&D units—positions that are frequently rotated, as previously mentioned. The local general manager (possibly the previous owner) may remain indefinitely, maintaining relationships with local customers and suppliers, but plant managers, technical directors, and engineers are exchanged freely. High-performing plants often provide experienced personnel to low-performing and new plants. The network created by rotations leads to an exchange of ideas from high-performing plants.

One other effective practice is due diligence: a group of engineers studies the newly acquired factory, searching for superior practices at the new site as well as opportunities to transfer the company's superior practices to the acquisition. This due-diligence group spends several weeks to several months at the new plant and builds networks across the plants. The group—likely consisting of engineers from different plants in different countries—spends a lot of time talking to each other about running plants and a lot of social time together at the end of the day. They build relationships and learn about the network of plants, which can subsequently be used in everyday problem solving. They also meet and talk with people from the new plant. Everyone's networks are enhanced in this process.

As the company expands its number of plants, size becomes a scale advantage. First, the number of plants increases the number of experiments done searching for improvements; twenty-five experimental sites generate more ideas than six. When an improvement is discovered at one of the plants, it can be transferred to twenty-four other plants versus just five plants in Australia. In this way, the company generates more ideas and more savings per idea. Second, the company becomes increasingly attractive to equipment vendors; more plants means larger-scale orders, which can benefit both the company and the vendor. Third, suppliers like to work with leading-edge customers, and the constant generation and transfer of ideas qualify these companies as such.

The authors of the Australian study just described were not specifically addressing the informal organization, but it is not difficult to extrapolate some ideas. Central to the competitiveness of cement and brick plants are kilns; to experiment with the latest technologies, the companies have quite probably created research centers—ideal places through which to rotate engineers from the plants. A company may also have a training center, a "Kiln Institute of Technology," where managers, engineers, and operators learn the latest technology and build their kiln personal network. At the annual meeting, top managers and engineers probably meet and discuss issues; equipment suppliers present their new technologies; and industry gurus speculate on future developments. Besides learning the latest technologies, the attendees establish new and refresh old relationships; these connections are best built and maintained when people meet outside of their formal roles.

Today there would probably be a kiln Web site, posting all the measures of the manufacturing process on a daily basis—if not in real time—for all kilns in the company. The latest experiments could be listed and reported; discussion groups about issues could be started; conferences on standardizing a new piece of equipment could be initiated, to be continued at the annual meeting. This intranet application is a powerful extension of the personal relationships and network knowledge that the company has built.

A number of lessons can be drawn from these Australian companies. One is the effect of history and country of origin. To be effective in Australia, companies had to perfect small geographical businesses to serve the scattered population centers. The winners were those who learned to acquire other small businesses and leave them alone except for process technology, which was subject to the transfer of innovations to bring the lowest-performing plant up to the level of the highest. This transfer can take place over long distances and across borders and is the advantage brought to new geographies.

The businesses are also good examples of the so-called multidomestic type. Each geographical unit is an autonomous profit center, with the strategic factors requiring little cross-border coordination: products are not transportable; business is not driven by R&D and new-product development; and customers and competitors are local. This type of business is, in fact, handled as a local business except for the key area of manufacturing-process technology.

One further lesson involves how personal networks across multiple geographical profit centers generate and transfer improvements. An informal organization is generated across sites through a combination of controlled competition, incentives, information-sharing values, rotational assignments, due-diligence teams, meetings, process training centers, and Websites. This informal organization results in everyday communication and dialogue across borders. The outstanding feature of these companies is not their multidomestic organizational structure, but the cross-site networks that generate and transfer best practices in key manufacturing processes.

Summary

The easiest lateral organization to create is the informal or voluntary organization. This organization is initiated by company employees who have discovered an issue requiring cross-border communication and coordination. In order for these people to resolve their issues, they need to know whom to contact. This "know-who" results mostly from personal networks of the individuals in the company. A richly connected company network is an important source of social capital; in order to use this capability, companies increasingly utilize design thinking to build interpersonal networks. These networks serve as the foundation for the informal organization, as well as for the more sophisticated forms of lateral organization, which will be the focus of the next chapter.

Chapter Eight

Formal Cross-Border Networks

The previous chapter described the process of coordinating activities across borders by voluntary communication or organization. Management's role in these self-organizing processes is to create the appropriate context and remove any barriers to free-flowing contacts. In the next level, described in this chapter, management—building on the informal networks—designs formal cross-border groups to manage shared functions, coordinate business units, and create global products. These activities require close coordination across countries and increased accountability from group members; these formal groups have charters, resources, and goals.

The chapter first describes what makes the groups formal, then discusses the design issues involved in creating formal groups that coordinate across borders. Several examples are given of cross-border teams. Finally, the capacity of formal groups to shift power to the cross-border or cross-business dimension is discussed.

Formal Groups

Coordination across subsidiaries becomes formal when management creates cross-border groups and then strives to give them power and legitimacy. Management's action is intended to increase the firm's ability to coordinate activities across country subsidiaries. For example, a bank may need to coordinate services delivered to a customer in several countries; within its borders the bank may have used self-organizing processes, but when multiple countries are involved, a formal customer team may be required. Or a manufacturing company may need to reduce time-to-market and launch a product simultaneously in all countries. Such close coordination usually requires a dedicated cross-border team. The leadership of a firm is active in creating the cross-border mechanisms to coordinate customer or product activities; leaders appoint staff and evaluate them on their group performance. Management usually takes the initiative to implement the groups by delineating objectives and goals, defining charters, and making some resources available to them.

Priority conflicts usually arise when serving customers and launching products across borders; not all countries see the same customer or product as a high priority. Such conflicts require the involvement of top managers, who conduct the discussion of issues and then decide what course of action is best for the corporation.

The Design of Groups

The writing on teams (Cohen, 1993; Snow, Davison, Snell, and Hambrick, 1996), team building and effectiveness (Dyer, 1988), and design issues in creating teams (Galbraith, 1973) covers topics that are valid, so they will not be treated extensively here. Instead, a brief summary of the design issues will be given, with some examples. The design of groups involves using all the organizational dimensions described in the Star Model in Chapter Two; there are considerations of structure, information, staffing, rewards, and leadership for all types of teams.

Basis

The design of groups requires the same balancing of pros and cons as does the choice of organizational structure (Galbraith, 1995, chap. 3). Groups are created around the same dimensions as the hierarchy; if the hierarchy is geographical, then teams can be functional, business, supplier, or customer based, to name some of the choices. The strategy for the organization is the guide to the choice of the basis of the formal group.

Charter

The scope and authority of the groups need to be defined. They must be compatible with the hierarchical structure and augment it. The decisions, issues, and resource levels within the group's scope should be defined for clarity of purpose and to avoid conflict and overlap with other efforts.

Staffing

The choice of a group's participants is central to its effective functioning. Representatives should be chosen from each affected unit; they should have a level and position that affords them information relevant to the issue and sufficient authority to commit their unit. Participants must possess the information and authority to collectively decide on an action, and the time to commit to the team's task.

Conflicts

Because each participant comes to the group seeing a different part of the elephant, so to speak, inevitable differences in point of view will arise. The group must develop its own process for resolving differences and focusing on problems and results. Some of the many team-building approaches will be useful for creating a process to manage conflicts and resolve them on a timely basis.

Rewards

Participants will have little motivation to confront conflict and to solve problems if they perceive few rewards for their efforts in the group (Lawler, 1990). Therefore, group outcomes and performance should be included in the total evaluation of participants on cross-unit teams and tied to the rewards system.

Leader Role

Does the group need a leader, and, if so, from what unit should the person come? For some groups with a reasonable number of members and some self-management experience, a designated leader may not be required; a different lead role may emerge instead, contingent on the issue at hand and who in the group is most competent to handle it. Most multinational organizations, however, designate a leader to plan the agenda, convene the group, lead discussions, and communicate with others about the group's work.

The leader may be chosen from the unit most affected by the group's work, or management may select a leader from the dominant or lead unit. Often, the business unit from the home country or the largest country supplies the leader.

Another model is the rotation of leadership. Dow Corning rotates the leader role in new-product groups as the product progresses from design to implementation. In the early phases, when R&D is most active, the leader comes from R&D in the home country; when the product moves into the factory, the leader comes from manufacturing in a factory that has taken the lead; when the product moves into the marketplace, the leader comes from sales and marketing. During all phases, the group is multifunctional and multicountry; members stay with the group throughout, and only the leader role rotates. The group gets the benefit of a general management leader over this period but gets it sequentially, through hand-offs from leader to leader.

For the difficult-to-manage groups handling important strategic factors, however, a permanent and neutral leader is necessary. The leader role is then expanded into a full-time coordinator role, which is discussed later in the chapter.

Functional Teams

The single-business firm begins to coordinate across borders with functional teams, which communicate and share best practices. These teams also promote standardization of practices, processes, and equipment, which allows best practices to be transferred most easily. Standardization can also reduce duplication and allow volume purchases of common equipment and materials.

Heineken employs functional councils for these purposes, with at least three councils—for manufacturing, distribution, and marketing. Each of the councils is chaired by one of the four managing directors that make up the leadership committee. The manufacturing council consists of the manufacturing directors from all countries, who constantly share ideas about brewing technology and practices. They also convene to discuss where and when to add new breweries or close old ones and how to combine purchases and reduce costs for materials and equipment. The distribution council was active in the redesign of the logistics system following the creation of the European Union; the council members decided how many warehouses would be needed and which breweries would supply which warehouses and markets. Their agenda includes the use of information technology in distribution. The marketing council concentrates on coordinating around the Heineken and Amstel brands.

Even in multibusiness companies, some functional groups coordinate across countries and across businesses. Certainly R&D, finance, and, increasingly, purchasing—functions that usually require a great deal of cross-subsidiary coordination—have cross-border teams or councils. Businesses whose portfolios are not very diverse will also have a lot of coordination across the businesses.

Business Teams

Manufacturing firms and some service firms need to coordinate business units across countries. When supplying customers in another country, launching a new product in many countries, or using the same brand in multiple countries, a firm may attempt cross-border coordination through business teams. The methods of forming and enhancing power—for example, information, P&L measures—are similar for different teams. The team structure at Black & Decker (Figure 8.1) is provided as an example. The structure of the teams, a hierarchical complex, contrasts with that of the functional teams, which are single-team structures.

Black & Decker's organizational structure, which is geographical or regional, is typical of companies with large domestic markets, where 50 percent or more of sales is in the home market. Instead of there being a North American region, the businesses report to the CEO, who is the de facto regional head. There is a modest need for cross-border coordination: customers and consumers are local, with considerable differences across countries; the household-products business—the unit of interest in the Black & Decker structure—varies greatly across countries because the home is one of the most culturally defined places, with variations in household-appliance usage and consumer attitudes about products; the business spends only 2 to 3 percent of sales on R&D; manufacturing plants are not capital intensive; and although the company has some global competitors, like Philips, it also has many local and regional competitors.

The company has some need to coordinate across borders for new products and global brands. The company has growth goals of 8 to 10 percent per year. The household-products unit has as its own goal that 35 percent of its revenue come from products less

Figure 8.1. Black & Decker Organizational Structure.

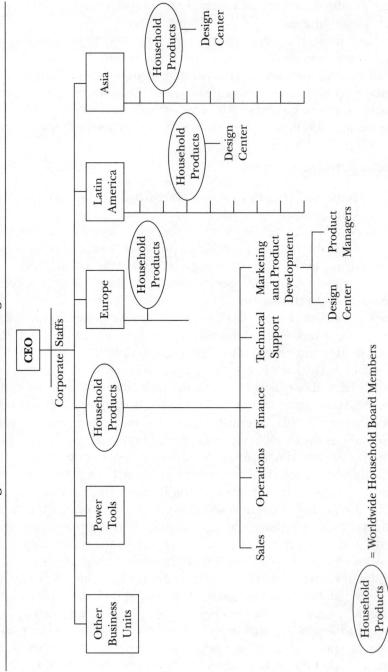

Source: Based on Graber, 1996.

than three years old. Some household products have one- to two-year life cycles; others have cycles of three to five years. A constant stream of new products is needed; some have global potential, and others can be easily modified to meet varying regional requirements. Considerable savings on new products are possible by utilizing cross-border coordination in the new-product-development process.

The cross-border coordination takes place through a hierarchy of product business teams, as shown in Figure 8.2. The top level is the worldwide household board, which consists of the heads of household products in all four regions. This board meets twice a year to formulate the global business strategy for the product line, approve product plans, and allocate resources to new-product initiatives. The board (identified by circles in Figure 8.1) is chaired by the business head from the largest market, which is the United States.

The next level is composed of the global-product business teams, one for each major line of products (lighting, garment care, and cleaning). These teams are staffed with product managers from each region, who meet four to six times annually and communicate constantly. The primary task of a global business team is to create the global plan for its product line. This plan covers a mixture of regional and global products and addresses major and minor changes. A minor change is one in styling or color or is a modest improvement in features; a medium change is a line extension or a next generation of an existing product; and a major change is a new product, like the flashlight (SnakeLight). Each year the board puts out guidelines for investing in each category of change.

Teams begin work on plans to change product lines by becoming familiar with their regional consumer markets. They use the customary market-research techniques and focus groups and, increasingly, actual observations of consumers using products at home. The other dimension of the plan that they consider is the global-regional split in new products. Teams operate with certain rules concerning this dimension: first, always start with the consumer; second, global products are desirable; third, do not make a product more global than it really is; and fourth, make as much common as possible without compromising the product. When these rules are applied, some products (like irons) become regional and some (like flashlights) become global.

Figure 8.2. Hierarchy of Product Business Teams.

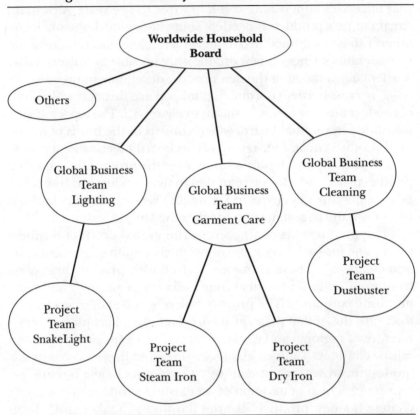

Irons are managed by the business team for garment care, which is chaired by the U.S. product manager. To the extent possible, the team attempts to share information, best practices, and parts. Such sharing is not extensive with the product line for irons, which is regional: in the United States, the preference is for steam irons; in Asia and Latin America, the preference is for hot, dry irons. The dry iron is managed out of Asia using the Singapore design center, with manufacturing split between the Malaysian factory for the Asian market and the Mexican factory for Latin America. The execution of the dry-iron program is managed by a project team led by a product manager from Asia. On the team are representatives from the factories, the Singapore design center, a Latin American product manager, and others as needed. The project is reviewed by the global business team. The steam-iron project is led by the U.S. product manager and staffed by representatives from the U.S. design center and factory. It, too, is reviewed by the global business team.

The global-product successes from Black & Decker have been the Dustbuster (led by Europe) and the SnakeLight flexible flashlight (led by the United States). Both products are portable and battery-powered, and so the firm can bypass the redesign necessary to accommodate regional differences in electric power. Dustbuster was a next-generation product capitalizing on new electronic technologies. The effort was led by the European product manager, who first coordinated market analysis in all regions. Three different product concepts were made into prototypes, which were tested in eight countries on three continents until a winning design was chosen. A team was then established consisting of product managers from three regions and manufacturing people from the U.S. design center and the two production factories.

The flashlight was a truly new product for Black & Decker, which had no other products in that category. Through an initial global market assessment, it found a common worldwide need for portable lighting, which suggested the possibility of a global product design, and it also found that no leadership brand existed. The project team was led by the U.S. product manager, along with product managers from the other regions and representatives from the U.S. design center and the U.S. and Mexican factories. The product design innovation is the flexible body of the flashlight, hence its brand name, SnakeLight. The product was introduced in the United States with a commercial using the 1960s rock-and-roll song "The Wanderer," which was subsequently used to introduce the product around the world; it has been Black & Decker's most successful new-product launch to date.

Black & Decker has been able to achieve considerable savings by developing new products that can be used across borders. The product-team structure, overlaid onto the basic regional organizational structure, provides the cross-border coordination.

Business Coordinators

The next level of cross-border integration comes with the creation of full-time coordinators for the business units (Lawrence and Lorsch, 1967; Galbraith, 1973, 1994). A full-time, neutral coordinator is enlisted to pursue strategies requiring extensive cross-border communication and coordination; this level of coordination can be necessary if cross-border customers request the same standards of service and warranties in all countries or if products need to be standardized on a regional or global basis. The key organizational-design issues for the integrator position are the types and amounts of decision-making power to build into the role and how to grow and develop qualified candidates. The structure of the business-coordinating roles at Nestlé is shown in Figure 8.3; it can be contrasted with the simpler worldwide business boards used by Black & Decker (Figure 8.4).

While the boards at Black & Decker consist of the managers who run the businesses in the four regions, Nestlé's business-unit managers (their term for coordinators or integrators) are full-time and neutral. They do not manage a business in a geography but rather concentrate on the global business and its integration. As with Black & Decker, Nestlé's profit centers are still the countries, but the business-unit managers have been increasing in power; at Nestlé several brands have been selected as global brands, to be managed by the business-unit managers.

The other strategic force at Nestlé is new products. In order to distinguish its products from private-label store brands, real product differences must be created. As R&D increases, so does the power base of business managers overseeing the new-product-development process. The launch of new product categories (such as nutrition, as shown in Figure 8.4) also strengthens the global business-unit managers.

Even if coordinators have no formal authority, they can exert influence. Discussed below are several mechanisms that companies like Nestlé use to increase the power base of the coordinator role; these can all be used individually or in combination to create the horsepower needed for effective integration. In each case, the organizational designer tries to match the power to coordinate across borders with integration required by the strategy.

Figure 8.3. Nestlé's Regional Structure with Business Teams and Business Coordinators.

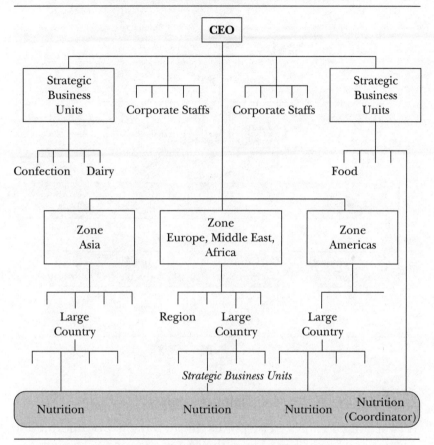

**Figure 8.4. Black & Decker's
Regional Structure with Business Teams.**

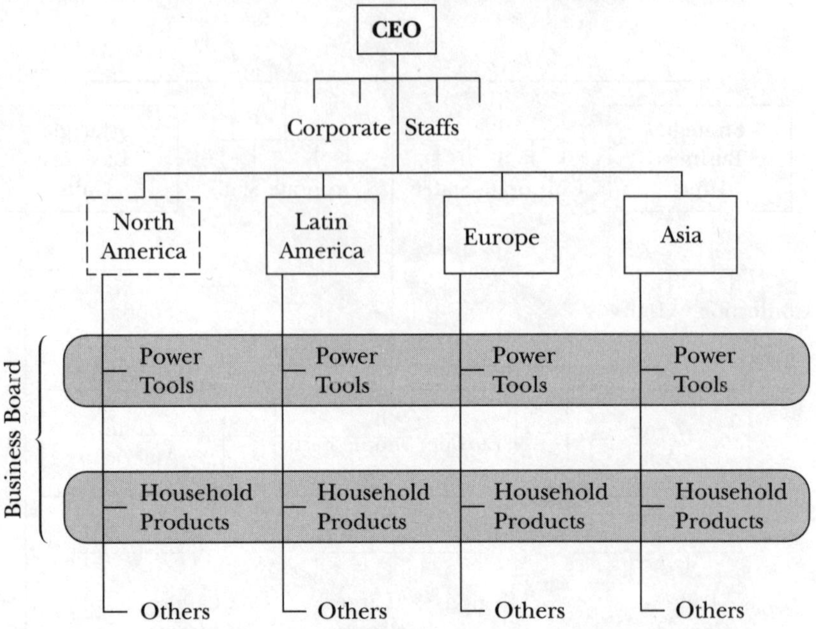

Use of Information and Planning Systems

A coordinator can exercise power through the use of information systems and by participation in the planning process. The business dimension is strengthened when business revenues and profits can be measured across countries; the visibility alone can empower the coordinator. Countries may be performing well in total while a business is losing revenue and market share; a coordinator can use these statistics to initiate action in the countries, as well as for the planning and budgeting processes. Most companies use a spreadsheet such as that in Figure 8.5 for coordinating business units and regions to arrive at a plan for the upcoming time period. This plan, as the basis of measure, causes zone and country managers to be held accountable for meeting their goals. To the extent that coordinators can in-

Figure 8.5. Sample Company Spreadsheet.

	Food	Nutrition	Dairy	Confection	Others
Zone Asia					
Zone Europe					
Zone Americas					

fluence this plan through participation in the planning process, they can influence business direction, goals, and outcomes.

The use of information systems gives coordinators necessary leverage. Without cross-border business systems that measure revenue, profit, and market share, coordinators can press their case, but it will simply be their opinion against that of the country managers—and country managers will dominate. The information systems create the opportunity to look at the world through business lenses as well as country lenses; more and different issues can be seen by incorporating both views.

By using the formal planning and budgeting systems, coordinators have a forum to make their case and to have it receive a fair hearing. If the country managers then disagree, it is incumbent on them to make a sufficiently compelling counterargument. Leadership has the responsibility of converting the formal system into a forum for debate; this forum allows management to focus on the key issues and create appropriate solutions. The astute leader can throw her or his weight onto the side of the business manager within the debating forum. More authority to the coordinator, as well as a superior plan of action, should result from the debate.

Staffing of the Role

The power of the role is also influenced by the selection of people to perform it. Some are quite effective at influencing the behavior of others with or without authority; they are persuasive and interpersonally competent. These people can bring their personal power to the role of coordinator. The effectiveness of the role can be enhanced by a concerted recruitment effort.

Besides this interpersonal persuasiveness, a number of other attributes are associated with effective coordinators. First, they have expertise in the business or product lines; they need expert power if they have no position power. Second, they have good networking ability and good networks, which they use to get information and to get things done. Third, they have credibility, either through a proven track record or by some other means. But the key is still the ability to influence without authority.

Most companies find it best to grow their own coordinators. The first step can be a test role that discerns coordinator aptitude. In chemical companies, testing is done at a scale-up or pilot plant before transferring a new product from the laboratory to the factory; the pilot plant has attributes of both a lab test and of a real plant. Those who perform well and like the pilot-plant stage become good coordinators; they then get international assignments, positions on cross-border teams, and, ultimately, a test in a coordinating role. Each assignment is an opportunity for them to develop and for the company to observe their skills. The network and the track record develop along the way.

Delegated Responsibilities

The coordinator can be delegated specific cross-border responsibilities, which typically concern new products, R&D investments, brands, customers, suppliers, and capital investments. At Nestlé, brands receive the most attention, with business units managing the global brands. The coordinators create teams—like the Black & Decker product teams—to gather information and manage the brands on a global basis, and they may also have the final say on the global advertising agency used, the global copy for the ads, and the common packaging. To be sure, the integrators gather as much input as possible, but they have the ability to make the final choice. Management must be clear about these responsibilities and involve the country managers in their establishment. Responsibility charts can be useful for delegating these roles and responsibilities (Galbraith, 1995, chap. 9).

Control of Resources

In addition to having the final choice, coordinators may have control over budgets for delegated responsibilities, with a budget for some portion of the R&D, product development, advertising, or packaging spending. In the pharmaceutical industry the global development manager has a budget for conducting the clinical trials, and the countries compete for the opportunity.

Dual Authority or Matrix

An additional step can create a power balance between the business manager and the geographical manager. The business coordinator can be given dual authority over the business manager within a country. This country business manager then has two bosses, as shown in Figure 6.7(a) for the ABB organization.

The adoption of the matrix form occurs when there is a strong need for cross-border coordination as well as coordination within borders; the business and geographical managers need to be equally strong. In a successful matrix most decisions are made by one manager or the other, but a few decisions are made jointly. These joint decisions concern the employees with two bosses. The effective practice is to jointly hire, jointly agree on goals, and jointly evaluate performance. These joint decisions result in a unified direction for the person with dual superiors. They also force discussions between the two sides of the matrix and encourage agreement about the general conduct of the business. A lack of joint decisions and communication leads to the dysfunctional conflicts that have resulted in discontinuing use of the matrix form.

Regarding "custody" of other decisions, the business manager usually decides on R&D priorities, where to invest, which factory supplies which market, capital expenditures, and so forth. The geographical manager decides on customer strategies, pricing, local relationships, local employees, and so on. Many of these are not independent decisions, and they require a dialogue; but one or the other manager ultimately decides. It is usually preferable not to take the issue to a higher level for resolution unless an important strategic issue is at stake; ABB was guided in this area by a twenty-four-page "bible" that defined roles and responsibilities.

The balanced matrix, such as that used at ABB, is becoming rare. Many companies—like Nestlé and Hewlett-Packard (HP)—have business and geographical managers reporting to the CEO, but one dimension or the other dominates. The disappearance of the matrix is due, in part, to the trend toward more cross-border integration and stronger businesses (as at HP and Shell). Also, newer forms, such as the transnational model and the front-back model, are being adopted where the matrix would have been used in the past. On still other occasions, the matrix is avoided because it is too difficult or is not believed to work.

Shifting Power Across the Network

The previous chapter and this chapter have described the use of lateral mechanisms to coordinate across borders. The assumption is that economic conditions cause firms to adopt strategies requiring increased cross-border integration. The simplest type of integration is the informal or voluntary organization. Building on these personal networks are the formal groups, coordinators, and matrix; in each case more cross-border coordination is achieved at the additional cost of more people spending more time communicating and coordinating across countries. Adding coordination mechanisms shifts the distribution of power toward the business and functional dimensions; these power shifts are shown in Figure 8.6. On the left are the Australian building-products companies, which require little cross-border coordination; they make heavy use of the informal networks. Next are the formal groups used at Black & Decker, with more power in the product groups. Then comes Nestlé, which has stronger businesses than Black & Decker because of the use of full-time, neutral business coordinators. ABB is still further to the right, at the power balance between the country and business dimensions in the matrix form.

A company may remain at any one of these levels of coordination; the Australian firms have used the voluntary form for some time and will probably continue to do so. Nestlé moved to its current position in the early 1990s; previously its power distribution

Figure 8.6. Power Distribution Between Country and Business.

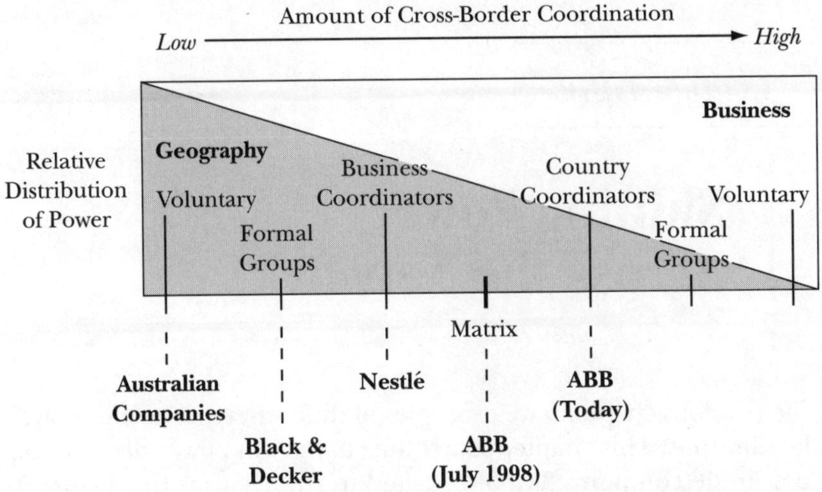

was similar to that of the Australian companies but with some strong functions. ABB has increased the power of its business areas, which are the sole profit centers. It retains the country managers, but today, as coordinators, they have reduced power.

A company may move across the diagram in either direction; power can be shifted to or from the countries. The 1998 financial crisis, which resulted in increased protectionism and less cross-border trade, brought a return of the country manager as the profit center. The trend, however, has been to shift power to the businesses. In the next chapter, the example of 3M Europe is used to illustrate the evolution from country to business profit centers.

Summary

This chapter completes the presentation of the coordination mechanisms that constitute the networking portion of the multidimensional network. The best summary is represented by Figure 8.6. Different companies with different distributions of power are shown along the appropriate type of network. The next chapter describes a single company, 3M, as it moves from country-based profit centers to coordinators to business-unit profit centers.

Chapter Nine

Shifting Power Across the Network

The previous chapter gave examples of different cross-border power distributions. This chapter charts the changes in power distribution in a single company, 3M. 3M started in the 1950s with an organization like that of the Australian building-products companies (Ackenhusen, Muzyka, and Churchill, 1996); over time 3M shifted power to the business units. First, it created business teams and co-ordinators; then, about a decade later, 3M shifted to a business-unit structure, with the regional managers as coordinators. These power shifts were made as the company evolved strategies requiring more and more cross-border coordination. In addition, the chapter reviews 3M's process of internationalization, tracing the transition of 3M from a national company to a globally integrated, differentiated network. After 3M's journey has been detailed, the chapter examines reasons for choosing a differentiated network.

The Case of 3M

Most people are familiar with 3M and its many products, like Scotch tape and Post-It notes; approximately sixty thousand products have emerged from 3M's coating and bonding technologies. Like most U.S. companies, 3M established some foreign operations

---

Note: The 3M case presented in this chapter is based largely on a presentation and discussion facilitated by Katherine Grenz of 3M's human resources department at the Sponsor's Meeting of the Center for Effective Organizations (CEO), Los Angeles, May 1993.

as long ago as the 1920s, but its serious international expansion began in the 1950s. Following World War II domestic growth began to slow, and many U.S. companies looked to Europe and its newly established Common Market as a new source of growth.

A National Company with Exports

As first steps, 3M created an international division and country-based sales companies; in some countries this step involved buying distributors and in others it involved building distribution from scratch. Several top executives went around the world recruiting local entrepreneurs to start and develop these new ventures. These entrepreneurs came from the parent but were dedicated to international assignments; with some administrative personnel they constituted the international division in charge of the subsidiaries, as shown in Figure 9.1.

The country subsidiary organizations, called CSOs, were always run by a managing director (MD) from the United States, who had the responsibility of imparting 3M culture and providing a link to U.S. headquarters; nationals from the other countries would later become MDs. CSOs were staffed by local nationals, with the MD holding the organization together; regular financial reporting was

Figure 9.1. 3M Structure Circa 1955.

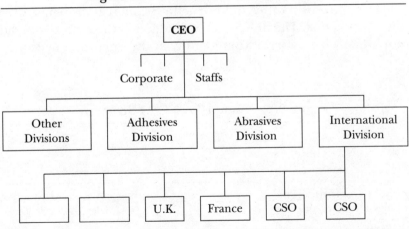

required, and visits from top executives were common. This minimal level of management was sufficient because there was little need for cross-border coordination.

The CSOs were quite autonomous, each developing its own match between local culture and 3M culture; the local language prevailed. Each CSO chose the products from the 3M portfolio that would sell best locally; given a choice of sixty thousand products, no two CSOs had similar portfolios. The start-ups were motivated to become profitable quickly because of 3M's conservative policy of not investing heavily in new businesses, which were expected to fund themselves.

As volume grew in a country, the CSO structure evolved and mirrored the divisions whose products it sold. Figure 9.2 shows the structure of a CSO with local sales and marketing divisions. This structure helped facilitate informal links between local sales and marketing divisions in the CSOs and the U.S. product divisions.

European Region

The internationalization process continued, with 3M adding more countries and more value-added activities to those countries. Expansion began to overload the management of the international division, so a European office was added to monitor and provide advice to the CSOs in Europe. Initially, this office had no formal authority and was viewed warily by the MDs.

The European office did not achieve any real influence over the CSOs at first. The unit, which was added in the early 1970s, did not initially have a significant identity in the organizational struc-

Figure 9.2. Example of a CSO Structure.

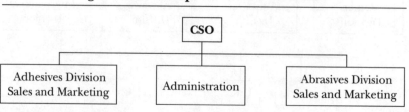

ture, and inevitably it became an extension of the international division. If the CSOs needed advice, they went directly to the U.S. divisions; they did not want to go through any regional obstacles. Although, in principle, the CSOs would all want a European to be the managing director of the region, one CSO or another always objected to a French or a German or a Briton in this position. In the end, 3M, like most U.S. companies, staffed the position with an American who had little understanding of Europe but had regionwide acceptability.

The European regional unit eventually evolved into a real headquarters unit; it began by acquiring a financial role. For 3M the regional manufacture of some products became economical as volume reached minimum efficient scale for a factory. Factories were built in certain countries and reported to the MDs of their respective CSOs. However, a factory was to supply all the countries in the region at the set transfer price. The regional unit created a manufacturing staff unit to help coordinate the supply across countries. Manufacturing expertise was seen as useful and needed by people in the CSOs, who were mostly sales and marketing types, and their respect for the regional unit increased. Also, the CSOs all wanted the next factory to be located in their country, and the manufacturing staff could advise on the best European location for a product. This manufacturing staff unit became a good illustration of a full-time, neutral integrator using expertise to influence decisions affecting countries and product divisions.

Another form of value-adding activity was the implementation of labs, which first supplied limited technical assistance to the factories and subsequently also to customers. Initially these labs were placed close to the factories and also reported to the MD of the local CSO. This addition caused the European unit to then add a technical staff function. By the late 1970s, the region had evolved into a profit center, with its own finance, manufacturing, and technical staff departments (Figure 9.3).

In the late 1970s international areas—Europe in particular—became an even higher priority at 3M. The company began to value and insist on international experience among its managers. To become MD of a CSO was seen as an excellent developmental assignment, and international began to receive an inflow of talent from the U.S. divisions.

Figure 9.3. 3M's European Unit.

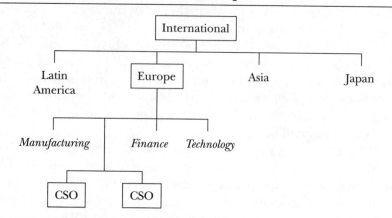

It also became evident that further growth in Europe would require products designed for the European market. Labs were up-
graded, and senior technical directors from the United States were
sent to Europe to build in the 3M culture and networking practices. The labs became more dedicated than they had been to
product development, customizing some products for Europe as
well as working with U.S. labs to design new products to be compatible with European tastes and requirements.

By the early 1980s the labs became a source of tension; they
had a charter to serve pan-European needs for new products and
to work with the U.S. labs, but they reported to the MDs in the
CSOs. MDs were interested primarily in products for their country
and in their own revenues, so there was a constant priority conflict,
especially in large countries, where large volumes could often justify the effort. The priority conflict was resolved by having the labs
report to their counterpart labs in the United States. This policy
made sense; because 3M is a product-driven company that spends
around 7 percent of sales on R&D, it cannot afford to have each
country promote and fund its own R&D direction. Thus, the labs
were physically connected to the factories but reported to and were
funded from the U.S. labs.

The technical function continued to grow to some fifteen hundred scientists in seventeen laboratories in seven countries. Each

lab eventually specialized in a different technology. Their role comprised about 20 percent factory support, 60 percent technical service for customers and product customization, and 20 percent new-product research. Scientists began to rotate among the European labs for periods of six months to a year; some transferred between Europe and the United States. These transfers helped break down barriers across countries and businesses, promoting the free flow of technology.

By the early 1980s, 3M had achieved a high level of cross-border integration within the finance, manufacturing, and R&D functions, with the businesses coordinated through informal contacts between divisions in the various countries. This informal coordination, however, was being reevaluated because of the growth in Europe, which now provided 20 percent of total sales. Many believed a more formal, more powerful form of cross-border business integration was needed.

European Business Teams

The head of 3M Europe in the early 1980s, a Scandinavian, having decided that there was a need for greater integration of product lines across Europe, created teams consisting of the product managers from the largest European countries. Called European management action teams (EMATs), they were to formulate integrated product strategies across Europe by linking to the various countries' marketing units and to the manufacturing units and labs that were appropriate for their product.

Two other changes to the organizational structure, implemented in 1982, supported the EMATs (Figure 9.4). In the United States, key people were moved from the international division to the previously domestic product divisions, which were given global charters. The product divisions were now not just to serve the U.S. market but to be responsible for all regions where their line was sold. Each division created its own international unit run by an international director.

The second change occurred at the European level with the creation of product coordinators, who functioned as the leaders of their respective EMATs. These people, who had regional coordinating roles, had no formal authority over their divisions in the

Figure 9.4. 3M Structure Circa 1982.

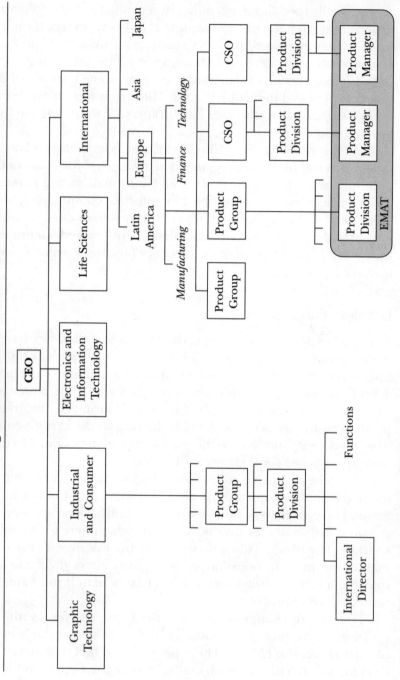

Source: Based on Ackenhusen, Muzyka, and Churchill, 1996.

CSOs. All European managers went through a training course to explain the change and build relationships across the CSOs. The U.S. structure was mirrored in Europe; 3M Europe was organized into sectors, like industrial and consumer, with each sector broken down into product groups, then divisions. The mirroring structures allowed one-to-one interfaces and promoted informal contacts and relationship building. The product coordinator served as the interface with the international director in the respective U.S. division. Initially, these roles were staffed mostly with Americans but, over time, Europeans from the CSOs were used; giving them these roles provided a good way to expose them to pan-European responsibility.

In 1986, a task force that evaluated the functioning of the EMATs found that they had greatly increased communication and contacts across the CSOs and with the U.S. divisions. On the issue of integration, however, the situation was mixed. Some EMATs achieved integration, usually because their leader spent a lot of time persuading the MDs of the CSOs to coordinate their activities, with the leaders sometimes getting help from their U.S. international director. EMATs with integrated businesses and global competitors—for which integration was the only way to survive—found that their CSOs were compelled to cooperate. Other EMATs were merely forums for discussions and fell short of providing the necessary cross-border integration.

Given the variable performance of the EMATs, the task force recommended that European business units be formed. The proposal to abandon the CSO structure was opposed by the MDs and was rejected by the leadership of the U.S. international division. As a result, the EMATs continued in their current form. The rejection of the reorganization proposal may have been appropriate for 1986. Without creating the proposed cross-border businesses, though, 3M lost an opportunity to upgrade the EMATs to be more effective and achieve more integration. What could have been done?

1. Upgrade the staffing of the European product group and division roles by appointing people with more status and credibility; former CSO MDs could have been persuaded to take these positions.
2. Upgrade the staffing of the EMATs; division managers rather than product managers could have become the team members.

3. Formally include manufacturing and laboratory representatives, with teams becoming fully functional business teams; charters could have been expanded to include new-product development.

4. Use the planning process as an integrating device; each EMAT would generate a business plan by country, and each CSO would generate a country plan by business. By using the spreadsheet shown in Figure 9.5, the planning process could have become the conflict-resolving process to integrate Europe; businesses needing more product integration could have attained an aligned set of business goals across countries. (The managing director of the European unit could have played a more active role in promoting those EMATs needing extra coordination.)

5. Form a business unit from one of the most regional of the product lines like the data business. Then learn from this pilot.

The planning option would have required a strong and active head of 3M Europe; the process involves managing the MDs and product-group heads as a team and mediating the heated discus-

Figure 9.5. Sample Spreadsheet for 3M.

	Adhesives	Abrasives	Tape	Other Products
U.K.				
France				
Italy				
Other Countries				

SHIFTING POWER ACROSS THE NETWORK 151

sions in order to arrive at the aligned goals. The major advantage of this process would have been the increased awareness of cross-country and cross-business issues. Additionally, the CSOs would have become accountable for business goals. However, the EMATs continued as is for another four years, when another task force was convened to look at cross-border integration.

European Business Units

In 1990, a task force comprising MDs from the small countries and some Americans with European experience reviewed the European situation. They found again a lack of product integration in many of the EMATs. Several other factors had also become important. First, decreasing product life cycles and development cycles heightened the need for cross-border integration for new products. Second, customers like Ford and Hewlett-Packard wanted to buy in one European location but be supplied at factories in various countries; 3M, however, had separate order-entry systems in each country, with price differences across them. These customers, who were buying in the lowest-cost country and shipping across borders, were coordinating cross-border supply themselves and complaining that they were incurring costs that should have been borne by 3M. The third important factor concerned high overhead. General and administrative expenses for most companies are always higher in Europe than in the United States because of duplication of administrative activities in each country. Some expenses, such as language and legislation costs, cannot be reduced easily; others, like seventeen different pricing processes and policies, can be reduced by integrating product lines across Europe. With these arguments, the task force again recommended a business-unit structure across Europe, this time recommending that the divisions in Europe and the United States form a single integrated business group for the Western world. And this time, with the retirement of the longtime head of the international division, the recommendation was accepted.

The task force delivered its report in January 1991. That same year a new executive vice president of the international division was appointed, whose task became that of implementing the new European structure. After extensive discussions in the United States and Europe, the new structure was announced in January 1992. The structure was put into place and launched in February 1993.

The structure for the integrated businesses is shown in Figure 9.6. It features several changes, the heart of which are the European business centers (EBCs), fully functional product businesses in Europe. All the product divisions (sales and marketing units) from the former CSOs—organized by customer and geography—have been relabeled European business units. These units, as well as the manufacturing units and technical labs associated with the product lines, report to the EBC. The European business units also report to their corresponding product division in the United States (shown by dotted line); this arrangement replaces the (now-eliminated) international director. The EBCs report to product-group leaders in the United States, as well as to the managing director of Europe (shown by dotted line); EBC leaders have the same status as U.S. product-division managers. In all, eighteen EBCs were created, replacing the seventeen CSOs as the basic profit centers in Europe.

Another change was the creation of ten regional subsidiary organizations (RSOs), which also took the place of the CSOs and consolidated the administrative activities, such as human resources, financial reporting, tax administration, and logistics. The four largest CSOs (the United Kingdom, France, Germany, and Italy) became single-country RSOs, while the smaller countries were grouped together to create more affordable administrative units; the RSOs reported to the European head. These regional managers were the new coordinators. (The former coordinators, the product-line heads, had become the new line organization.) The RSOs represented the company in their regions; they managed relationships with local governments and institutions as well as executing administrative functions. The EBCs and RSOs formed a European operating committee that was chaired by the regional head of Europe.

Staffing was an important consideration; it was desirable to have Europeans run the EBCs, and in large measure they do, showing the progress in developing local talent. The other important issue was the location of the headquarters for the EBCs. One view was to locate them all in the European headquarters in Brussels; the other option, which was adopted, was to locate the headquarters near the factories and laboratories. Most business heads moved to new headquarters, which were distributed across Europe. Business teams,

Figure 9.6. 3M International Structure 1992–1993.

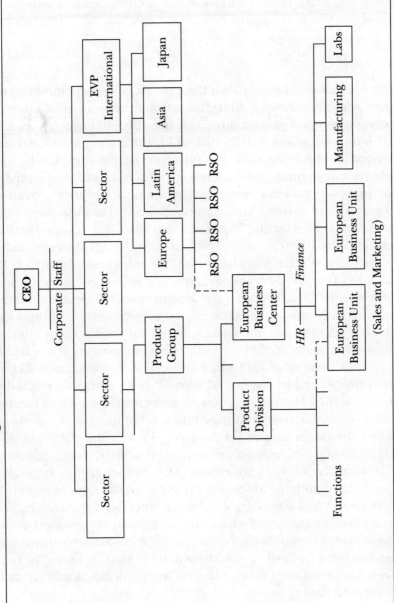

Source: Based on Ackenhusen, Muzyka, and Churchill, 1996.

however, were a special consideration; the best candidates would not necessarily want to move from their home countries. In most cases, the best staff was chosen and allowed to remain in their home countries, resulting in a greater need for team building and travel.

Review of Changes

The 3M case is an example of the process of internationalization as power shifts across a multidimensional network. The internationalization process also illustrates the effect of history, a feature 3M has in common with Shell and Philips. Being a 100-year old company, 3M initially built strong country subsidiaries (CSOs) outside its home country; the speed of its international development to business units was constrained by the legacy of strong country managers and a strong international division. The large size of the home market—a feature 3M shares with Black & Decker—also factors into the internationalization process. Companies with large home markets often form business units at home while organizing the rest of the world by geography. The business units serving a large domestic market often see the international business as a distraction; only when they need revenue growth, get an international charter, get credit for international revenue, and acquire international experience do they seriously focus on international markets.

The transition of 3M from a national to an international company proceeded in stages. 3M started with exports through distributors, then entered an international growth phase and created sales companies, first in Europe and then in the rest of the world. When volume in an area hit the level of minimum efficient scale, 3M built a factory to supply that market; labs were then added to provide technical support. Finally, with further growth attainable only by designing products for the local markets, more scientists were added and the labs got a new product-development charter. In a stagewise process such as this, additional value-added activities are created outside the home country, in contrast to the process used by firms from small countries that are starting up today; Logitech was mentioned previously as a company that began virtually as a transnational.

If 3M had been a company with little need for cross-border integration, it could have proceeded by adding more CSOs and more regions for control purposes, and it would have evolved into a structure like Nestlé's. But 3M spends 7 percent of sales on R&D and has a corporate goal of 35 percent of revenue coming from products less than four years old, with product lines subject to shorter and shorter life and development cycles. The result is high fixed costs for new-product development, which U.S. sales alone cannot cover; products must be designed from the beginning to sell in multiple countries. 3M also had to contend with the evolving customer demand for pan-European—and even global—supply contracts; this demand necessitated cross-border coordination for product development and supply. The United States was already organized by product lines, so the next transition involved mirroring this structure in Europe, shifting power away from CSOs to product lines.

The distribution of power between business and geography is represented in Figure 9.7. At the far left, in the beginning the power was in the geography, with only informal coordination between divisions in the United States and divisions in the CSOs until the creation of the EMATs in 1982. Some power was then shifted from the CSOs to the European region and to the global technical function.

The first big shift toward cross-border business integration came with the creation of the business teams, the EMATs, and of product-group coordinators at the regional level. These coordination mechanisms accomplished some integration but, more important, built communication channels and interpersonal networks across borders. Along with the training, they created a pan-European readiness that set the stage for future changes. The mechanisms also gave 3M management the opportunity to see who could become the leaders of future cross-border initiatives; the EMATs were auditions for future EBC leaders. The figure also shows the possible enhancement of the EMATs that could have been implemented in 1986.

Finally, in 1993, the P&L was put in the businesses within Europe. The task force noted the need for more cross-border coordination: product strategies had to be coordinated to reduce product-development cycles and to create global products, and

Figure 9.7. Shift in Power to Business-Unit Profit Centers.

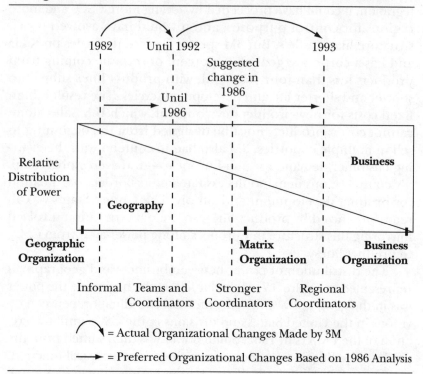

products needed to be delivered to cross-border customers de-manding a common European price and single interface. This cross-country business integration was best achieved with a business structure as the line organization; the geographical dimension became the integrator and the RSOs became the coordinating roles. The earlier organization moves to EMATs and mirror-image structures set the stage for this latest shift; they built the infrastructure, changed mind-sets, and developed the talent.

Although continuing to develop its international presence, 3M is still a heavily U.S.-oriented company; about 50 percent of sales, 60 percent of assets, and 70 percent of employees are in the United States. The company's next moves will depend on future developments. If free trade and deregulation continue, 3M will probably create additional value-added activities outside the home country.

In Europe, the RSOs might disappear, with the administrative work consolidated and placed in a shared-services unit or outsourced to Price Waterhouse or Ernst & Young. The manager with the largest responsibility in a country could take on the country-manager role, as at DuPont or Roche. However, if the reaction to globalization continues to be negative and protectionism increases, the need for cross-border or cross-regional trade and coordination would decrease, and the RSOs or, more likely, the European region could strengthen and become the P&L center again.

Today, 3M is organized by product groups in the Western world; this structure gives the cross-border product integration needed to generate new products and supply cross-border customers. However, in Latin America and Asia, where 3M is less internationally developed and where host governments are more active and cross-border trade is not as significant as in Europe, 3M is still organized by geography. 3M is thus a good example of differentiated organizational structures; the motivations for choosing this organization will now be examined.

Reasons for Differentiation

When a single company such as 3M incorporates multiple strategies, the result is usually a differentiated network—the same company organized in different ways in different parts of the world and across different businesses (Nohria and Ghoshal, 1997). This structure will be employed for several reasons: first, a company can be at different levels of development in different geographies; second, different businesses and different functions may require different amounts of cross-border coordination; and, third, the governments of different countries participate differently in the economic process.

Organizational designers need to understand these differentiating factors and then create and defend the differentiated organizations that are required. These factors, although usually well recognized, do not always lead to the implementation of organizational differences; a conflicting mandate may be to simplify the complexity of the global environment. Companies prefer a uniform application of business processes, control systems, practices, and structures; these preferences simplify the work of headquarters but complicate the work of subsidiaries that do not fit the dominant logic of the company's systems. However, tailoring the structures, practices, and systems of the company to the differing requirements of the subsidiaries frees them to deal with the complexity of customers (as should be the case), while headquarters deals with the complex reality of a global business. Simplifying the internal relationship for subsidiaries and complicating it for headquarters results in greater effectiveness for the company (Nohria and Ghoshal, 1997); the global network, therefore, should be multidimensional and differentiated.

Different Levels of Development

Different organizational forms are appropriate for different geographies if the company has different levels of development in those geographies or the different locales have market conditions requiring different strategies (or both). Headquarters must tailor its relationship with the subsidiaries appropriately.

If a company is at different levels of international or geographical development in different parts of the world, different types of organization should match those levels. The Ford situation mentioned in Chapter Three provides a good example. Ford has integrated the operations of North America and Europe, with Europe taking the lead on small- and medium-sized front-wheel-drive vehicles and North America taking the lead on large cars. These operations are organized as a matrix, with product lines or platforms as one dimension and functions as the other. In Latin America and Asia, however, they are organized geographically. Until the late 1990s Ford had joint ventures in these regions, teaming with Volkswagen in Latin America and with Mazda in Japan. The joint venture with Volkswagen has since been dissolved, and Ford has taken effective control of Mazda; Ford is now expanding in both regions, effectively in start-up mode. With such differing strategies it makes good sense to organize as a transnational in Europe and North America and by geographical division in the other regions. The ultimate intention is to integrate the other regions into the global network after they are developed and after North America and Europe have been effectively combined. It is also possible for a company to pursue different strategies even though it is similarly developed in different parts of the world, as in the 3M case.

Different Business Units and Functions

Business units can also require differentiated organization. The key issue is the amount of cross-border coordination required, and different businesses may require different amounts of coordination. For example, a pharmaceutical company may produce a compound for both prescription sales through physicians and over-the-counter (OTC) sales through mass merchandisers. The prescription business usually develops the compound first and pays for the R&D; it is a global, R&D-driven business, which spends 12 percent or more on R&D. The OTC business invests in advertising, promotion, packaging, and distribution; it is a marketing-driven business, local in character, with geographical and country managers as the profit centers. The power distributions of both businesses can be compared in Figure 9.8. The figure illustrates the principle that different businesses should be organized differently: the greater the cross-border coordination, the stronger the business manager; the less the cross-border coordination, the stronger the country.

Figure 9.8. Differentiated Business Structures.

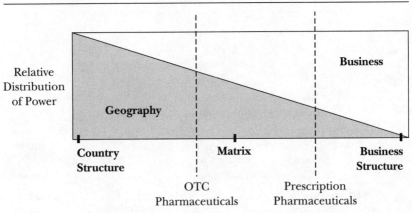

A similar situation prevails for the functions within a business. For example, the prescription pharmaceutical business (described in Chapter Six) is a global business whose pattern of power distribution is different for different functions (Figure 9.9). Research or discovery is clearly a global function; a firm cannot afford to duplicate research costs. Development, which is responsible for clinical trials, is also a global function, but country managers need a certain amount of influence so that opinion leaders in key countries run some of the trials. The manufacturing of basic ingredients, another global function, is a capital-intensive, quality-control-intensive, and multistep synthesis process. The filling and packaging function is local and regional, and sales is an entirely local function run by country managers. The situation for marketing is more complicated. One set of issues involves pricing, promotions, and ads in the local market, which are mostly country decisions or government-regulated decisions. The other issues are related to new-product development and product priorities, which are generally global functions. Marketing is often split into local marketing and global or strategic marketing; the power distributions are also shown in

Figure 9.9. Differentiated Function-Geography Structure.

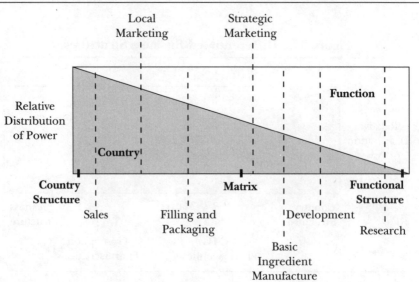

Figure 9.9. Thus, even within a function some activities will be more local than others.

The complexity in these examples is apparent. Headquarters must hold the business manager accountable in the prescription business and the country manager accountable in the OTC business; if several additional businesses are factored in, headquarters can lose sight of who is responsible for what. Country managers must also be clear that they are more responsible for OTC and less responsible for prescription and understand why they have little say about budgets even when a manufacturing plant and a research laboratory are in their country. Country managers believe that they manage all the company's activities in their country; headquarters needs to clarify for all managers why and how the functions are differentiated. A logical, reasoned argument will be necessary to explain why sales and marketing are localized in the prescription business, which is a global business.

Creating differentiated power distributions across a company's network is absolutely appropriate, but it is complicated. Discussions will need to be held, and disputes will need to be settled by the leaders in order to clarify the situation for everyone. Understanding the facts concerning the logic of differentiation is part of acquiring a global mind-set.

Different Levels of Government Participation in the Economic Process

The activity levels of different host governments are another factor in differentiation. If a government makes demands on the multinational and is active in the economic process (as a customer or as a regulator or both), more power is delegated to the country manager than to the business manager, even when strategic factors indicate that the businesses are global.

Citibank and Motorola, for example, both manage separate global businesses. Citibank's global consumer bank and global corporate bank are separate global businesses, as are Motorola's semiconductor and mobile-telecommunications businesses. In Japan, however, each company has combined its businesses under a Japanese country manager, who serves as the profit center. In Japan, a company has to be integrated into the local institutional framework;

in this key market, it is more important for the Japanese businesses to be integrated into the Japanese business environment than to be integrated with the other global businesses. Banking and telecom are regulated businesses; semiconductors is a strategic industry (and Japan often initiates technology consortia, in which Motorola may find it important to participate). It is important for both Citibank and Motorola to be seen as Japanese companies.

A related reason to combine businesses is the large subsidiary that is created. With their expanded Japanese subsidiaries, both companies have more local clout and can recruit senior Japanese managers to integrate them into the local Japanese institutional framework. Motorola recruited a senior executive from NEC to run Nippon Motorola; Citibank was at one time attracting staff from the Ministry of Finance. These recruits have negotiating leverage with the active host government.

A similar situation prevails in other countries that have large attractive markets and follow the Japanese model. India, China, and Indonesia are well aware of their large domestic markets and offer access to multinationals in exchange for value-adding investments and technology transfers. The initial entry may have been negotiated by the home-based CEO, but negotiations rarely stop and may get intense after the fixed investment is made: profits may not be repatriated as planned, imported goods may have trouble in customs, and so forth. A senior country manager, preferably a local national who does not have to check with headquarters (considered a loss of "face"), is invaluable in these extended negotiations. Different levels of government participation and market attractiveness lead to different amounts of power being conferred on the country manager.

Summary

The 3M case is a good review of the concepts presented so far in this book. 3M illustrates the process of internationalization—moving from being a national company to being an international company. It made the transition from country profit centers to business profit centers. In doing so it created various multidimensional networks by adding functions and growing regions and by introducing business teams and coordinators. The case shows how the integrating mechanisms can be used to build organizational capability. 3M could have built more cross-border coordination capability than it did. Its transition from country profit centers to business profit center would have been smoother. Finally, 3M illustrates the differentiated network because it is differentially developed in different parts of the world.

As a firm's international complexity increases and subsidiaries begin to take an ever greater role, one further level of international organization can be employed. This transnational form, Level V in the sequence, is addressed in the next chapter.

Chapter Ten

The Transnational Form

The last level of international development is the transnational form. As with the multidimensional network form, a significant portion of the transnational's assets and employees are outside the home country. The different and distinguishing feature of the transnational is the role that the subsidiaries play. In the multi-dimensional network, subsidiaries implement advantages and strategies generated in the home country; in the transnational they take leading and contributing roles in generating advantages. These advantages are then transferred to other subsidiaries and back to the home country itself. In addition to creating resources in other countries, the transnational shifts power to those sub-sidiaries exercising a leadership role; this transfer of power results in a distributed power structure. The challenge for the transna-tional is to supply the coordination and communication needed to hold the distributed network together. The chapter begins with a discussion of the factors that are creating this organizational form. The organizational-design issues are then elaborated in an example. Finally, a case study of a new transnational organization is analyzed.

Note: This chapter is based on several sources. Key understandings come from presentations by Hatim Tyabji to the International Institute for Management Development MBAs in summer 1996 and by Eugene Buechele to the CEO Con-ference on Global Organizations in April 1997. The Verifone.com Website pro-vided many documents and references. Two cases—Galal, Stoddard, Nolan, and Kao, 1995; and Stoddard, Donnellon, and Nolan, 1997—were also helpful.

Why a Transnational?

A number of factors led to the transnational form. One was the growing awareness of location-specific advantages and lead markets outside the home market. When the level of competition began increasing, companies searched for every possible advantage; lead markets and competencies in subsidiaries became new sources of competitive advantages and competitive necessities. Awareness of location-specific advantages and lead markets was furthered by Porter (1990).

Location-specific advantages were always recognized when firms sought abundant raw materials, cheap energy, and low wages. Then firms began to recognize competencies that developed through the accidents of geography or history: Swiss skills in precision mechanics, Japanese competence in miniaturization, Italian design, British finance, and so on. In order to capitalize on these location-specific skills, most companies needed a change of mindset. Headquarters and expatriates had thought of themselves as teachers; now the teachers needed to be taught. Also, most differences across countries had been seen as negatives, as obstacles to global programs and policies. Now the differences were positives that could enhance the competitiveness of the company.

Competition was more intense and more advanced in certain geographical markets; companies desiring a leading position in their industry had to have leading positions in these markets. In financial derivatives, New York is where the competition is intense and innovation the greatest, but London has the largest volumes of foreign exchange, which make it the leading foreign-exchange market. Financial institutions with strategies in these product lines needed a presence in these markets. Most companies, however, found that they needed more than a presence; they needed their people in these lead markets to take control of the resources, with sufficient autonomy to compete in the market. Only in this way could a firm learn and develop the competencies it would need when the home market caught up with the lead market. Today, companies are trying to develop the means to enter these advanced markets without an advantage. (This mode of entry may take some time—witness European firms trying to establish themselves in New York.)

The trend today for many companies is to place the leadership for a business in the lead market, irrespective of where that market is located. Lead markets tend to have the toughest competition, the most demanding customers, and the most advanced technology. It is also possible for a lead market to change: The United Kingdom was one of the first to deregulate and open its telecommunications markets, becoming the lead market; today, however, the most competitive and open telecom markets are in Scandinavia, and Nokia and Ericsson are benefiting. California, by passing legislation on the level of auto emissions permissible in the year 2000, became the lead market for environmentally friendly cars; if the Green party comes to power in Germany, perhaps Germany or the European Union will become the lead market.

Another factor that played an early role in the creation of transnationals was regionalization. In global industries where local governments insisted on local value-added, the transnational was a solution. This is exemplified with the countries of Southeast Asia, which formed a free-trade group, the Association of Southeast Asian Nations (ASEAN); each country, however, wanted its own car industry and as much value-added as possible. The auto companies explained that they could not create an engine plant, a transmission plant, a braking-system plant, and so forth in each country because automotive is a scale business. In order to achieve scale, ASEAN agreed to have Toyota assemble in all the countries but specialize the manufacture of all engines in Indonesia, transmissions in Thailand, and brakes in the Philippines. Thus each country got some value-added and exports, and Toyota got its scale economies. When a company specializes by country, each country gets a product with a regional or global mission; each country then supplies the others but must also engage in reciprocal purchasing with the other specializing countries.

This form of the transnational, though, has not always been successful. When the European Union and the Maastricht Treaty came into being, the European regional headquarters of multinational corporations were given the task of coordinating supplies across borders. Many companies, however, did not centralize activities in a European headquarters but instead gave each country a product mandate for the region. In other words, the German subsidiary would supply one product for all countries in Europe, the French would supply another, and the United Kingdom a third. This arrangement had great appeal because each country got a European mandate, yet each was dependent on the others for its own supply; it had great political appeal and perceived fairness. Many of these arrangements, however, have not been successful. One reason is the inability to coordinate the logistics of distributed-supply arrangements, but the main reason is the unwillingness of subsidiaries to become dependent on other subsidiaries that are unqualified to supply at a competitive standard; it is one thing to give a regional or global mandate to a world-class subsidiary with leadership in the product category but quite another to give a mandate for political reasons. Giving all subsidiaries a mandate creates fairness, reciprocity, and balance, but it works only if they all also have a leading competence. Today, fewer transnationals are being created for political purposes.

A more popular version of the transnational occurs when the contributing role is given to subsidiary activities like R&D labs. A number of Japanese companies have created software and multimedia labs in the United States; some have created audio labs in the United Kingdom, which has attained world leadership in high-end audio research. These labs take the leadership in their respective technologies, with the results of their work transferred back to the labs in Japan. From there, the technologies are commercialized by the Japanese product divisions.

Transnational Organizational-Design Issues

The issues of coordinating the transnational can be illustrated with an example. A U.S. company in the medical-diagnostics business had grown by acquiring a European company and by forming a joint venture in Japan (gaining majority control over time, it treated the Japanese venture with respect but as a subsidiary). The company initially made x-ray machines, then added CT-scan machines, and then magnetic-resonance-imaging (MRI) machines. When the industry subsequently experienced increasing costs of developing the digital technologies for its products, it became necessary to develop these expensive products in one place for use throughout the company. However, medical equipment is politically sensitive, and, in many countries, the government is often the customer. In these countries, to be selected as a vendor, a company would have to supply local value-added.

The company decided to specialize: each region would be given a product line and a global mandate to develop the product for all regions, along with responsibility for manufacturing and exporting any scale-sensitive components. The final assembly, sales, and servicing of all products would take place in each individual region. Every time a next-generation product was introduced, its specialization was assigned to one region. Over a period of years, the company migrated to the transnational form: the North American unit took the leadership for MRI machines, Europe took x-rays, and Japan took CT scanners.

The specialization greatly lowered costs; there was one development process for each product—not three—and no more duplication in the manufacturing of expensive components. Although specialization lowered costs, it also lowered morale for those who "lost" the product to other regions. This loss was felt most strongly in the United States, where engineering believed it should lead on all products. Conversely, the morale in Europe and Japan went up in those areas where they received a global mandate; they now felt more like a true partner than like a subsidiary. Some of the engineers were willing to take assignments in other countries and aid in the transfer and integration. The government ministries accepted the change and liked the exports.

The organizational structure did not change; the North American, European, and Japanese regions still reported to the U.S.-based headquarters. However, the supply and communications relationships changed enormously. The original hub-and-spokes model, shown in Figure 10.1(a), was a simple, decentralized model with self-contained regions; headquarters managed finances and transferred technology and people. In the peer model, or transnational, shown in Figure 10.1(b), there is much more interdependence; decisions are still made in the regions, but much more communication and coordination are needed to reach them. Each region is dependent on the others to supply products for their customers. In order to coordinate this high level of interdependence, the company used four practices.

Figure 10.1. Communications Relationships Between Subsidiaries and Headquarters.

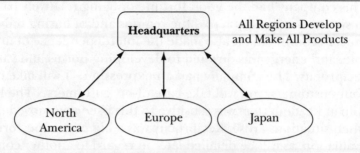

All Regions Develop and Make All Products

(a) Original Hub-and-Spokes Model

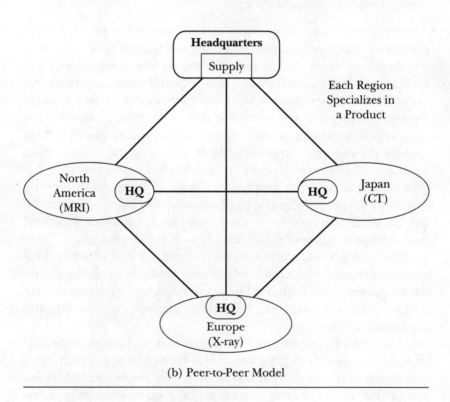

Each Region Specializes in a Product

(b) Peer-to-Peer Model

Norms and Values of Reciprocity

This company had the good fortune of being relatively balanced in size and capability across the regions and of having only three units to coordinate. It also made the interdependence of units visible, and energy was devoted to developing norms and values of reciprocity. The company had an expression: "I will take care of your customers; you will take care of my customers." The leadership at headquarters was sensitive to this issue and moved quickly when situations arose. Reciprocity was a big part of performance evaluation, as will be detailed later in regard to another company.

Global Order-Fulfillment Process

The order-fulfillment process—one of two global processes the company implemented to coordinate work across the regions—was designed when the company began its migration toward specialization. A cross-functional, cross-regional team was created to coordinate the new design; the team consisted of representatives from sales, assembly, and component manufacturing selected from each region and two representatives from corporate headquarters. One of the corporate representatives was the leader of the team, known as the "process owner" (this person would eventually become the leader of the supply-coordination function). A consulting team supported the effort; these team members were chosen for their ability to coordinate their own North American, Japanese, and European offices for the duration of the project.

The new process was put on an intranet, with all orders, schedules, inventories, and component flows available to all the appropriate parties in all regions. The transparency of order-flow status and the norms of reciprocity helped facilitate the coordination and communication effort.

The order-fulfillment process was further supported by the supply-coordination function, which was launched at the corporate center when the new organization was fully implemented. It was led by the "owner" of the process and the other corporate representative on the process-design team. In addition, two employees from each region's supply function spent two years in the unit; half of the six—one from each region—were replaced on a yearly basis.

This unit coordinated supply decisions (like exports to Brazil), maintained the process, and conducted seminars on it.

The design of the central supply unit has several interesting features. First, it re-creates the organization in microcosm, with representatives from the three regions supported by the formal information system. These eight people constitute a global decision-making unit, which becomes a powerful, neutral integrating body. Second, it builds informal networks among those who run the order-fulfillment process throughout the world. Third, it provides international and global experience for the participants. Fourth, management has a chance to see high-potential candidates in action and interact with them. A two-year stint in the unit has become a desirable assignment.

Product-Development Process

The other global process for facilitating coordination across regions was a redesigned new-product-development process. The nine-person design team for the process consisted of representatives for each region from product marketing, manufacturing, and engineering. The team was supported by the corporate information-technology function, and the completed process design again made use of the company intranet. The engineering head of the North American region was the "owner" of the product-design process, with the position rotating every few years. The entire engineering group in a region had ownership of the process for its products.

From the beginning of the process start-up, the company's engineering units standardized on a CAD system; three-dimensional digital representations of new products were subsequently accessible in all regions, and preliminary designs could be tested on lead customers before an architecture was chosen. All products were designed to consist of a modular platform that could be adapted with local modules for different regional markets; a subteam headed by the region responsible for a product led in creating its modular structure.

Networks across regions for product lines were created and maintained by the region responsible for the product line. The product marketing managers from each region, plus the engineering managers from the lead region, made up the core team for developing products. Face-to-face encounters—rotational assignments, exchanges, visits, and seminars on the product-development process—were the primary means of building relationships and sharing information; the CAD system and other electronic means were used in between face-to-face events. Another relationship-building tool was the debriefing after each new product launch; the team members, along with those who worked with them, reviewed the experience and determined what was learned, what should be different next time, and what changes should be made to the process and the CAD system.

The Management Team

Some of the biggest changes affected management team members, whose whole style of operation had to change. They needed new processes, measures, and rewards, along with a different type of regional manager. The changes in management style can be inferred from Figure 10.1: Under the old system (a), the leader could manage with a one-on-one style; each region was independent and self-contained; and a regional manager did not need to know much about the other regions. Under the transnational form (b), however, the now-interdependent managers needed to work as a team, reviewing the whole operation together; each new product launch affected all of them. The leader needed to sit around the table with the three regional managers, as they solved problems and confronted conflicts together; a problem-solving style that transcended different nationalities took a long time to evolve.

One of the tools that they used was the region-product spreadsheet shown in Figure 10.2, which gave a factual foundation for discussions and became the basis for planning and review. It displays sales, profits, market share, and other relevant data for products in regions and was available to all members of the team. Finer divisions of the data—broken down by product lines and countries, for example—were also made available.

The measures of performance also changed. Previously, managers had been responsible for the revenues and profits in their region; now they were additionally responsible for their product line across all regions. Simple bottom-line measures for a self-contained region were not possible; performance was more sub-

Figure 10.2. Region-Product Spreadsheet.

	North America	Europe	Japan
MRI			
CT			
X-ray			

jective and required discussions with other regions and the CEO. As a result, the new bonus system for the top team was based on total global revenues and profits.

The transnational ultimately required a new team composed of regional managers who knew not only the local market but also the global situation for a product line. They also had to work well with other regional managers and, perhaps most important, be able to contribute to global and local problem-solving sessions. These are rare qualities; a transnational must ultimately grow its own people for these key roles.

Challenges

The difficulty in designing a true transnational can now be appreciated. It is not simply a matter of distributing regional and global mandates. Rather, it involves the creation of global management teams for the top group, as well as other key groups like product-development teams; the design of global business processes and information systems; the creation of new measurement and reward systems; and, finally, the use of managers with a global mind-set and team skills. These are the policies necessary for coordinating distributed but interdependent power centers.

This example has illustrated some of the difficulties of moving to and managing a transnational. The change process can be painful; shifting power out of the home country and vesting it in a subsidiary is always resisted by those who will lose power. A debate at one multinational to determine whether the home-country business unit or a subsidiary business unit should take the leadership led to genuinely bad blood between the two groups. To avoid such conflict, some companies have backed away from the transnational. The medical-diagnostics company in the example used time, the fairness argument ("everybody gets one"), and natural change opportunities (from new-product redesigns) to help make the transition.

Another challenge is the lack of candidates with the requisite skills and mind-set. The top team needs experience, cross-regional knowledge and understanding, teamwork skills, and, probably, computer proficiency. Building cross-regional processes and developing new products can result not only in new processes and products but also in new transnational managers; the company cited above used a transition time of several years to develop the talent.

One further challenge, a never-ending one, is managing the interdependence across regions. Under the old system, a product delay in Japan was a problem for Japan; with the transnational, it is a problem for the whole company. Once a transnational has been put together, it must be managed to stay together.

For all these reasons, the transnational is being adopted on a measured basis. They also illustrate why the contributor role is popular: it is a halfway step that may generate advantages for the network, give pride to the subsidiary, and avoid the home-country backlash. However, companies will continue to move to the transnational form when it is required. It is in a company's interest to use it to capture location-specific advantages and to flex its power centers as lead markets change. Real advantages accrue to the firm with the organizational capability to utilize the transnational form, as evinced by young companies. New companies or new divisions in old companies do not have the history and existing constituencies that slow old companies. The next section analyzes a new company that started with a clean sheet of paper and created a transnational.

Case Study: The Verifone Company

Verifone designs and makes the hardware and software used to verify credit-card transactions. It is a young company that expanded internationally after 1986, moving directly from a national to a transnational; it seems that when companies have no historical constraints or existing power structures, they move quickly and naturally to the transnational form.

The hardware that Verifone designs is the device through which the retailer swipes the credit card, which reads the information on the magnetic strip. Verifone also writes the software used by credit-card companies and the banks that issue the cards. Upon verification by the bank, a hardware device prints out a bill that the card member signs. Verifone defines itself as a transaction-automation company; it makes hardware and software for smart cards, debit cards, and, increasingly, electronic-commerce transactions over the Internet. It is also moving into the services that support the installation of such systems—for merchants, health care groups, oil companies—and also sells customer education, systems integration, consulting, and financing for e-commerce systems. In the spring of 1997, Verifone was acquired by Hewlett-Packard and is now a relatively autonomous subsidiary.

The company, started in 1981 by some entrepreneurs, made products that were popular but profitless; in late 1986 they hired Hatim Tyabji, who, over ten years, took the company from $31 million in sales with nothing outside the United States to $475 million and 40 percent outside the United States. Verifone now has direct sales in fifteen countries and regional distributors in seventy; it has sold products and received certification in ninety countries. Half of the twenty-five hundred employees are located outside the United States.

Verifone calls itself a virtual company because it has no headquarters and has multiple development centers around the world. There is a nominal headquarters in Silicon Valley, but the CEO lives elsewhere in the San Francisco Bay area; the chief information officer, in Santa Fe, New Mexico; and the head of human resources, in Dallas. The company was started in Hawaii (which defines itself as the farthest spot from anywhere else in the world); because they could not do much in Hawaii, the founders, and then

Tyabji, started developing hardware and software in other locales. Hardware was initially developed and manufactured in Costa Mesa, California, but manufacturing was quickly transferred to Taiwan, a center of excellence for electronics manufacturing. A development center for hardware has now been created in Taiwan, and a low-cost manufacturing plant was opened in China in 1996.

The development of software and applications is distributed. Initially sites in the United States took the lead in developing software for credit-card applications; the United States was, and still is, the credit-card capital of the world. Sites were created at Redwood City (California), Washington, D.C., Dallas, and Atlanta. Tyabji returned to his native India to start a development center in Bangalore; India is still regarded as the most cost-effective site for software development and has taken the lead in developing some systems software. Another center was created in Paris; the Europeans in general, and the French in particular, are the most advanced in smart-card technology and applications, and the French center has the global mandate to develop software for smart-card applications. Another center was started in Singapore, which is the leader in applications for stored-value cards, like phone cards. Stored-value cards are popular in Asia, where, in many regions, the telecom infrastructure is not well developed and on-line credit-card verification is difficult. With the value stored in the magnetic strip of the card, the merchant device extracts the value from the card without requiring verification through the telecom system; when a card's value has been spent, the customer acquires another. A development center in the United States, which is the lead market in the use of PCs and the Internet, has taken the lead in the development of applications in electronic commerce; a U.S. center has the global mandate to learn about and develop the applications and to teach the rest of the company.

Verifone identifies location-specific competencies and lead markets and locates its activities in these areas. If, for example, the British Health Service started an application using smart cards for health records and payment services, Verifone would establish a development center in that lead market by working with the center in Paris to develop the technology and also working with the Health Ministries, banks, telecom companies, and hospitals to create a consortium to support the application. By identifying lead customers in lead markets, Verifone builds new competencies for new applications; the challenge for the company is to coordinate all these physically dispersed yet interdependent activities. The various characteristics and qualities that make Verifone a successful transnational will now be examined.

Organization

The largely functional structure of the organization is nothing extraordinary: field sales is spread around the world, with some application specialization in the United States where volume merits; an operations function does all purchasing, manufacturing, and distribution; engineering is divided between hardware and software, for the telecom systems to link to the banks and for applications; and there are the usual marketing, human resource, financial, and legal functions. The advantage of a functional organization is common standards and practices; even though activities are located around the world, common standards and processes facilitate communication and coordination.

The functional organization is the standard way to structure a single business, and as Verifone increases the number of applications and products, the need for cross-functional coordination and cross-product priority decisions increases. At Verifone, one of the functional managers is chosen to lead an application or product division; the head of information systems, for example, is also the general manager for the development of the Smart Fone (a mobile phone that can complete financial transactions over the Internet). Each functional manager is also a general manager for a product or application and provides cross-functional leadership. As a group, the functional and divisional leaders make up the top team for setting cross-division priorities. As volume increases, along with the number of divisions, some of the larger divisions will probably be separated out and made profit centers.

Strong Culture

This far-flung company is held together by a combination of strong culture and e-mail; all companies have a philosophy statement and an e-mail system, but Verifone works hard at their continued use and development in order to hold this distributed organization together. The strong culture is based on the Verifone philosophy, a statement that reads like those of most other companies; it addresses excellence, the customer, the individual, teamwork, and ethical behavior. But the statement then elaborates on each of these items, giving concrete examples of behavior at Verifone. The leadership then tries to instill in all employees an obligation to conduct themselves professionally according to the philosophy; leaders also strive to create an open climate in which people can point out when behavior, even that of the leadership, does not match the philosophy. To the extent that the obligation is felt and openness is achieved, the culture becomes self-policing.

Building the culture starts with the hiring process, which is the same in every country; the written hiring procedure is available in the database. The interview presents a realistic picture of life at Verifone, emphasizing that not everyone will like it. The negatives are described and emphasized, as well as the philosophy and the expected behavior. New hires are trained in the philosophy; training at Verifone is one part socialization into the culture and one part skill development. Those who do not buy into the culture leave or are encouraged to leave; those who stay are comfortable with the philosophy and make the obligation to live by it.

The culture and philosophy are reinforced through the e-mail system. Stories and ideas that bring the philosophy to life are published; employees submit their thoughts and observations on the achievements of others. These anecdotes are repeated to reinforce the culture and are made available to everyone via an internal Website under sections called "Excellence in Thought" and "Excellence in Action." One "Excellence in Action" entry described events surrounding an important appointment Tyabji and the French sales manager had with a French bank. On the rainy morning of the appointment no taxis were available, so both men put on raingear and traveled to the bank's offices on the sales manager's motorcycle, arriving on time after some unorthodox driving. The bank leaders were impressed; the sale was successfully made. This story is used to illustrate commitment to the customer.

Tyabji himself is an inherent element of cultural support. He sees his leadership task as that of living the philosophy, carrying the message everywhere that they practice what they preach. He travels four hundred thousand miles per year to all sites, bringing the message home.

The culture of Verifone is not one that everyone likes or buys into, but it is a strong one that is shared among the several hundred leaders of the company. It provides a bond among them and helps hold this transnational together.

E-Mail and Electronic Networks

In addition to its usefulness in reinforcing the company's culture and philosophy, Verifone's e-mail system is a powerful integrative device for several other reasons. Verifone's system is unique because there is no other choice; there are no secretaries, and paper is banned. All company communications take place via e-mail; managers submit their budgets via e-mail. Face-to-face meetings and telephones are still in use, but documented information travels exclusively through the e-mail system.

Leadership believes that this is the best way to be a twenty-four-hour transnational; with e-mail and voice mail—tools that overcome time and distance, with the added benefit of speed—it does not matter where people are. Development projects follow the sun and are twenty-four-hour projects: software code is developed in Bangalore and sent to Atlanta; it is tested in Atlanta and sent to Hawaii; the systems engineers in Hawaii integrate the code into the master file. Development projects are purposely structured to be conducted at three sites in different time zones, permitting twenty-four-hour development and short cycle times.

Speed is emphasized in information dispersal. Several stories describe a rumor concerning a competitor's new tactic or strategy. A call goes out to the field to verify it; if it is true, response ideas are brainstormed, selected, and communicated to everyone in the field by the next day. One story describes a salesperson trying to close a big sale to a bank in Europe. At the end of the day, the bank voiced reluctance to close the deal because it had been told by a competitor that Verifone had no experience with debit cards. The salesperson sent out a call for help to others in sales and, by the next morning, had sixteen responses and ten names of customers, with phone numbers, to use as references. (Verifone had no debit-card functions in that particular European country, but it had four hundred thousand debit-card terminals installed around the world.) The local salesperson downloaded the information that had been gathered and presented it to the bank; Verifone received the order. The story emphasized that when a competitor lies about Verifone, a sales call becomes a call to arms.

Verifone provides universal access to company information; a central database is maintained with updated financial information that can be accessed by any manager in any location. Executives in different countries can work together on the same spreadsheets and overheads. One new manager said he became a believer when four managers from different countries put together a marketing plan for small retailers in less than a week; at his former employer, it would have taken three months, plus wait time for CEO approval.

On a daily basis, the head of information systems records and interprets revenues gained, big orders received, products shipped, and milestones met, and sends out a summary of the previous day's events for everyone to see. There is a database called "Today" that reports news, events, jobs available, and other daily happenings. "Skills" is a listing of skills like languages spoken, programming languages known, experiences gained in various countries, and applications made. Employees describe the e-mail network as the heartbeat of the company; it is where the firm's main business takes place.

Tyabji uses the network to pass on stories and perpetuate the culture and also as a means of recognition. After big wins, he congratulates those involved, sometimes giving recognition publicly and sometimes privately via either e-mail or voice mail.

Virtual Teams

The transnational was created to capture location-specific advantages, and virtual teams are the means by which the capture is accomplished and integrated. Virtual teams are formed to tap the best people regardless of location, with members working together at different times and different places. As mentioned above, the teams can also work around the clock, for speed and efficiency. Verifone's use of virtual teams is made possible by the team-based culture, the electronic tools, the interpersonal network, and the modular architectures.

The team-based culture, one of the dimensions of the Verifone philosophy, is presented to employees during their orientation and continuously stressed thereafter. Before working on a team, everyone goes through a forty-hour class on the subject, with part of the week devoted to learning the expected team behaviors, as listed here (Buechele, 1997):

Mutual Accountability

- I feel responsible for what my team members do (or don't do).
- I ask for help when I'm in trouble (quickly).
- I'm willing to help out when someone else appears stumped.
- If something's going wrong, I let people know. I escalate quickly.

Personal Ownership

- It's not acceptable to say, "I can't do my job because they didn't do their job."
- I have a work plan and a backup plan in case it doesn't work.
- Other people know what I'm doing (or NOT doing).
- I work the hours I need to make sure I do what I've committed to others.

Talking and Listening to One Another

- I speak with candor and frankness, but with respect for others' feelings.
- I validate that what I hear is what was intended.
- Agreements that must be shared are written down.
- I do NOT take things at face value (I apply my own experience and judgment).

Everyone has a copy of this list, and employees pull it out during a meeting and question whether these expected behaviors are being followed.

It is said to take about six months to learn the process, after which it becomes natural. While the forty-hour course emphasizes the team-based culture, it also gets reinforced through the performance-evaluation system. Each manager gathers data on an individual's teamwork and contributions (with 20 percent of the performance evaluation based on the person's work on teams). Periodically, management meetings include an assessment of the quality of the group's teamwork, with actions taken and improvement goals set when changes are needed.

Besides teaching the team behaviors, the forty-hour course is also devoted to teaching the virtual-team process used at Verifone. Every team follows the same documented procedures. These procedures are accessible on-line from Verifone's "virtual university," which contains the virtual-team course. The first step in the process is to define a team's purpose and put it in writing; this purpose becomes the team's charter or mission, and every meeting starts with its being read. A checklist of team start-up procedures guarantees that everyone at Verifone knows and uses the team processes. The team leader recruits the appropriate and available people for membership; diversity is sought among the members, as well as representation in three different time zones to facilitate the twenty-four-hour strategy. Once formed, the team makes its plan and sets a schedule and milestones to completion.

An important element of the course is instruction in the use of communication tools. Employees are taught not only how to use the company's 160 different tools and databases but, more important, when to use which tool. Beepers, mobile phones, and voice mail are used to keep in contact remotely; e-mail, fax, and application sharing over the network are used to disseminate or discuss information. For decision making and conflict resolution, audio or video conferences are recommended if face-to-face conferences are not possible. The course sensitizes employees to the pitfalls and psychological traps of remote communication, an important one being that subtleties are lost when communicating across cultures and in second languages. The following list is a ranking of levels of interactivity—from lowest to highest—of some of the tools and normal media. (Source: Hossam Galal and others, *Verifone: The Transaction Automation Company [A]*, Case 9-195-088. Boston: Harvard Business School Press, 1994. Copyright © 1994 by the President and Fellows of Harvard College. Reprinted by permission.)

U.S. mail—P-mail (snail mail)

courier P-mail

e-mail (addressed)

e-mail (bulletin board)

fax

voice mail

electronic "chat"—1:1

electronic "chat"—many

one-way broadcast audio

one-way broadcast video

store-and-forward compressed audio-on-demand

audio annotation to files (e-mail)

store-and-forward compressed video-on-demand

one-way broadcast audio with audio back channel

point-to-point telephone call (standard telephone)

point-to-point telephone call (full duplex audio conferencing)

multipoint telephone call (standard telephone)

multipoint telephone call (full duplex audio conferencing)

live board with point-to-point audio

live board with multipoint audio

one-way broadcast video with audio back channel

point-to-point video conference (56–112 KBytes)

point-to-point video conference (>112 KBytes)

multipoint video conference (56–112 KBytes)

multipoint video conference (>112 KBytes)

virtual-reality meeting

face-to-face meeting

How and when to communicate is a primary issue for newly formed teams; the course in virtual teams is key to sustaining a team-based culture and learning how and when to use different communication tools.

Personal Networks

Verifone invests time and energy in building the personal networks on which the virtual-team process depends by using the standard means mentioned earlier: rotational assignments, training courses, meetings, social events. The team process itself builds on an employee's network; the more teams on which people participate, the more their networks expand.

Travel at Verifone—to visit customers and work sites—is extensive, encouraged, and part of the culture. For managers in the upper-third echelon, an average of 50 percent of work time is spent away from home base. One of the databases charts where traveling employees are visiting and staying. Travel is a key means of meeting new contacts, building networks, and engendering face-to-face discussions.

Another tool that encourages personal networks is the use of mirror-image structures across development sites. The structure for the software-engineering function is shown in Figure 10.3. Software is broken down into categories for the merchant's site, the merchant's server, and the bank's server, as well as connections with the telecommunications systems. Each of these is a specialized group at a separate development site, but each site has an identical structure. One-to-one relationships between the heads of telecom software are easily established and maintained; then a few quick calls or voice mails can staff a project.

Modular Architectures

Another facilitator of virtual teams is modular architectures for hardware and software. This architecture allows a complete module to be assigned to a site. A complete module gives the site the greatest amount of communication and coordination internally and minimizes the need for information across sites. The process of developing new products at remote sites is thereby simplified and the need for continuous communication is reduced.

The software component of a product employs object-oriented programming that features software objects as modules. For example, in an e-commerce product there is a software object for the cardholder to run on his or her PC, a software object for the merchant, a software object for the merchant's bank (which also connects to the Visa network), and an interconnection object for using the telecommunications system. Each object has a subobject section that allows country-specific customization for different currencies, banking laws, and telecom standards. The cardholder and mer-

Figure 10.3. Software-Engineering Global Structure.

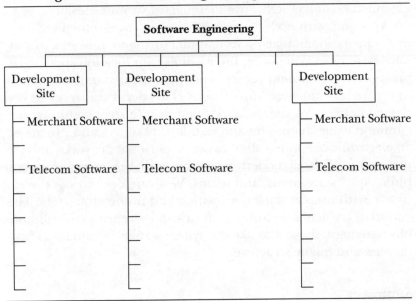

chant objects are assigned to the Redwood City site, the bank object to Atlanta, and the interconnection object to Bangalore; an overall architectural team in Hawaii maintains the integration. The architectural team has built a simulation test program against which each site can test its object. This simulation tests the connection and operation of the object with the other objects; the architectural team also tests all objects as a system. The object-oriented architecture and the simulation test allow each site to work concurrently and as autonomously as possible. Other teams, which were subsequently created to provide country-specific and bank-specific customization, add additional modules as required.

The overall team for one software product, for example, consists of a core team, subteams for each object, and a sales and marketing team; the core team is made up of the six leaders of the subteams, with a team leader in Redwood City. Members of the sales and marketing team, led by a manager in Costa Mesa, handle bank relationships, customization, hardware interface, training programs, and sales programs; the hardware-interface team is in

Taiwan; and training is handled by human resources in Dallas. The extended team has eighty-two members at various sites.

Verifone, with no history or existing assets, essentially started as a transnational, placing its manufacturing in Taiwan and software systems in Bangalore, India—sites with location-specific advantages. Development centers were then created in lead markets to create leading-edge applications. This decentralized and dispersed network of sites is held together by a strong culture and common values, common and standard practices and processes, an electronic communication network, personal networks, and virtual teams. While all modern organizations have computers, e-mail, philosophy statements, and teams, Verifone operates at the extreme, with no secretaries, no paper, and no headquarters. The culture is particularly strong, with strict adherence to the philosophy statement; those who like this system stay and maintain its fragmented and fragile structure.

Summary

The Verifone case illustrates the rapid internationalization that is pursued by the new multinationals. They establish presence quickly in all markets, some of which are lead markets and some of which are not. These transnationals establish presence in lead markets and at sites that have location-specific advantages, transferring power and leadership responsibilities to these lead sites. They then use shared values, personal networks, and electronic networks to hold these distributed centers together, and they employ electronic cross-border processes and modular architectures as the new coordination technologies. These cultures and technologies manage the complexity of the transnational form.

For many companies, the organizational complexity presented thus far—up to and including the transnational—will be sufficient for their situations. Many others, however, face further challenges; the following chapters address this added complexity.

Chapter Eleven

The Multidimensional Multinational

Reconfigurable Organization

The previous chapters dealt with the complexity of managing two dimensions simultaneously. The single-business company balanced functions and geographies; the multibusiness company balanced business units and geographies. However, many companies must also deal with the demanding global customer; in this and the subsequent two chapters, organizing around the full complexity that these companies face will be addressed.

The full complexity facing many companies involves simultaneously managing functions, geographies, product lines (or business units), customers, and solutions—at the very least. These companies must use multidimensional structures, with the dynamics of global business requiring that these multiple dimensions be reconfigurable. Different customers require the services of different combinations of business units and country subsidiaries; to be competitive, a company must be able to configure and reconfigure its profit centers to create value for customers.

This chapter presents the framework for organizing around multiple dimensions, with the next chapter focusing specifically on the customer and customer solutions. Chapter Thirteen deals with an evolving hybrid form of organization: the front-back structure. This organization contains both a front structure—either local country subsidiaries or global segments—which organizes around customers, and a back portion, which organizes around product lines or global-scale-efficient activities.

Requisite Complexity

The effective global organization needs to be as complex as its business. If the business environment has a dozen ways to affect a company's performance, its organization needs a dozen ways to respond or counter; otherwise, the company is vulnerable. This idea is taken from control theory and is usually called the law of requisite variety (Ashby, 1952). When applied to organizations, it has been called requisite complexity (Nohria and Ghoshal, 1997, chap. 11). The organization must be able to configure and reconfigure itself easily along a number of different dimensions so that it never falls behind the pace of the business. These are the two main capabilities of the reconfigurable organization—matching the company's organizational complexity to that of the business environment and changing as quickly as the business environment does.

Besides developing a capability to manage it, a company can reduce the complexity it faces by reducing the number of different businesses that make up its portfolio (Sadtler, Campbell, and Koch, 1997); choosing the type of customer that it serves best, thereby avoiding the complexity of serving different customer types (Treacy and Wiersema, 1995); maintaining a low profile in the environment (Simon, 1995); and avoiding "strange" countries like China and India. The idea of requisite complexity applies equally to companies choosing to be more or less complex; companies do not want to miss emerging opportunities while reducing organizational complexity.

Procter & Gamble provides an example of a major campaign to simplify businesses. For the Pringles product line, Procter & Gamble greatly reduced the variety it was managing by standardizing on a single factory design, common equipment, common products, a standard process, and common maintenance programs. Procter & Gamble has found that the common Pringles factories greatly reduced costs because they provided buying leverage for equipment and raw materials; reduced inventories of spare parts; allowed for a single training program for all plants; and improved transfer of ideas, practices, and people among plants. The new organization is focusing on further reducing variety in its businesses.

Procter & Gamble also simplified its marketing; it reduced the number of product lines by dropping low-volume and low-profit lines and minimized variations in packages, sizes, and extensions of the remaining products. It has also reduced the number of promotions, specials, price changes, and ads, effectively lowering the price for customers and making their choices simpler. Therein lies the key: by reducing unnecessary complexity within the organization—an advantage in itself—a company can provide the customer with simpler choices and lower everyday prices.

On other occasions, making things simple for the customer results in complexity for management. When a global customer wants a single global partnership around the world or wants solutions or global warranty support regardless of where a product is purchased, complexity for management is created. It is not, however, unnecessary or needless complexity; on the contrary, it creates value for the customer. In the case of Procter & Gamble, special units have been created to coordinate across P&Ls for Wal-Mart, Ahold, and Carrefour, who want global supply agreements. The requisite complexity could involve configuring a network of profit centers for one customer and reconfiguring another network for a different customer—all at the speed at which the customer and technology change. IBM calls this capability "integrated speed in front of the customer."

Figure 11.1 shows an array of profit centers. At Nestlé these could be the German confectionery business, the U.K. confectionery business, the U.S. dairy business, the U.K. dairy business, and so forth; at ABB, these could be the Swedish transformer business, the Swiss transformer business, the German power-generation business, the U.S. robotics business, and so on. If these profit centers had no relationships they could function independently, and corporate headquarters would then be a holding company that would have to justify its existence fiscally.

But there are relationships. At ABB the businesses share common products, manufacturing processes, and technologies, with profit centers configured into business areas to prevent duplication and harmful competition, as shown at the top of Figure 11.2. The ABB profit centers also share common local customers (like electric utilities), so they are also configured into networks within commonly served countries. Figure 11.2 shows this common—and, in an age of reconfiguring and change, relatively permanent—way of configuring profit centers into business and country networks.

Figure 11.1. Profit Centers.

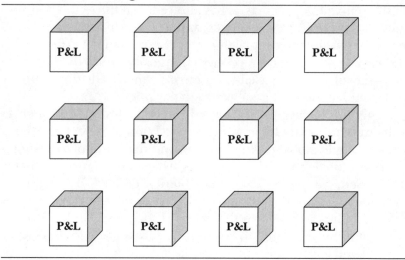

Figure 11.2. Networks of P&Ls for Businesses and Countries.

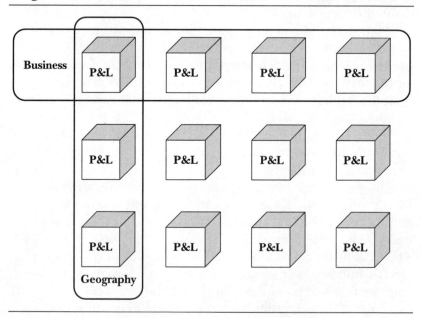

Nestlé, in its configuration, puts the power and responsibility along the geographical dimension, with geographical zones and countries the line organization and strategic business units the second priority, except on decisions about global brands. Conversely, Hewlett-Packard (HP) puts the power along the business dimension, with countries the second priority, except on human resources issues like salaries and pensions, where country differences and legislation prevail. Until July 1998, ABB used a balanced power distribution across the two dimensions, with the business primary on individual decisions like product development and the country primary on customer relationships; since then, ABB has transitioned to an HP-type structure. Many companies use the HP model in developed countries and the Nestlé model in emerging markets. In general, the trend, as evidenced by ABB, has been a shift in power to the business dimension as more cross-border coordination becomes necessary.

The business-country grouping has been the most stable configuration of profit centers, but the increasing complexity and speed of change has necessitated an increasing amount of reconfiguring within the geographical and the business networks. The geographical dimension has been the most stable; geography does not change much. In the past contiguous countries were usually formed into regions (Europe, North America, Asia); grouping together countries with similar levels of development and somewhat common cultures and time zones minimizes travel and communications problems. However, as the number of countries and size of country businesses grew, changes occurred in numbers of levels and groupings. A Scandinavian subregion might be formed, as well as a German-speaking group (Germany, Austria, Switzerland) or an Iberian group; sometimes a country, such as Japan, would be targeted for priority and report directly to headquarters. As a rule, these were minor changes—except for those directly involved— that did not change the basic geographical structure.

Today, contiguous grouping is being questioned. For businesses in which logistics is an important activity, grouping by contiguous countries still makes sense for sharing factories, warehouses, and distribution. But other businesses find that contiguous countries at different stages of development have different features, and coordination is difficult. These businesses find more similarity, for example, between Vietnam and the Ukraine, which are moving from Communist regimes and have poorly developed economic infrastructures, than between the contiguous Vietnam and Japan; these businesses have created emerging-markets groupings that simplify administration and the sharing of practices and ideas. The commercial-banking business at Citibank divides countries into a developed-country grouping (known at Citibank as OECD, or Organization for Economic Cooperation and Development) and two emerging-market units. The OECD unit is the JENA region (Japan, Europe, and North America), which is driven by capital markets and where Citibank focuses on products for global customers; in developing countries, where financing is bank driven, Citibank makes money on loans to local and global customers.

As companies reach the point where they have over one hundred countries in their portfolio, they question what is the best grouping for managing these countries; they are, increasingly, finding alternatives to geographically contiguous regions. Oil companies, for example, have traditionally grouped oil fields into geographical units for their exploration and production business; this grouping makes sense in regard to logistics and pertinent government regulations. However, other alternatives seem to make more sense when companies, such as Shell and British Petroleum, have fifty to one hundred such fields, and technology becomes important. Perhaps all deep-water fields companywide have more in common than deep-water and land-based fields in the same country or region. Or perhaps all fields using horizontal-drilling technology should be grouped into the same unit, regardless of proximity. McKinsey is investigating the feasibility of creating a unit that would manage all of Shell's mature fields because it has found that the small, independent oil companies generate great profit by purchasing mature fields from the large oil companies and operating them with low overheads. Why not, instead, set up a separate unit within the large oil companies, structured to have low overheads? A mature field grouping is therefore another alternative to the geographically contiguous model; it exemplifies the idea of reconfiguring geographical units as their situation changes.

The Tetra Pak packaging company has been exploring a reconfigurable approach that is more dynamic than McKinsey's idea.

Its Argentine subsidiary has captured a large market share by packaging wine in paper and plastic bricks, and other country subsidiaries with a wine industry—such as South Africa, Australia, and Hungary—are interested in learning from the Argentine subsidiary, as well as pooling their R&D efforts to develop wine-specific packaging. Instead of a Latin American group of countries, why not form a group around their common interest in wine? Another group of countries, led by Japan, is interested in new packages designed specifically for vending machines, while in the United States milk has been put in a new single-serve container called a "chug"; these advances have generated interest in several countries for an adult, single-serve beverage grouping. Tetra Pak is exploring whether to group country subsidiaries around common product-development interests. When the current product needs of a country are met, the country and the groupings can change, configured and reconfigured into more business-relevant networks.

The business dimension has been a bit more reconfiguration-ready than the geographical. Most companies have more businesses than can report directly to the CEO, so they form groups or sectors of subportfolios of businesses, which are often reconfigured. Most companies have had difficulties establishing organizational layers between businesses and the CEO; no group executive wants to be a mere span-reducer, so synergies and ways to add value have been sought. Most of the time, however, these layers have destroyed value (Campbell and Goold, 1998). Many companies, like GE, have expanded the office of the chief executive and eliminated intervening layers.

At some companies, an important role for group executives has been reconfiguring the product-market charters of business units. As change increases and product life and development cycles decrease, technology companies constantly shuffle charters among businesses (Eisenhart and Gallunic, 2000). HP has a tradition of moving product-market charters around its divisions. In the past, HP consistently split divisions in two when they reached a certain size; as a result the company grew from ten divisions in the late 1950s to approximately fifty divisions in the mid-1980s. Today, there is less division formation but more movement of charters between divisions. For example, a division may develop three different product lines and lose focus. One product line is then taken away, and a new division is started. Or, more likely, the product line is given to a division that needs a new charter; its market may be disappearing (like defense), and it can put its skills to work on the new product line. The group executive makes these moves; they do not happen naturally, as no division likes to give up its "children."

Charters are reconfigured for a number of other reasons (Eisenhart and Gallunic, 2000). A division may introduce a new product for a market opportunity that it sees, but the product may better fit the skills of another division. The group executive migrates the product-market charter to the other division. Or a market may mature, with cost becoming more important than new technology for a next-generation product, and a division with high overheads and advanced technological skills may not have the needed low-cost manufacturing competencies. (HP has addressed this situation by creating a Singapore division for high-volume, low-cost manufacturing.) In another case, two or more divisions may see the same market opportunity and introduce competing products. Product divisions for television broadcasters and computer servers may both begin projects to create video servers; these competing experiments are allowed to continue until one is preferred by the customer. The group executive then consolidates the charter in the best division. In companies with fast-moving markets and technologies, configuration and reconfiguration of product-market charters assigned to businesses are continual, with group executives trying to match the competencies of divisions or businesses with the product-market needs in changing situations.

Reconfiguring profit centers within geographical and business networks may have its challenges, but the greater challenge is that of configuring networks across profit centers in different geographies and different businesses, with a third dimension—functions—representing different networks for finance, human resources, purchasing, and R&D. Figure 11.3 shows networks that cross several businesses and countries. One network could represent all profit centers with significant purchases of steel, another all profit centers with significant purchases of semiconductor memories. A third is a network for all R&D groups working on digital signal processing, and still another for all groups working on superconductivity. These networks need to be constantly reconfigured as new tech-

Figure 11.3. Networks for Five Dimensions.

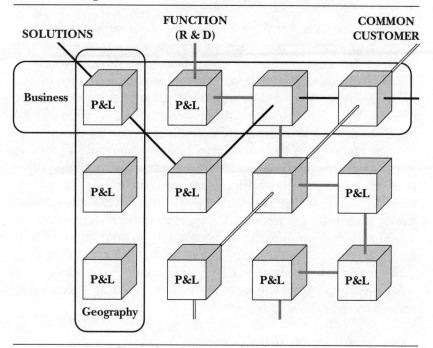

nologies arrive, new materials are ordered, and new businesses and subsidiaries are added.

Add, then, to these functional networks those desired by global customers. ABB focused initially on seven global customers that wanted to centrally coordinate their purchases; the number subsequently grew to fifty key accounts desiring central coordination of purchasing and a simplified interface with ABB. There is a different network for each customer, with configuration of profit centers requiring constant updating as customers expand into new countries, form joint ventures, and buy and sell businesses. The last network shown in Figure 11.3 represents a customer solution. For ABB a solution could be a turnkey power plant or a waste-treatment power plant; for H-P a solution would be a trading room for a bank. In all cases, however, networks of profit centers must be configured and reconfigured for different products and different solutions. This type of complexity is challenging the leading multinationals.

Organizing for Complexity

Managing complexity involves balancing the requisite complexity of the business with management's capacity to coordinate across units. Globalization, currently driven by foreign direct investment, has generally increased the level of requisite complexity. In this section, a framework for analyzing how to manage the complexity is described; the framework was developed from observation of leading firms dealing with the current challenges.

The challenge is to manage the multiple dimensions inherent in the business. A firm must have an organization capable of responding along as many dimensions and through as many networks as there are important issues in the global business—in other words, it must have a network for every important dimension. Yet most firms have trouble with the normal three dimensions of business, geography, and function. The firms that are expanding their capacity to manage customers, solutions, channels, processes, and so on—in addition to the normal three dimensions—are characterized by the following features:

1. A reconfigurable network mind-set
2. An ability to prioritize the various dimensions
3. Timely decision making regarding strategic priorities
4. An ability to match the strategic priority with the appropriate level of coordination
5. An ability to flex the priority and the level of coordination
6. The use of reserve capabilities
7. The use of the new coordination technologies
8. Clean interfaces

The next sections describe each of these features.

Reconfigurable Mind-Set

The most important component of managing complexity is having a leadership that thinks in terms of flexibility and uses its organization as a competitive weapon. This organization is one that can combine and recombine its profit centers to serve different customers and create different solutions for them. This flexible model is the antithesis of fixed, simple, and autonomous profit centers. When leadership sees that its organization can be a source of competitive advantage by creating value for customers, the next steps are easier.

Strategic Prioritizing

When priorities are set, communicated, and understood throughout the organization, decision making becomes clear in the multidimensional structures. Managers can deal with the complexity of their business issues without the added complexity of having to deal with internal unresolved conflicts. Yet, in many multinationals, these priorities are not set, and unresolved conflicts are a major reason for the failure of matrix and multidimensional structures.

Citibank's institutional banking business is a good example (Malknight and Yoshino, 1992a, 1992b). Until the mid-1990s, Citibank had no explicit strategy for prioritizing the country, product, and customer profit centers. Instead, Citibank wanted growth and the entrepreneurial pursuit of opportunities; it tried to do everything and say no to nothing. The de facto priorities were countries first, then products, customers, and, finally, functions. The power resided in the traditional country manager, with loans made in each country's own currency; a few product centers, such as foreign exchange, were strong; customers had still less power (it not always being possible to get customer profitability measures across countries); and the corporate staff functions had always been weak.

This system pleased no one. With each unit measured on its bottom line, there was competition and tension rather than cooperation between them. The least satisfied were the customers, who did not want six or seven aggressive Citibank units calling on them. The cross-border customer often felt well-served in the home country but ignored in countries with a smaller operation. The corporation was not satisfied because of customer complaints and low profitability. Even country managers were dismayed, often finding themselves unaware that product specialists were in their country and proposing deals to their local customer.

Then, in the mid-1990s, Citibank, having recovered from its problems with Latin American debt and U.S. real estate, began a thorough analysis of its strategy. It became clear that Citibank's advantage, which stemmed from its visibility in nearly one hundred countries, was its ability to take deposits and make loans in the local currency, thus eliminating Citibank's exposure to currency fluctuations; the nearest competitor was Hong Kong–Shanghai Bank, with visibility in some forty countries. This advantage could not be matched, so Citibank focused on being a cross-border bank, prioritizing multinational customers and their global-product needs, like cash management and foreign exchange. The strategic priorities became: (1) the customer, (2) products, (3) countries, and (4) functions (with the exception of risk management).

Explicitly setting priorities focused the business and clarified the relations among profit centers. Countries were to serve the priority global customer, not the more locally profitable local customers. Products were to provide service to global customers, be measured by customer satisfaction, and serve other customers only if volume helped lower the cost for the global customer. Priorities were set, communicated, and understood throughout the organization.

The ability to set and reset priorities is a key capability of today's multinational, although it remains a difficult decision-making process for a number of reasons. First, some managers believe that it is wrong to set priorities or make statements about which dimension is more important; they believe that if they say customers are first and products are second, the product staff will lose motivation. But this position simply avoids the decision, and, as a result, it is passed somewhere else in the organization. By definition, whenever the demand for resources exceeds the supply, priorities will be set; leadership's choice is *how* to set priorities, not *whether* to set them. If customers are the appropriate priority, the product staff will lose motivation only if they have not had the opportunity to debate the issue and understand the rationale of the customer-first strategy. As a rule, it is preferable to face reality, have the debates, and decide on and communicate the priorities; employees then have a context in which to make daily decisions.

A second reason that managers do not set priorities is because they are unable to manage conflict and reach a decision. Despite decades of recommendations from researchers who have identified conflict resolution as a key organizational capability (Lawrence and Lorsch, 1967; Galbraith, 1973; Eisenhardt, Kahwajy, and Bourgeois, 1997), most organizations fall short of effectively managing natural conflict. (Multinationals have the added challenge of setting priorities in different cultures with different beliefs about managing disagreements.) Whether management is unable or unwilling, the result is the same: an unresolved conflict falls through the organization until it reaches someone who does not have the choice to avoid it. In a pharmaceutical company it is easy to find disagreements between the global head of development and country managers; the global development head usually favors global-product clinical trials in a country, while the country head prefers trials or reformulations of profitable local products. The preferred decision-making method has the heads of the function and country—with input from the country development people—reaching a single, joint-priority decision in the company's best interest. If the two heads do not resolve their differences, the priority decision falls to the head of development in the country.

A third challenge facing multinationals is the constantly changing environment; priorities need not only to be decided but to be redecided in a timely manner, with strategic decisions that used to be made every three or four years now being made yearly.

Timely Decision Making

How do companies cope with the complexity and speed of decision making? The emerging pattern appears to involve a process rather than a plan, with companies expeditiously testing and experimenting instead of forecasting, predicting, and planning. They put a concept or prototype in front of a customer or run a simulation, then, based on the data from the simulation and feedback from customers, they modify the concept and test it again (Eisenhardt, 1989; Eisenhardt and Tabrizi, 1995). Eisenhardt's work shows that adaptive processes are superior and more timely than forecasts and plans, and they create more data (especially real-time data) on which to base conflict resolution. Predictions create disagreements between one forecast for the future and another; rather than argue, managers should test the forecasts. To be sure, the resulting data are subject to interpretation, but these interpretations can be tested as well. Thus, leading companies appear to be using more facts and fewer opinions than they have in the past for resolving their differences.

The top performers also consider more alternatives simultaneously than the poor performers do. The slower decision makers work with one or two alternatives sequentially, one usually being the CEO's preferred alternative; the quality of the debate is therefore questionable. Having to choose between two alternatives polarizes the participants, and when one alternative proves to be inferior, they usually have to scramble for more. Conversely, four or five alternatives generated by the organization's many dimensions give a wide range of options, with fall-back positions readily available. Generating the alternatives can be a fun, creative exercise: integrative solutions are more likely to be discovered; and the participants can change alternatives without losing face.

Eisenhardt's work also confirms past research on conflict resolution. Conflicts are best resolved when groups can get agreement on a higher-level goal; when deciding on actions to take, Lou Gerstner at IBM tries to establish priorities with the customer's interest first, the company's second, and the business unit's third. The other feature of effective companies is decision by consensus, which is not necessarily unanimity; the minority supports the consensus of the majority. These kinds of consensus decisions engender a sense of urgency and allow everyone to be heard up to a point. If there is not unanimity, the CEO decides, and everyone supports the decision.

Many companies have stated values and beliefs to guide timely decisions. The belief at Sun Microsystems is, "The best decision is the right decision. The second-best decision is the wrong decision. The worst decision is no decision." Implicit in this belief is the view that it is best to make a decision while the window of opportunity is open; if the decision is wrong, follow up quickly and correct it. This process of timely decisions and rapid mistake corrections is also followed by ABB. The effective practice therefore appears to be to give everyone a say but to have leadership decide on a timely basis, followed by an appeal to a higher-level goal to get support from the minority opinion holders; if the decision is incorrect, the plan is to quickly redecide and get on the proper course.

Other decision tools are evolving to support strategic decisions in an era of speed and uncertainty. The use of scenarios, which have been around for some time, is increasing. Whether the scenarios are accurate or inaccurate is less important than opening minds to possible futures; as events unfold, managers can see possibilities in a new light. Similarly, options are being applied to strategic decisions, not just financial ones; rather than predicting a future, real options provide in various ways the flexibility to respond to new information. Some see strategic planning as the creation of portfolios of options.

All these tools increase the set of alternatives, provide choices based on real-time information, and open management mind-sets to a range of options and probable change. The techniques are intended to create a capability for management to resolve conflicts and establish priorities among the strategic dimensions as well as to reprioritize on a timely basis.

Coordination-Priority Matching

A company should match the type and amount of network coordination with the priority that is assigned to the strategic dimension and choose the least costly and least difficult coordination process to meet the required objectives. As discussed in Chapter Seven and shown here in Figure 11.4, the rule is to start on the bottom step and go up another step only if necessary to achieve the necessary coordination. For example, a company could maintain the status quo for businesses, geographies, and functions and add

Figure 11.4. Levels of Coordination.

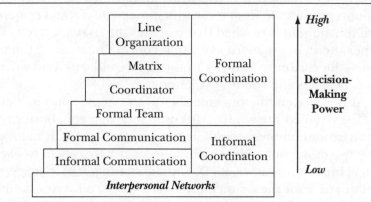

informal networks for customers, channels, and common partners. (The more dimensions that can be managed through informal networks and self-organizing processes, the greater the company's capacity to handle complexity where it is needed; this use of informal networks decentralizes the coordination across units and involves additional people in the process.) In all likelihood, there will be networks on all the steps, the step assigned to a dimension depending on its strategic priority.

Moving up the steps can facilitate the resolution of conflicts; disagreements about priorities are easily generated across profit centers. In the earlier example of Citibank, a good global customer had a small presence in another country, and, as a result, the country manager in that country assigned a low priority to this demanding but low-revenue, low-profit customer. When coordination was informal, this customer's subsidiary was not likely to receive service. However, after the bank created key accounts and key-account management teams, an employee in the country was assigned to the customer's small subsidiary and could make a case for the customer. The creation of a formal team such as this one increases the likelihood of service but does not guarantee it. The probability of service could be further increased if there were a champion for key accounts—like a vice president—at corporate headquarters. The vice president, whose status is probably at the country manager's level, could try to persuade the country manager to give a higher priority to the global customer's small subsidiary and could possibly do a favor at headquarters for the country manager in exchange. Moving up the steps provides the dimension with increasing amounts of attention from those with more authority and resources until the amount is reached that matches the strategic need. The higher the step, the more likely that coordination along the network—the customer network in this case—will exist and will cut across business and country dimensions.

ABB was operating on a number of the steps shown in Figure 11.4. As detailed previously, ABB used to assign equal priority to countries and businesses and, in fact, was famous for its matrix of these two dimensions. Next lower in priority were functions like finance, human resources, R&D, and purchasing; staff managers at headquarters for these functions served—and still serve—as their champions at the leadership level. The dimension for solutions and mega-projects is managed at a similar level, with a senior manager who is the champion for these projects. For the customer dimension, formal teams were created for the key accounts; the account manager in the customer's home country with the largest amount of revenue acts as the global account manager. Finally, there are informal and formal networks for various technologies.

Network Flexing

As described in the previous section, each dimension is assigned a level of coordination that matches its strategic priority. When priorities change, the level of coordination changes. For example, if ABB achieves a breakthrough in superconductivity, the R&D manager may rise in power on funding decisions for new-product development; formal cross-country and cross-business teams will form to implement the technology and exploit a technological lead. When the technology is adopted by competitors, it will cease to be a source of competitive advantage and instead will be a normal source of competitive necessity. The R&D manager will then return to the champion position, below the business managers and equal to other functions, countries, and projects. Formal teams will be disbanded, but formal communication and informal coordination between the researchers will remain. With this reprioritization and reconfiguring, the company develops a capability to shift power to internal networks as technology competencies provide an advantage and until they are matched by others.

Changes can occur in any of a company's constituencies. Overcapacity can shift power to the customer; this book has detailed the increasing global presence and power of the customer, which are matched by internal changes in the power of customer networks and global account coordination. If the Internet explodes into a profitable channel, it may become the focus for another network. Should an industry's key raw material become scarce, the purchasing function and commodity teams would then escalate in importance until the scarcity subsides.

The task of leadership is to monitor these issues and see that the organizational networks respond to them; if the organization does not naturally change, leadership must intervene and remove the barriers. These changes need to be made at the speed at which the business changes. The globalization of the customer has been achieving critical mass slowly since the mid-1980s; companies strategically focusing on the global customer have been evolving their customer networks over this time period. The Internet phenomenon occurred much faster; it had been around for many years but became suddenly accessible to everyone with the appearance of the World Wide Web and Web browsers; many businesses are now trying to move at Internet speed.

The ability to shift power to and from networks is another reconfigurable feature of the capability. Matching the level of coordination across profit centers with the strategic priority of the network dimension is a dynamic challenge of organization design.

Reserve Capabilities

Another method for managing complexity is by creating networks for coordination but holding them in reserve. Some strategic dimensions may be important but do not require continuously active networks; for these, the relationships along a network can be created and maintained but used only when required. For example, a company could create a network for responding to a boycott of its U.S. consumer products.

The best analogy is the office-building crisis team, which takes charge in the case of an earthquake, a fire, a bomb, or whatever disaster may strike. All these people do their regular jobs, but they are a trained team; they know each other and know how to work together. This team can swing into action at the sound of an alarm, although most of the time this capability is held in reserve.

Winter and Steger (1998) note that stakeholder groups take actions against special projects, including the launch of new products, new scientific discoveries, new sites, and so on. If a company is beginning a project that may be controversial, Winter and Steger suggest creating two groups—one for the company response to the pressure groups and one to role-play how an active stakeholder group will react. The company-response group then prepares a plan to respond to the stakeholder group's input, conducts a simulation, and stays in contact until notified. This response group is a reserve capacity, giving the company the ability to manage a variety of stakeholders without the complexity of coordinating multiple networks simultaneously.

Coordination Technologies

Sanchez (1995) has stated that advances in software capabilities and modular designs constitute the new coordination technologies. These technologies allow a simplification of manager duties by embedding some of the complexity in the software and product design.

A number of experts have stated that software will absorb much of the coordination and communication now conducted by managers. Haeckel and Nolan (1993) suggest that executives will "manage-by-wire" in the same way pilots of high-performance aircraft "fly-by-wire" by flying a digital representation of the plane; if the pilot decides to fire and turn left, the computer system takes care of the coordination commands and details. Similarly, digital representations of products and markets and the use of simulations allow managers to leave the detailed communication to the software; managers can then focus on the remaining complexities.

The use of modularly designed products and object-oriented programs (their software equivalent) is certainly not new, but they have received new emphasis with digital convergence. For example, solutions can be managed more simply if standard interfaces are agreed on; with a server designed by the server division and a printer module designed by the printer division, communication between the divisions is simplified and reduced once the interface is chosen. In the broader sense, standard interfaces and common operating systems are essential in a world of connectivity. The digital revolution is both increasing complexity and providing tools to manage it.

Clean Interfaces

During discussions of complexity at IMD, one of the managers stated, "It's the interfaces that kill you." The successful management of complexity requires simple communications at the interfaces; when interfaces between dimensions are numerous and unclear and when the interests of the parties are not aligned, the amount of coordination and communication is overwhelming. An important organizational-design task is to simplify coordination across the interfaces.

Few, Clean Interfaces

The minimum number of interfaces is one per organizational unit participating in a particular dimension (the basic organizational unit may be a subsidiary or a business unit in a subsidiary). For the top-priority dimensions, the managing director may be the interface, but that person cannot play that role for all dimensions. Figure 11.5 shows the interfaces for an ABB business in a subsidiary. The managing director handles the two dimensions of the ABB matrix (the geography and the business unit), and then there are single, clear interfaces for the other three dimensions (global functions, global-customer accounts, and mega-projects). These interfaces provide the dimension coordinator—or a peer in another subsidiary—with a single clear point of contact for communications. This design minimizes the number of interfaces for communication between the basic units; the person serving as the interface coordinates between and within the units. For example, activities within a unit may require coordination with other units. Minimizing the number of interfaces simplifies between-unit coordination, as is shown graphically in Figure 11.6.

In creating a single interface to the rest of the corporation, the organizational designer has a choice for the basic unit. It can be a structure like that in Figure 11.5, where the roles are simple but the structure is complex. Or it can be a simple structure with complex jobs, as shown in Figure 11.6. In this design, the sales manager handles local sales and global accounts; the R&D manager handles local R&D and serves as the interface and local voice for company R&D and mega-projects; and the operations manager handles local manufacturing and purchasing and serves as the interface and local voice for corporate purchasing coordination. In both designs, the corporation has a single interface with the basic unit. If there is not much communication to and from the basic unit and the workload is small, the multiple-job model is probably most efficient; it is also appropriate for small subsidiaries and lesser-priority dimensions.

As the priority given to and the amount of global-accounts and mega-project work increase, it becomes efficient to create a full-time role for execution of the dimension. In addition to having one interface in each basic unit of a dimension, each basic unit must have an interface for each of *its* relevant dimensions. As seen

Figure 11.5. Interfaces for ABB's Five Dimensions: Complex-Structure Model.

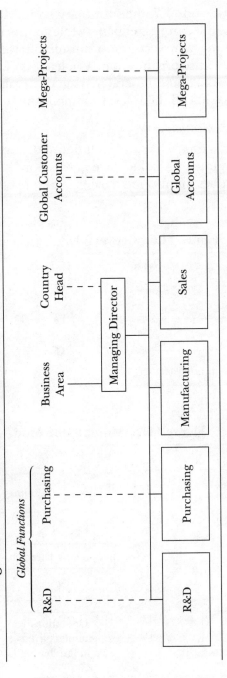

in Figures 11.5 and 11.7, the subsidiary business unit can become as complex as the parent company; while some subsidiaries will not have R&D or mega-projects, most subsidiaries will mirror the complexity of the entire organization. The leaders of these subsidiaries need to be broad-range general managers, capable of understanding and managing all the relevant dimensions.

Ease of Communication

Even if interfaces are few and well defined, communication and coordination must still take place across borders and businesses. Several practices mentioned earlier facilitate communication: if

Figure 11.6. Between-Unit Interfaces.

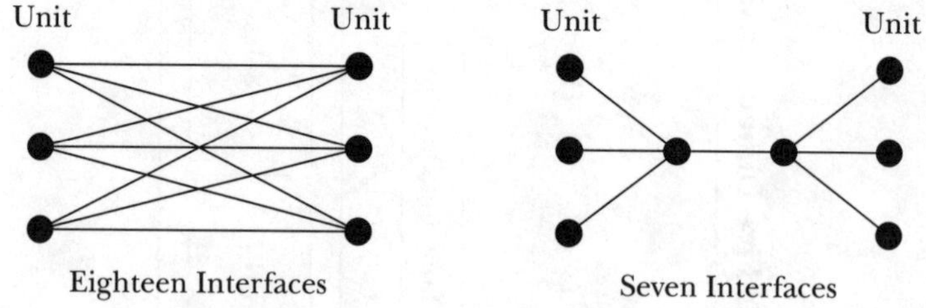

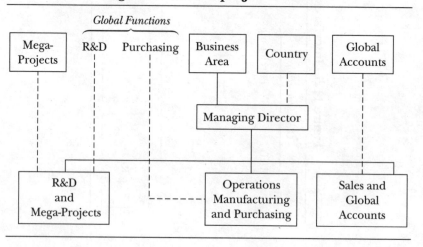

Figure 11.7. Multiple-Job Model.

there is extensive participation in strategy formulation, people share a common understanding of direction; if management builds networks and creates shared values around information sharing, people know one another and communicate; if there are common systems and common processes, people can communicate because of a shared language and common practices; and if products and services are created as modular designs with common, known standards, the need to communicate during design and manufacturing is greatly diminished. All these practices contribute to making the interfaces manageable.

It is also important to achieve some goal alignment for the parties on either side of the interface. For this to happen, the company needs an information system and a process for completing the spreadsheet shown in Figure 11.8. The first rows provide the standard business-geography two-dimensional planning matrix; into these boxes are entered the revenues, profits, and growth targets for businesses in the particular regions. The planning process that leads to the targets results in aligned goals and shared goods across businesses and regions (Galbraith, 1994, p. 97). For other

Figure 11.8. Spreadsheet for Multidimensional Planning.

	Europe	Japan	Middle East	North America	Other Regions
Business 1					
Business 2					
Business n					
Global Customers					
Mega-Projects					

strategically important dimensions, such as revenues from global customers and profits for mega-projects, other categories can be provided. Information collected about performance in these dimensions can be reported to all participants.

Firms will be discovering features to add to the eight described above. For the moment, however, these eight are the practices used by leading firms to increase their capacity for coordination in the face of complexity and change.

Building Capacity

It is natural to question whether companies have the capacity to manage all this complexity. Throughout this book, it has frequently been stated that companies have difficulty with the three dimensions of countries, businesses, and functions. Is it possible to manage four, five, or more dimensions? Is it necessary to manage all these sources of complexity? Let us address the second question first.

Several references have been made to authors who counsel that simple organizations are best for implementing strategy. In this book the position is that simple organizations are appropriate for simple businesses. Companies can simplify their businesses by avoiding complexities in the ways already described; simplification is always an option. But advancing technology and globalization are increasing the connections between businesses, countries, and markets, with an increase in requisite complexity. How many of these new opportunities and connections can a company forego? The new growth opportunities are at the convergence of industries, as with solutions; at the emergence of new channels, like the Internet; and with global customers who want suppliers to be present at all their locations. How long can a supplier avoid the requests of the global customer? Some organizations are seizing the opportunity to serve this customer and to pursue new opportunities in solutions, and so on. Will it be possible for them to coordinate across business units, countries, and functions without becoming consumed with internal conflicts?

This book is based on the belief that it is possible to develop the capacity to coordinate activities to capture the new opportunities. It should be noted that the criteria for success are relative: ABB does not have to effortlessly and perfectly execute mega-projects, just execute them better than Siemens and Mitsubishi; to serve Carrefour's interests, Procter & Gamble only has to execute better than Unilever and Colgate-Palmolive. What is feasible is determined by relative standards of success. However, the customer, satisfied with a little seamless service, will demand more.

The multinational can respond to requests for increased coordination by developing the capacity to serve *while* service is being provided. Each of the steps in Figure 11.4 represents more coordination for the customer *and* the further development of a coordination capability. For example, a move to formal communication among units serving global customers is likely to increase the global service received by the customer, and it will also begin educating employees in cross-border service. Another move up, to the step of formal customer teams, actively involves team members from different countries in preparing a customer plan and executing it; the customer receives more service, and the team members receive more experience in working across borders and serving a global customer. Management can observe which employees like to participate in cross-border teams and which are effective at working in customer teams. Those with both attributes can take future leadership positions in the customer network, while others learn that they do not like this type of work. Management can then expand the number of teams, the number of employees involved, and the number of customers served; more is learned about global customers and more capability is created. Next, a global-accounts coordinator is appointed, probably one of the early enthusiasts discovered during the first steps; this person then builds customer information systems, customer accounting systems, and customer planning processes. In this step-by-step process, the capacity to coordinate is developed while the firm is delivering increasing service to the customer. Management needs only to beware of the developmental consequences for people in the process of coordination and manage the situation accordingly.

The caveat for management is not to push coordination attempts ahead of capacity; internal conflicts will consume an organization when it tries to execute a coordination approach that far exceeds its current capability. In the 1980s, companies that moved from informal coordination to matrix were usually overwhelmed and concluded that matrix did not work. Moving up the steps and learning the lessons in a measured way keep the learning within the capabilities of the company and within the expectations of the customer. Clearly, the faster a company can learn, the faster it can build capacity—and the further ahead of the competition it can move.

Summary

This chapter has set the groundwork for managing the new complexity. It started with two premises: first, that the company needs an organization as complex as its business and, second, that it needs an organization that changes as fast as its business. Because both complexity and rate of change are increasing, organizations need to be adaptable along numerous dimensions; those with this capability have been labeled reconfigurable organizations or networks.

Management needs to think in terms of reconfigurable networks to capture today's opportunities. It then must recognize and prioritize the strategic dimensions, matching the level of priority with the requisite level of coordination. Management subsequently needs to reprioritize and rematch coordination levels at the rate at which the business moves; this reprioritization requires a management capability to make speedy strategic decisions and manage the natural conflict that accompanies priority setting. All these features support a reconfigurable organization and must be developed. In the next chapter, professional-services firms are presented as leaders in developing reconfigurable capabilities.

Chapter Twelve

Organizing to Serve the Global Customer

This chapter focuses on organizing to meet the challenge of the global customer, a challenge that arises from the customer's increased global presence and interest in fewer, closer supplier relationships. Professional-services companies have experienced this challenge for some time, and they provide a good example of the capability to reconfigure organizations. When a customer opportunity appears, these companies configure a cross-border team to bid on it and execute the project if they win. A different team is configured for another customer with another project. These firms have developed skills and tools for assembling and disassembling these global-customer teams.

The chapter illustrates the levels of coordination that were shown in Figure 11.4. The self-organizing step will be elaborated first, followed by formal teams, customer-coordinating units, and matrix options. Several companies, such as Citibank and IBM, have taken the next step and organized around the customer as the primary profit center. (These customer-product hybrid structures will be described in the next chapter).

Organizing Around the Customer

The reconfigurable organization is illustrated by professional-services companies and the field organizations of manufacturers such as computer companies. These companies face the same three-pronged challenge. First, the global customer may want one auditor, ad agency, bank, law firm, and systems integrator to serve every global subsidiary. Second, many customers want solutions, not just stand-alone products or services. Companies do not just borrow money today; they want financial solutions involving help with foreign exchange and management of interest-rate and exchange-rate risks. The third factor challenging these companies is the knowledge explosion underlying their professions. Each profession needs an increasing number of specialists for particular services—such as mergers and acquisitions (M&A), securitization, and derivatives—and must marshal these resources when a global customer wants a solution. Because each customer and each deal are different, the professional-services firm must be able to easily and quickly configure and reconfigure customer teams.

The challenge for these firms occurs because they have been organized geographically; even within large countries like the United States or the United Kingdom, they are structured around geographical offices, with the country typically the profit center. After geography, the second organizational priority pertains to the specialists, who are typically located in regional centers like New York and London and serve all offices; the specialist groups are also profit centers. Functions like finance, human resources, legal, information technology, and risk management are the third priority and the third dimension of the organization. The global customer then becomes the fourth dimension, requiring coordination across offices and specialty profit centers. That is the challenge.

The practices used by all the professional-services firms are quite similar. The variation that is observed is related to the size of the firm—both numbers of people and number of countries—and the size, duration, and complexity of the customer's opportunity. Some investment banks, for example, do deals that affect two or three countries and require the services of five or six people for two months; conversely, a consulting firm may employ 250 people on an enterprise software project costing $300 million and carried out for five years in over one hundred countries. Fast-moving investment banks use mostly self-organizing networks among specialists to form and re-form customer teams, whereas big consulting firms like Andersen Consulting have organized by customer groups—usually broad industry groupings—on a global basis and use regional resource pools of specialists (tapped by full-time scheduling units) to form customer teams. The practices of other firms are distributed along this size-and-complexity spectrum. To explain how these teams form and re-form, the smallest and least complex opportunity is studied here first; the chapter then moves along the spectrum to the large, long-duration, and complex projects.

Self-Organization

Self-organization is a process for rapidly assembling and disassembling customer teams across geographical and product profit centers; it is used by professional-services firms under the following circumstances:

1. The deals are mostly transaction-based rather than relationship-based.
2. The deals are short (usually several months).
3. The firms are small (one thousand to two thousand people).
4. The teams are not large or complex (typically four to six people, two to three countries, and three to five specialties).
5. Supporting processes are put into place.

All organizations use self-organizing processes to a greater or lesser degree; investment banks, with their fast-moving environments, are renowned for them (Eccles and Crane, 1988). A U.S. investment bank provides a good example. With approximately seventeen hundred employees, about 80 percent located in New York City, the bank has the structure shown in Figure 12.1. There are three main geographical offices, in New York City, London, and Hong Kong. Each office serves its region with product specialists, back-office administration, and relationship managers (RMs), who call on customers.

A deal typically starts with an RM. For example, the New York RM has a customer that wants a working-capital loan of $1 billion to finance the Christmas season in both North America and Europe. The RM contacts the syndicated-loan product manager (PM), as well as the customer's London RM. These three put together a deal team of four people: syndicated-loan specialists from both London and New York, a foreign-exchange specialist from London, and a derivatives specialist from New York; the syndicated-loan PM becomes the deal captain. The RMs usually step back and represent

Figure 12.1. Investment Bank Organized by Region and Specialists.

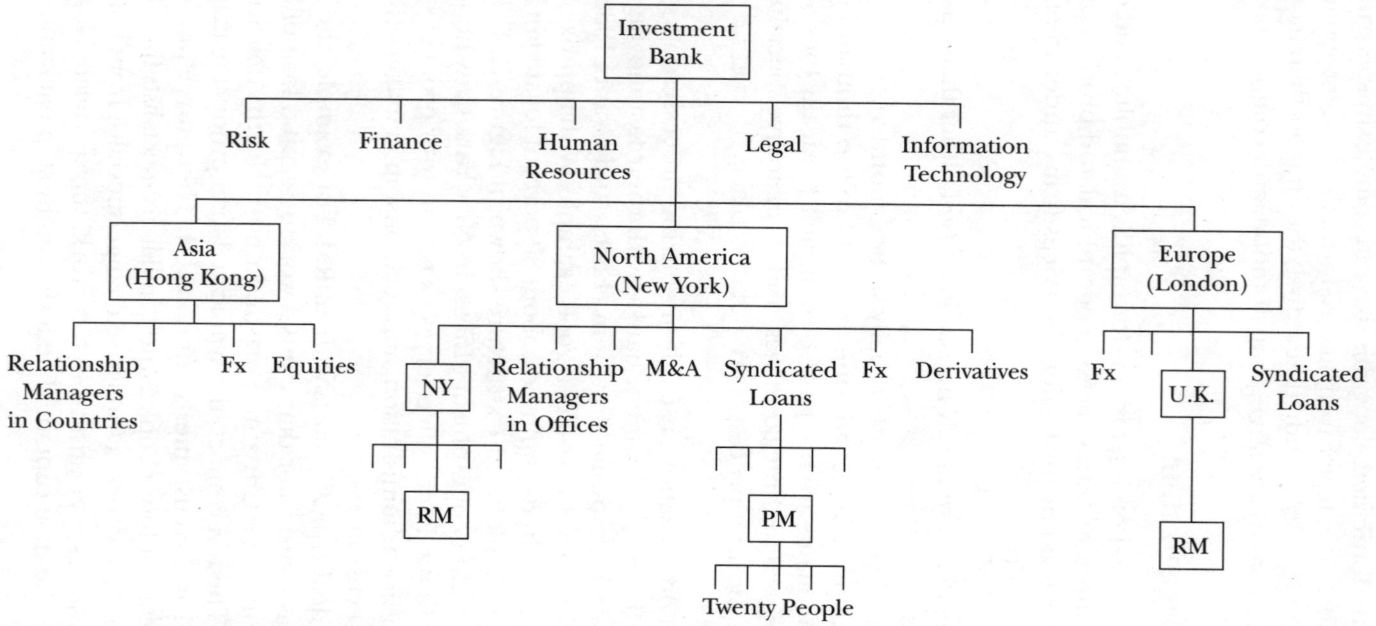

the customer's interests, although the London RM, if new to the account, might participate on the team in order to learn the account.

The team is put together by first-liners like the RM and PM, who try to find the people with the skill, experience, and chemistry necessary to serve the client and to work together. The PM with the biggest piece of the deal is typically the deal captain—in this case, from syndicated loans. (Another deal, for an acquisition, may find the PM from M&A as the captain.) The captain calls the first meeting, assigning duties and detailing the major milestones, and subsequently keeps the deal on track and maintains communication with the participants. A deal typically takes two months from first call to close. The first-line PMs typically have twenty to twenty-five people in their departments and do twenty to twenty-five deals per year, with ten ongoing at any specific time; it is a hectic and fast-paced environment.

Forming teams in this manner is usually referred to as a self-organizing process. The RMs and PMs, with their direct customer and product contact, have the best information for the organizing decisions. These decisions, however, can be made effectively and quickly only if they are supported with some organizational practices. The investment banks have evolved a number of practices to expedite the self-organizing process across profit centers with a minimum of friction.

Personal Networks

The self-organizing process, as mentioned in previous chapters, works best when the key players have extensive personal networks. At the investment banks, the key players are the RMs and the first-level PMs, who are vice presidents (at least) and have ten to twenty years experience with the bank. It is known around these banks that the best deal managers are those with the best networks; they have the experience, credibility, and knowledge of their organization necessary to put together a group of people who will work well with each other and the client. In a bank staffed with seventeen hundred people, probably eighty or ninety key people are in the self-organizing network. All these people may know one another; the bank usually brings this key group together at the annual meeting to build bonds and strengthen relationships, as well as to pursue the annual agenda.

Networking is regarded as central to the functioning of the self-organizing process, so human resource practices also support networking behavior. In addition to the appropriate financial and analytical skills, the employees selected by banks that function in a solutions environment also have the behavioral skills needed in a fast-moving deal-team environment. Big egos get in the way, and human resources seeks instead to attract those who can work well with different specialties, nationalities, levels, ages, and customer types. Those who prove that they have these abilities on actual deals are rewarded and promoted; these firms value networkers. One experienced banker said, "We push out those who are not networkers, who can't work in a matrix and want control—even if they are good revenue producers."

The networks are built primarily through the deals; the teamwork is both the cause and effect of the networks. After ten deals a year for fifteen years, a skilled banker is quite well connected. In this demanding environment, however, there is not much opportunity for rotational assignments across specialties; it is not feasible to move from M&A to derivatives, given the need for specialists with in-depth knowledge. Bankers can, however, move from specialties to being RMs and then back to being PMs. These moves are encouraged, as are moves within specialist groups across geographies (everyone in foreign exchange wants an opportunity in London, the world's largest foreign-exchange market). So there is some opportunity to use rotating assignments as network builders.

Reward Systems and Performance Measurement

The self-organizing process is further supported by incentive systems that reward cooperation across the multiple profit centers. Allocating revenues, profits, and credit to the P&L centers is always an issue when multiple profit centers work together on a deal, and investment banks have experimented with a number of profit-measurement and allocation schemes. They additionally use a number of other measures, like customer satisfaction, to provide a total assessment of employee and department performance.

The current practice for dividing revenues and credit is best described with a quote from a banker: "If there is a clear and clean distinction in the contributions from different departments, we make the distinction. If the contributions are fuzzy, we count the revenues for both or all groups." The contributions of the RMs and the PM, as in the previous example, are often joint efforts, so the RMs and the syndicated-loan PM will all get credit for the $1 billion loan. The contribution from the foreign-exchange group, however, may be a standard fee for advice and the transaction. Similarly, a derivative may be a standard hedge on interest-rate and exchange-rate risk, and the firm may use a standard price for the transaction. The customer may also want to see the unbundled deal and is probably aware of the market prices. The foreign-exchange and derivative groups receive a market-based revenue credit for clear contributions, and most banks do not put much effort into allocations across RMs and PMs. What is considered most important is to do the deal for the customer and to get the fees for the bank. Any effort given to internal allocation of profits is thought to create no value for the customer, send the wrong message to bank employees, and possibly create animosity if seen as unfair. The typical practice is thus to double- or triple-count the revenues unless the contributions are clear.

The quantitative profit and revenue aspects are only part of the performance-measurement system. Customer satisfaction is probably the most important measure, with customers surveyed by professional survey firms or contacted directly by bank senior managers. The customer may also be interested in the bank's evaluation of the customer deal team, in which case evaluations are exchanged.

A team debriefing following the deal closing is considered a good way to interpret customer feedback and provide peer reviews. Because the deal environment is so fast-paced, however, most banks fail to take the time. For longer-term projects at banks and other professional-services firms, though, the time is taken; they are also likely to convene a group when a deal is lost and record the lessons learned. A senior partner may also debrief the team members and the customer following a deal; senior managers spend a good deal of time evaluating performance. The idea is to get a complete picture of performance, including customer perception and teamwork, not just revenue and profit. One bank uses internal surveys of the departments to discover how well they are working together; such peer ratings are an important part of the evaluation process. Negative relations between departments are taken seriously, and the leaders of these groups are usually given improvement targets as a result.

Flexible profit- and revenue-accounting systems and performance-evaluation practices are intended to support a self-organizing process, with all the factors then combined into a total assessment of the individuals and departments. The assessments become the basis for bonuses, and bonuses account for 80 to 90 percent of an individual's annual earnings. Needless to say, the effort devoted to performance is substantial and is taken seriously.

Leadership

The behavior of the bank's leadership plays an important role in building and reinforcing the self-organizing capability. The natural tendency in a multiprofit center is to fragment and focus on one's own bottom line; leadership must reinforce cooperation constantly and consistently to overcome this tendency. Leaders reinforce cooperation through how they spend their own time and how they distribute the bonuses. Employees become aware if peer and customer ratings are consistently being weighed and evaluated; team players need to be rewarded and offenders punished, with repeat offenders asked to leave. These actions can build significant value; in order to create integrated solutions for global customers, banks need full cooperation between product departments and relationship offices. Leader behavior builds this integration by valuing and rewarding networkers and cooperation and by removing any obstacles to effective integration.

All professional-services firms use self-organizing processes to a greater or lesser extent, and some have developed additional practices to enhance the ease and effectiveness of forming teams. For example, consulting firms make particularly effective use of their electronic networks and databases, with "electronic yellow pages" to locate skills, languages, recent experiences, availability, and unique attributes of possible team members. Other companies are building the information and knowledge bases of key organizers like the RMs and PMs; the more thorough the understanding of the firm and customer strategies, the more intelligently the RM can self-organize teams.

One RM from a computer company's field organization deduced that his power emanated from his ability to create new business for the profit centers, so he tried to find customer opportunities attractive to the product specialties. Through studying their strategies, he discerned the attractive pieces of businesses, which he then presented to the product lines. With the opportunities that would be viewed as marginal, the RM tried to unbundle a solution, giving the internal product line the right of first refusal and then going to an outside partner as needed so the customer would still be served. After securing some good business for a product specialty, he could then usually ask for its support on an opportunity it deemed marginal but that was a high priority for a customer. This efficient maneuvering on the part of the RM was possible because of his knowledge of the customer's and the firm's businesses and strategies.

The best understanding of a firm's business and strategy comes from participating in strategy formulation. Some companies are using extensive employee participation in the strategy-formulation process. EDS dedicated a core group of 150 people for one year to rethink the company's strategy, with 2,500 participating in the process overall; Nokia had 250 managers work quarter-time for six months on company strategy. These employees have a thorough understanding of the strategy because they created it and taught it to others.

Two techniques are evolving that permit this extensive involvement and also speed up the time frame. The first is the large-scale meeting, which involves fifty to five hundred people in one to three days of intensive strategy sessions (Wall and Wall, 1995). With the skillful use of a sequence of plenary and breakout sessions, the meetings can create strategies and an understanding of the logic of the strategies. The second technique is the use of electronic networks. British Petroleum held a strategy meeting off-site for its top seventy people, with employees sitting at the company's twenty thousand PCs also invited to attend electronically. Thousands from around the world had access to the presentation slides and live audio and could send in comments and questions that were fed to the discussion leaders. The response was overwhelmingly positive. According to the strategic-planning head, "We'll never do a conventional meeting again." The next sessions will feature a live video feed.

The written strategies are also being placed on the intranets, with strategic planners conducting electronic discussion groups around them. Employees from the field send in comments, questions, and experiences, and special issues are singled out for comment and discussion. Performance information is then tracked to see how well the strategies are being executed. The trend is to inform increasing numbers of people about and involve them in the decision making about a company's strategy and performance; these employees provide key inputs to those who make the organizing decisions.

Self-organizing is an important capability, present in all professional-services firms. But companies involved in large and complex projects complement it with formal coordination mechanisms. In the next section, the organization of firms that use formal teams are described.

Global-Customer Teams

Permanent customer teams are put into place when the service is relationship-based and the size of the professional-services firm and its projects is large. The big audit firms are a good example. The audit has changed from a six-week checkup to a continuous relationship; a customer may want one auditor to serve it in all thirty-seven countries where it requires an audit. Fulfilling this request requires staffing each country with a small audit team and a partner-in-charge, with all thirty-seven partners-in-charge forming the global audit team. The partner-in-charge from the customer's home country serves as the global team leader. The audit relationship is more complex than investment banking deals and requires a more formal coordination mechanism to manage.

The audit-firm structure for a large country is shown in Figure 12.2; audit firms have the same type of structure as the other professional-services firms with a few variations. Except for Arthur Andersen (which is one global partnership and not disadvantaged by country structures) audit firms have a small international office overseeing the independently owned country partnerships, with each country further divided into audit, tax, and consulting businesses. In large countries, the audit and tax practices are

Figure 12.2. Global Audit Firm.

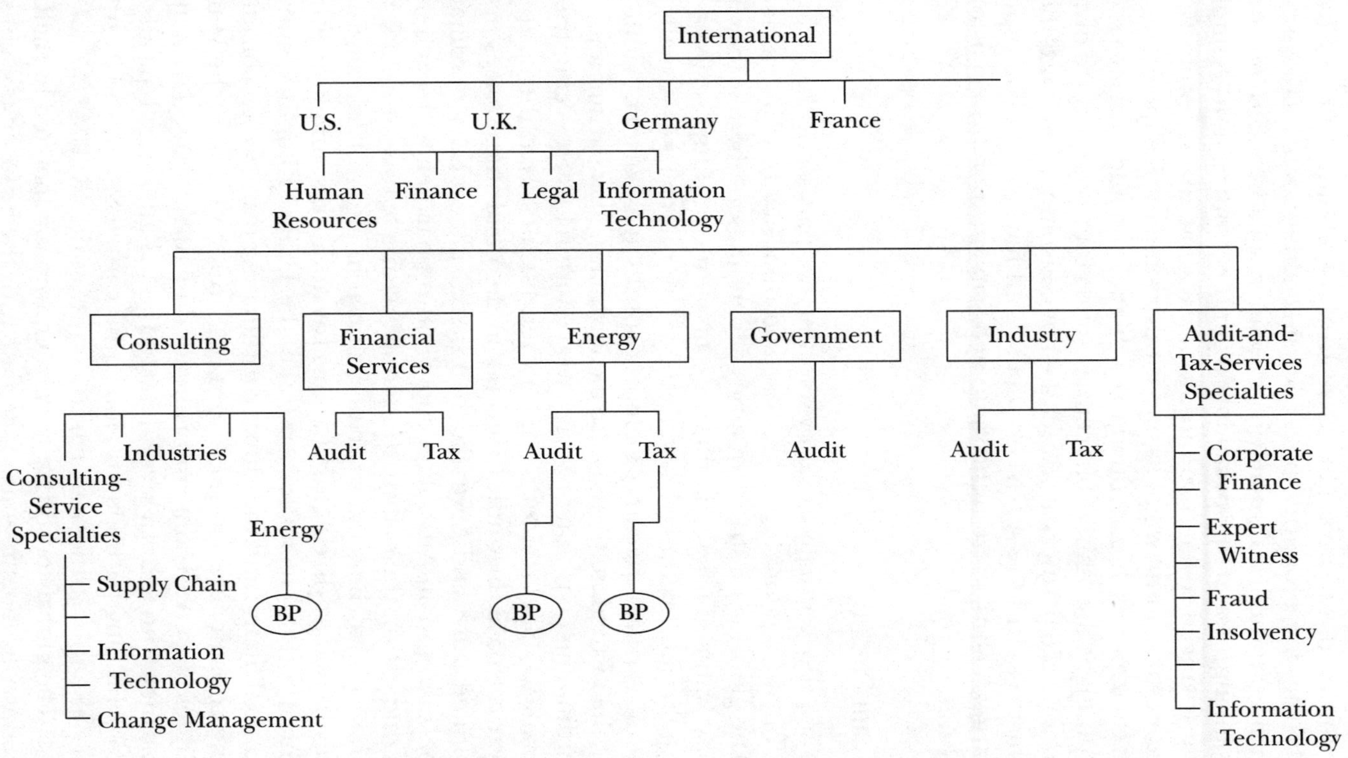

combined into broad industry groupings. In these cases, all in-dustries are supported by service specialties, such as corporate fi-nance (audit firms are moving into financial advice and investment banking), fraud for special investigations, information technology for financial systems, and insolvency for bankruptcy projects; the consulting business has its own industry and service specialties and is thus more self-contained than the tax and audit practices. The country is the main profit center—and country profits are divided among the partners at year end—but consulting, audit, tax, the in-dustries, and the service specialties all have revenue and profit targets. Thus, there is the same necessity for mobilizing customer teams.

Team Creation

The process usually works by selecting the partner-in-charge in the United Kingdom for a U.K.-based account like British Petroleum. The global-team structure varies depending on whether the client also wants to use the audit firm's tax and consulting services. If a total relationship is desired, the partner-in-charge—usually the audit partner—becomes a global coordinating partner. Within the United Kingdom there is also a coordinating tax partner and a co-ordinating consulting partner, who coordinate across countries to manage the customer team for their businesses. If the customer wants to use the audit firm's tax and consulting services in the United States and Australia, then there will be a U.S. coordinating partner and an Australian coordinating partner, with each man-aging within the country but coordinating across audit, tax, and consulting. The team structure, shown in Figure 12.3, consists of seven teams: three global teams for audit, tax, and consulting; three country teams for Australia, the United Kingdom, and the United States; and the global coordinating team, which consists of the coordinating partners for tax, audit, consulting, the United States, and Australia, and is headed by the global coordinating partner, who wears a second hat as the U.K. partner. Typically the coordinating partners for global, the United States, and Australia are also the partners-in-charge for the audit.

The global coordinating partner, who is appointed by the U.K. country leadership, must negotiate with the heads of tax, consult-ing, and the countries to appoint the other coordinating partners

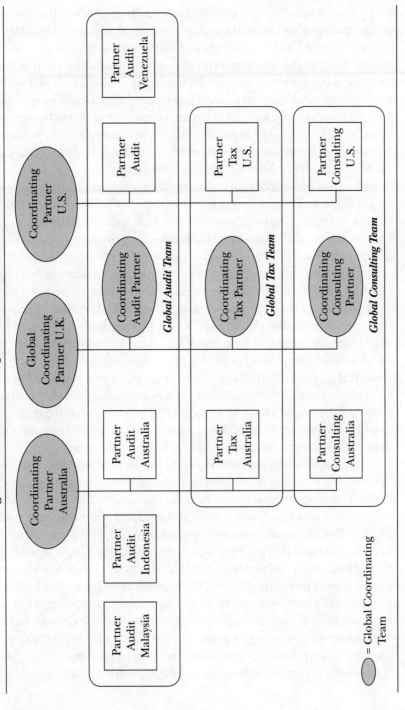

Figure 12.3. Team Complex for a Global Customer.

and partners-in-charge. During this staffing process the coordinating partner works in the same manner as the RMs and PMs in an investment bank, although staffing is a larger, though less frequent, task for the auditor. Typically, the coordinating partners use their networks, as well as the electronic databases, to learn whom to request. Candidates are listed by country, industry, and specialty, with résumés listing special skills and experience. A customer may have specific wishes—employees skilled in electronic-interchange, Internet transactions, or derivatives, for example—but the assignment must still go through the country heads.

The process works well in many cases, often inspiring reciprocity among countries; when the U.S. partnership has as many global clients in the United Kingdom as the U.K. partnership has in the United States, the attitude is "I will take care of your global clients, and you take care of mine." The strongest regulating factor, however, is the customer, who does not care how a partnership is organized as long as it provides seamless service across all profit centers (any problems that may occur are handled by the vice chairman from the international office on a case-by-case basis). The force of the customer comes to bear through annual customer-satisfaction surveys of the top two hundred accounts. The overall results—reported by country, industry, and specialty—are reviewed at the annual partners' meetings, and the coordinating partners' profit share is influenced more by customer satisfaction (future revenue) than by current revenue. Thus, the voice of the customer is the main driving force behind cross-border coordination.

In countries where there is no reciprocity or in emerging markets, where business is largely local, the staffing process can be difficult. The biggest issues arise in countries where the multinational customer has a small presence; the local partnership views this global client as low-revenue, low-margin, and overly demanding. Certain countries with a shortage of talent prefer not to service the foreign-owned multinational client at all; local clients are easier to work for and more profitable. The coordinating partner must negotiate with these country leaders to get a partner assigned to the multinational customer's account. It may be quite an effort, but coordinating partners are chosen, in part, for their ability to negotiate, exchange favors, and know which networks to use. The coordinating partner may have to negotiate with country heads all over again if the client objects to certain partners in certain countries. If no agreement can be reached, the coordinating partner may send an expatriate to serve as partner-in-charge in that country. Expatriates, however, are usually expensive, and there is then a negotiation about who covers the cost.

Negotiations are necessary to determine the price of the audit, the schedule, the services to be included, and the quality standards. There are also frequent asymmetries in costs and revenues. For example, the U.K. partnership may work hard to win an audit that has been tendered by a U.K. multinational. However, after winning the audit the U.K. partner may find that most of the next year's work will be done in the client's Canadian and Australian subsidiaries; the work was done and the costs were incurred in the United Kingdom, but the revenues will accrue to the partnerships in Canada and Australia. Although the partner can negotiate for some credit, the outcome is not automatic. When this process occurs in seventeen or eighteen countries, life becomes nonstop negotiation for the coordinating partner.

The fallback option is to use the aforementioned expatriates, who can usually be found by search engines seeking specific skills and availability. Some firms have an administrator who looks after staffing and supports the coordinating partners. The assignments for expatriates can vary from a few months to several years. Citibank uses a mobile group called the "international staff"; they sign on to travel the world and are paid in dollars. These third-country nationals are a flexible pool of talent that can move with the client deals. The last resort for the coordinating partner is to use people from the home country. With a lot of negotiation, the global-customer teams get staffed; all the firms are working to increase the speed and effectiveness of their formation.

Electronic Networks

Once the global teams are formed, electronic networks play an increasingly large role in coordinating their work. Various groupware systems are becoming an important source of coordination among partners on global-customer teams and are becoming important tools for building the teams, generating the proposals, and executing the project on a day-to-day basis.

Most firms have global standardization on PCs, laptops, and software. In one firm the intranet system is run by a chief knowledge officer; a staff of two hundred supports a system of three knowledge centers in North America, Europe, and Asia, and portfolios, which are designed at the centers and are standard throughout the world, correspond to the industry groups, specialty service areas, and multinational clients. Each portfolio has a partner who serves as the chief knowledge officer for the subject; this partner becomes responsible for the content and databases. In each country, a partner serves as the chief knowledge officer, usually with a couple of administrative assistants who train the partners in the use of the system and maintain the country's inputs. These country partners' task is to solicit content and encourage use of the system.

Once a global team has been created, the members can communicate and coordinate via the intranet system; standardized formats allow the team to work remotely and generate a proposal. They can also search the portfolios for supporting information. One informative portfolio contains a selection of winning proposals; the chief knowledge officers keep track of wins and losses, entering the wins (as well as the lessons learned from the losses) into the databases. There are also records of various tools that have led to client satisfaction; they provide information on how to contact the creator of the tool and discussions by others who have used, modified, and improved the tool under various circumstances (along with their contact information).

The system also supports the audit once the proposal has been accepted. Each client is listed within the multinational-client portfolio, with its organization charts, officers, detailed information about its business, and a listing of current work being done for the client in addition to the audit. The audit team has a secure-access account for the audit, which lists all the partners and teams working on the effort. The objective is to have each team report its progress and issues at the end of each day; these entries are then available to everyone, particularly the coordinating partner. Based on agreed-on criteria, a section for "hot items" is the auditor's early-warning system.

The hot-items system can be a real advantage for an auditor, but it must be handled properly because the auditor's information system works faster than the client's; the coordinating partner often has information that the client's CFO does not have or may never have. How, then, should hot-item issues be handled? The team and the client usually try to establish criteria for situations that warrant notifying the CFO, the subsidiary, and the audit committee of the board. For these reasons, the audit today is an ongoing relationship, and the coordinating partners—in constant contact with the companies dealing with hot items—are chosen for their relationship skills.

Hierarchical Decisions

The (electronically assisted) self-organizing process works well as long as projects are sufficiently staffed; today, there are shortages of talent. Even when overall staffing levels are adequate, there are still shortages of particular kinds of talent. (As stated above, audit firms need partners with relationship skills, which are in too short supply.) The professional-services firms are thus employing hierarchical decision processes to get a total view of the firm when allocating these limited resources.

One audit firm has introduced a central staffing board for global accounts that have tendered their audit. About twenty-five tenders per year merit centralized staffing and delegation of a partner-in-charge. These tenders, which are public statements about the current auditor and a big opportunity for the others, motivate the firm to consider the entire opportunity set and match it against employable resources; the discussions are delicate yet rich. An audit today is sold on the chemistry between the partner and the client: some clients are looking for a partner with "stomach" who will "blow the whistle" early on a problem; others want a diplomat who can handle the tension between the CFO and the audit committee of the board. Thus those making the formal decision consider information about personality, chemistry, competence, and experience, as well as the prospective partner-in-charge's interests and desires. They ask questions like "Can we move the partner from the current assignment, where the client is very happy?" After achieving a complete perspective of the firm's total opportunities and resources, a hierarchical decision process among a small group of senior partners can then allocate the limited resources and resolve any conflicts in a timely manner.

The firm's consulting arm employs ad hoc groups for allocating talent across borders on high-priority projects. The groups are ad hoc because the resource that is in short supply is subject to change; the resource is not just talent, but particular types of talent. The consulting arms of the Big Five auditing firms are all limited by the availability of SAP programmers; European systems integrators are limited by the availability of people who can do secure transactions on the Internet; all European banks are interested in implementing Internet-based systems, but when talent is scarce, they want to see the names of the people who will work on their project before signing a contract. European systems integrators want to get a group together to match limited resources to customer opportunities; they want a total view of the firm, information about resources, knowledge of customer applications, and the power to decide—all in a single group. These consulting operations also employ this hierarchical decision process to decide on priorities in a time frame that fits the cycles of the business; this hierarchy is a court of appeals in which priority decisions can be quickly escalated and made. As such, it is not a rigid hierarchy but a flexible, hierarchical decision process.

When projects get long, cover a large number of countries, and are staffed with dozens of people for a year or more, the customer teams become formal and utilize the tools and processes described above. In addition, some companies are developing coordinating units to create systems that make cross-border negotiations and coordination less onerous.

Global-Accounts Coordinators

The next step taken by professional-services firms focusing on the global customer is to shift additional power to the customer dimension by creating a coordinating unit for global-customer accounts. This unit, although it has a coordinating role with no formal authority, does have several important features that make the customer dimension more powerful relative to the country and product dimensions. They provide a voice for the customer dimension, they build customer information systems, and they build planning processes. The presence of a senior partner in the leadership gives the customer dimension a voice to promote the cause; this voice helps to create systems that make the negotiating task of coordinating partners easier.

The next task of the coordinator is to build and implement the firm's system for acquiring customer information. The firm's accounting systems support the profit centers, which are country- and product-specialty-based. In order for coordinating partners to know the total customer revenue and to set revenue targets, firms need the ability to account for revenue and profit by customer; partners on the global-customer teams can then make revenue commitments to each other. With this system in place, the coordinating partner can take responsibility for the global revenue and profits of the customer and get credit for increasing them, in addition to seeing which are the most valuable customers. The system gives firmwide visibility of the global customer.

The next task of the coordinator is to build a customer-focused planning process whereby the global teams can use the customer information system to generate a strategy and a plan for each global account. The global-account coordinator sets the guidelines and the steps for the process, so that the system is standardized across countries. The partners on each team then participate in the planning process, from which several benefits result. For one, the product specialties get a forecast of likely demands for their services and can add or take away staff accordingly. In addition, the planning effort builds an important link between the customer team, which is made up of RMs from around the world, and the product-specialty units. Each customer team establishes a contact person in each product-specialty group; there may be enough customer activity to dedicate a product specialist to a team, while some specialists may be dedicated to a group of customer teams for an industry. These contact persons will be mobilized when a customer opportunity appears and will also recruit additional people from the specialty when they are needed.

As well as being an important bridge-building process between RMs and PMs, the planning process is a team-building process for the global team, which gets to know the customer and each other. Even if the plan changes, the team is educated and prepared for making changes. The process also allows leadership to look at all the global accounts at one time. They can set priorities based on the profitability, growth prospects, learning opportunities, and other characteristics of the customers; when opportunities arise, the priorities can be used for assigning partners and talent. Finally, the plans can be set across countries and across customers, allowing goals to be set by country managers for serving local clients as well as global clients. Country heads can then be held accountable for serving the global clients, and the goals and interests of the co-ordinating partner and the country head can be aligned based on common goals and plans.

At this point in their development many professional-services firms strategically focus on global accounts rather than local ac-counts. The coordinating role is then expanded, along with the number of global accounts. They are usually grouped into cus-tomer segments similar to broad industry groups. Industry-segment leaders are appointed, and they participate in setting planning guidelines and customer priorities. The account manager for global customers is often given the power to set prices across coun-tries for some global accounts. This authority and having addi-tional people assigned to industries shifts power to serve the global customer.

Thus, the global coordinating role and the supporting systems reduce the negotiating burden and increase the power base of the coordinating partners, who must bargain with country managers and heads of the product specialties. In some countries, though, professional-services firms have taken the next step and created dedicated staff for the global customer.

Matrix Structure

In order to deliver seamless service to the global customer, some firms have created units dedicated to that customer within certain countries. These are often emerging-market countries with talent shortages and profitable local customers. The country organization is divided into units for the local customers and for the global ac-counts; an industry with a lot of business within the country may even have its own unit. The structure is shown in Figure 12.4. The countries are divided into units for local accounts, global oil and gas accounts, and other global accounts. These global-accounts units re-port to both the country head and the global-accounts coordinator for the region. Also shown in the figure are the product-specialty

Figure 12.4. Global-Accounts and Country Matrix.

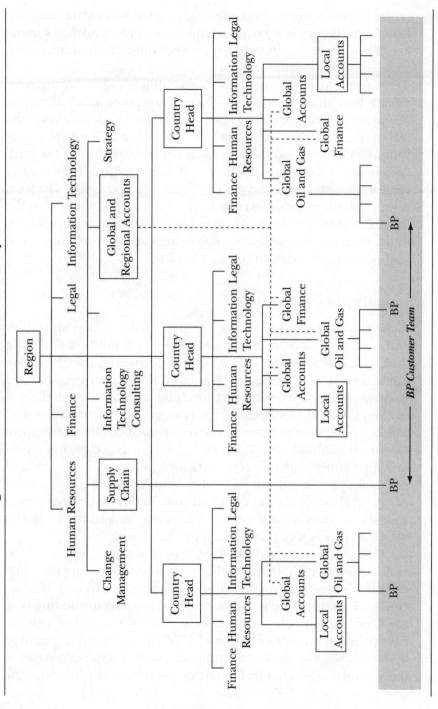

units for the region and the regional functions. A partial team for British Petroleum is shown working across the countries; a member of the supply-chain specialty is also a full-time member of this global-customer team.

In some firms, the country partnership is owned by the partners. When this is the case, the international company often creates with the local partners a joint venture dedicated to serving the global client. In one case, a Big Five firm created a joint venture in Indonesia to serve global clients; the venture was run by five partners from Australia and staffed with a few dedicated locals and some expatriates from the global clients' home country. The joint venture also bought services from the local partnership to handle fluctuations in workloads. In such cases, the global-accounts units in the countries are able to establish increased control over local staffing to serve the needs of the global client.

Organization by Customer

Some firms—such as Citibank's commercial banking unit, IBM, and Andersen Consulting—have taken the final step: changing their structure to support a strategy that focuses on the global customer. In terms of the steps in Figure 11.4, they have established a customer-focused line organization. The country units dedicated to the global customer now report to global-customer groups, which are the profit centers; in actuality, each customer is a profit center. At Citibank, the 1,703 global accounts are grouped into broadly defined industry segments such as financial services and consumer products. In developed countries, the country manager is not a P&L manager but rather an ambassador; in emerging markets, the country units service the local clients, and the global industry segments serve the global clients.

IBM provides a good example of how to organize around the global customer. In the early 1990s, IBM Europe was focused first on countries, second on service specialties, and third on global accounts. This priority changed when IBM lost an outsourcing contract from a valuable long-term customer who wanted a single vendor in all countries; some of IBM's country managers had opted out because the opportunity was small and not profitable in their country. The contract went to a competitor who was organized by industry instead of countries. IBM then reorganized its field organization by industry, grouping one thousand chosen customers into these industry segments. The service specialties, such as equipment maintenance, IBM credit, consulting, outsourcing, and software, had been profit centers within the countries; these units were placed into European regional profit centers. With no country P&Ls for these units, the employees stayed in their countries but were now available for pan-European assignments. These changes reduced country influence, emphasized the global customer, and made the specialties flexible for customer assignments on a regional basis.

Another major change was the implementation of the customer relationship-management process (CRM). After several attempts at improvement, the entire process was redesigned and placed on the company's value-added network. It was piloted in 1994 and made global in 1995, and there was a companywide one-week training program in 1996. The result is a common worldwide process for managing customers and customer opportunities.

The annual CRM process begins with plans for the one thousand global customers. Each customer has a global-accounts manager, local account managers, and sales representatives in countries with sufficient volume to justify the staffing. Specialists from the services are assigned to accounts when volumes justify the dedication. The customers receive the names of all those working on their team. These annual customer plans are accumulated into sectors, such as banking, and then into industries, like financial services. The industries then set quotas for the appropriate teams of people. (Team quotas are a big change from past practice.) The industries additionally assign priorities to accounts based on revenue from the account, profitability, the customer's expected growth, and share of customer spending. Each customer is also assigned an executive from IBM's top two hundred; the industry leadership is particularly active in dealing with select priority accounts.

The opportunity-management system, which is activated when a salesperson identifies an opportunity, is a major part of the CRM. All opportunities are identified and ranked through a series of filters, with each opportunity assigned an owner. Small opportunities are assigned to the local account manager; large and top-priority opportunities to one of the top two hundred executives, who serves as owner. The owner and the customer-account manager marshal a team from regional-service units, working through the contact person from the service unit assigned to the customer team. Top-priority projects may require pulling people off current assignments; it is important to get the right people to work on the large opportunities. These opportunities are usually decided at the customer's CEO level, and therefore IBM must have salespeople who can work with the customer's CEO.

After about two years, everyone at IBM was using the system. All functions—owners, staffing, quotas, opportunities being proposed and worked on, and so forth—are now visible. IBM aspires to achieve "integrated speed" in front of the customer, assembling and disassembling teams for customer opportunities with team members from different countries and different specialties. The CRM process is key to holding them together; all sixty to seventy team members—wherever they are located—have access to the same data, communications, and plans.

In order to quickly mobilize talent for frequent projects and long projects, firms such as Citibank, IBM, and Andersen Consulting have formed customer groups as the primary profit center, with countries and specialties becoming the secondary profit centers in support of the customer. These firms are discussed in detail in the next chapter.

Summary

This chapter has described how professional-services firms have organized to serve the global customer. Originally, these firms were organized first by country and then by service-specialty profit centers; their experience should be directly relatable to other firms organized by country and business unit. Some professional-services firms, like investment banks, were able to use self-organizing processes across countries and specialties. These deals usually lasted a few months and required few people. Formal structures were required by companies serving customers in a large number of countries. The audit firms' tax practices employ global teams for a customer; tax is still a local country business, but there are opportunities for cross-border arbitrage and problem solving, and the teams pursue these opportunities. The audit practice usually employs the next step, that of using global-accounts coordinators and industry specialization in addition to account teams. These firms' consulting arms usually go the farthest in pursuing integration across countries for the global customer; consulting uses joint ventures, matrix, and customer profit centers in order to serve the global client. It is likely that other firms will move along this progression for certain customers and for their different businesses; some have already moved to customer structures and created front-back models. This form is the subject of the next chapter.

Chapter Thirteen

The Front-Back
Hybrid Organization

The customer-focused structures created by Citibank and IBM provide two line organizations: one focused on the customer (the front end) and a second focused on products (the back end). Several other types of companies are also adopting this type of organization; the objective in all cases is to achieve a customer focus and responsiveness concurrent with global-scale economies. When the front end is based on countries, the objective is to achieve the elusive global-local combination, which results from solving the management challenge of effectively linking the customer front with the product back. This hybrid front-back structure has arisen in many other contexts as well (see Galbraith, 1993, 1995, 1998); this type of structure was originally described in Corey and Starr (1970) but has been undeveloped since then.

The first section of the chapter describes this type of hybrid organization, distinguishing it from other forms of organization such as the matrix. Next, the forces impelling companies to choose this form of organization are identified. The final section addresses the key issues of coordinating the front and back portions of the organization.

The Front-Back Structure

The front-back model is a type of dual structure in which both halves are multifunctional units. The front half, which is organized around the customer, can be a geographical or country structure, or it can be focused on some market-segmentation scheme like

Figure 13.1. Front-Back Hybrid Structure.

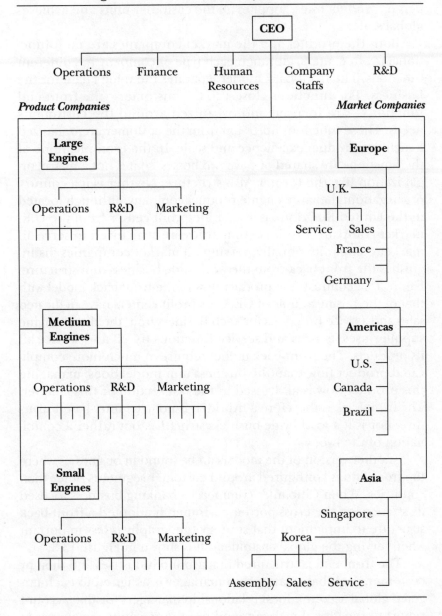

industries. The back half, which is usually organized around products or product lines, supplies all the customer units and achieves global scale.

Both the product and the market companies are multifunctional profit centers, although each type of company has different functions. The front-back model separates the value chain for the business. The functions closest to the customer—the front-end functions—are focused and organized around the customer's needs. Those functions upstream from the customer are organized to achieve product excellence and scale. In the example, none of the functions are shared or have two bosses, so it is not a matrix organization like the former ABB structure. Neither is it a country organization; the large-engine product company, although located in the United Kingdom, is a separate profit center from the U.K. market company. Product companies are structured to serve all market companies equally; serving all market companies distinguishes the front-back from the worldwide-business-unit structure. Figure 13.2 contrasts the product flow of the front-back model with that of the business units of GE. GE's profit centers have dedicated sales and service functions for each business unit; the diesel-engine supplier uses its sales and service functions to sell and service all its products. The front-back model requires a much more complicated product flow than the business-unit model does; managing this product flow is addressed in the last section of this chapter. The front-back is therefore a hybrid; it is not a country-based structure, nor is it a worldwide-business structure, but rather a combination of the two.

Another version of the model can be found in businesses where the front end is configured around customer segments other than countries. When Citibank's commercial-banking business focused its strategy on the cross-border customer, it adopted a front-back structure to implement that strategy (geography is less important when serving the global customer). It is shown in Figure 13.3.

The front end is structured first around industries and then by customer. A global relationship manager is assigned to each targeted global account; local relationship managers for that account report to the global manager and not to the country manager at their location. (Country managers have become site managers in

Figure 13.2. Front-Back Model Compared with Business Units.

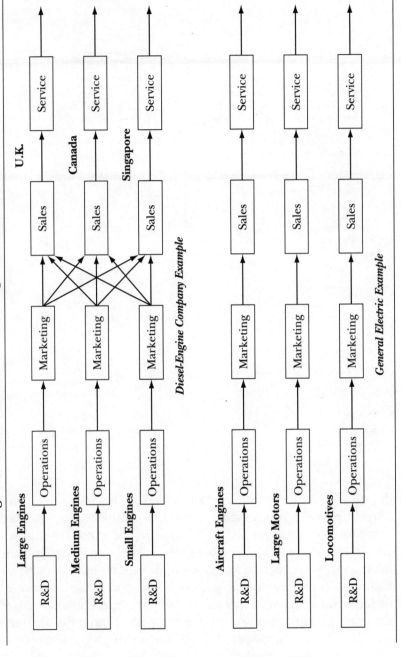

Diesel-Engine Company Example

General Electric Example

Figure 13.3. Global Products and Global Customers.

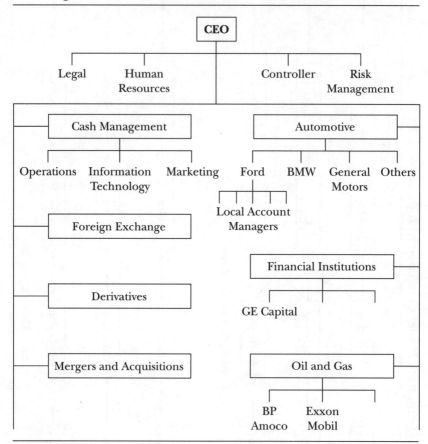

developed countries with no P&L responsibility.) The front end is therefore a cross-border customer-relationship structure, with the relationship managers selling all the products that the customer needs on a global basis. The back end is made up of profit centers producing global products like cash management and foreign exchange—activities that require product expertise and scale in order to be effective. They are usually organized around a product-management function that works with the relationship manager to sell their product. An operations function processes all transactions, and a technology activity keeps hardware and software current. Citibank has defined its strategy as serving the global customer with global products. To implement this strategy, it has divided its activities into relationship and product units, with each then organized to best execute its unique mission. The different missions are best executed by a front-back structure.

Some form of matrix is usually employed to tie the front and the back together; the diesel-engine supplier illustrates the concept. In the 1980s diesel engines began to be used to supply electric power, and some towns and factories found that they could use a smaller power plant than those supplied by power-generation companies like ABB (the diesel-engine company whose organization is shown in Figure 13.1 focused on this power market). A diesel-engine supplier could get an engine running and delivering power more quickly than a power-generation company could by making product modifications so that its engines could more efficiently generate electricity; fully half the current diesel-engine sales are to the power market (the remainder are for ship propulsion). Because the purchasers of power engines want only an electrical source and not all the headaches of running a power plant, the engine supplier started a service business to operate power plants for cities and factories, as well as to provide engine maintenance. The resulting organization is shown in Figure 13.4.

The diesel engine supplier has added two new businesses—power and service—to what was the lone marine-engine business. These global businesses link the product companies and the market companies, through shared activities that form a matrix organization. For example, sales in the market companies are now specialized and divided into the marine market, the power market, and the service market. The marine-sales unit in a country is shared and reports to the marine business manager and the country manager. In the product companies, product development, some manufacturing, and product marketing are now organized by power, service, and marine; within the product companies, there is sufficient volume to allow a business specialization. Purchasing and some component manufacturing remain separate and serve all businesses; the R&D and manufacturing resources are shared resources, collected into the businesses. The business manager within the product company reports to the global business manager and to the head of the product company. The businesses form

Figure 13.4. Combination of Front-Back and Matrix Models.

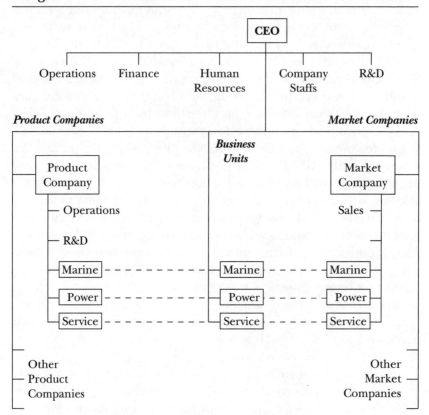

a matrix structure across the product and market companies, with the business resources shared.

In some industries the front-back hybrid form has been around for some time, although it was not referred to as front-back. The investment-banking business has always had relationship-management and product-management components, but the front-back model now occurs in all types of businesses. What is causing this organizational form to be the structure of choice?

Forces Creating the Hybrid Structure

A number of forces are pushing companies into the front-back structure, but the dominant one is the customer. A major effect of global competition has been a shift in the buyer-seller relationship to the buyer, who has learned how to use this power and now demands more value and more attentive service than previously. Sellers are responding to these demands by organizing their activities around customers and customer segments, although in many industries it is impossible to align and dedicate all functional activities to a customer segment and form a self-contained business unit; the semiconductor industry is an example.

Semiconductor manufacturers must now customize their products for buyers in the telecommunications, defense, computer, and automotive industries; these manufacturers have created sales, service, application-engineering, and product-design units dedicated to customers in these industries. However, a semiconductor factory now costs $1 billion or more, and it is impossible to build a factory for each customer segment. Therefore product units, which supply all customer segments, are created for the factories, as well as product-engineering and -supporting activities. These product units achieve global scale, while the customer units achieve focus and responsiveness. (This example would resemble the Citibank structure shown in Figure 13.3.) This is the primary objective of the structure: to simultaneously achieve customer focus and responsiveness as well as product excellence and scale. The local customer, with uniquely local needs, can be supplied by global scale; this structure permits the supplier to be simultaneously global *and* local.

Suppliers to the automotive industry provide a detailed illustration, as demonstrated by the changes taking place at a supplier of braking systems. Until the late 1980s, the supplier provided a relatively complete line of brake components to auto assemblers like Chrysler and Fiat. Manufacturing disk brakes and drum brakes for the front and back wheels and friction materials for the brake pads, and designing and manufacturing pumps and hydraulic actuation components for power brakes, the supplier considered the brake unit to be a multiproduct, single business. It was organized into regions for Europe, North America, and the remainder of the world; the North American region was a functional organization, while Europe was organized as a functional-country matrix structure (Figure 13.5). The only activities dedicated to a customer are circled in the figure. In addition to the usual sales representatives, there were liaison engineers—usually situated at

**Figure 13.5. Functional-Geographical
Structure for an Auto Supplier.**

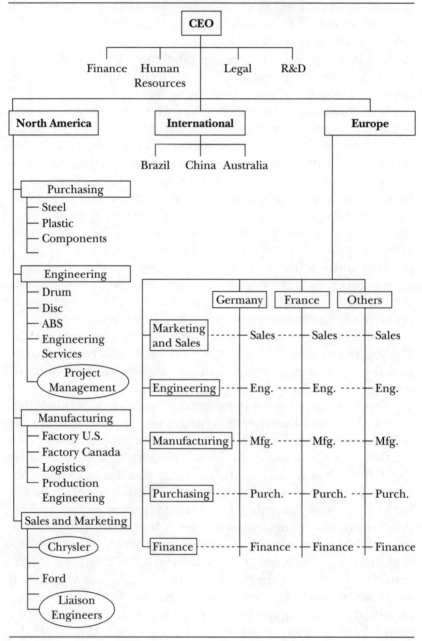

the customer facility—who rotated through the position every two to three years. A project manager usually led the design of the brakes for a new car model like a Chrysler minivan. Others had contact with Chrysler, but these were the only employees specifically dedicated to Chrysler in the old geographical and functional structure.

The auto industry then began to make changes requiring much greater cross-functional and cross-border integration from their suppliers. First, the auto assemblers, or original equipment manufacturers (OEMs), began to adopt the Toyota lean-manufacturing system in all its dimensions. As a result, they asked the supplier to do more design work than in the past and to manufacture braking systems, not just components; the suppliers began doing more systems integration and acquired competencies in antilock braking systems. Second, Chrysler and Fiat began selecting a brake supplier for each car or platform program, so there was now one supplier for Chrysler's Neon and one for Fiat's Punto, for example. Third, Fiat and Chrysler began using simultaneous engineering to reduce their product-development time and demanded the same of their suppliers. Fourth, the OEMs created strong platform-program managers for the Neon and the Punto in order to increase cross-functional and cross-border coordination on new-product platforms; again they demanded the same changes from their suppliers. Fifth, the OEMs began to operate on a just-in-time basis, asking their chosen suppliers to set up satellite plants to supply their assembly line on a just-in-time basis as well. Thus, when Fiat built a new plant in the south of Italy (Melfi), they asked their suppliers to occupy a portion of the new plant to achieve the new, tighter relationship.

The OEMs were additionally integrating their operations across countries. The national-champion structure had been breaking down in Europe: Volkswagen was integrating its operations in Germany, the Czech Republic, Spain, Mexico, and Brazil; Ford was integrating its European and North American operations; and Fiat was asking suppliers to accompany the company not only to Melfi in the south of Italy but to Poland, Turkey, Argentina, and Brazil as well. OEMs began to select suppliers on the basis of their ability and willingness to invest in new countries. In addition, they chose suppliers with the capability to integrate their own operations across countries.

The brake supplier changed its structure to meet the demands of its OEM customer. Reporting to the CEO are global-product units and global-customer units. The product structure was formed by combining the North American and European activities to get large volumes for each product; the functional structure was no longer needed to achieve scale. Each product unit is a fully functional global profit center; it develops technologies, manufactures components, and assembles them. The antilock-brake unit, which features the most advanced technology and is naturally integrating in its function, serves as the center for systems integration and R&D. A central purchasing function coordinates across product lines, using commodity teams to pool purchases and secure quantity discounts. All the back-end activities require global scale; they plan and position their products for the future while positioning them against those of competitors; they may also sell parts to other companies and to the "after-market" distribution in order to achieve additional scale.

The second structural change was the creation of customer business units for the supplier's long-standing customers. A Chrysler business manager and a Fiat business manager are shown in Figure 13.6. The business unit is a profit center managed by a multifunction general manager, not a sales manager; the Chrysler unit is actually managed by a former Chrysler executive who hired on with the supplier when Chrysler outsourced its braking-systems design and integration activity.

The Fiat business unit is shown in detail; it reflects the fact that all product development now takes place within the customer business units. Strong program managers lead the efforts for the Punto program and the Brava program; design engineers, manufacturing planners, and manufacturing engineers all report to the program manager. Staffing for the program is done by the product-engineering and manufacturing functions in the product units; some team members remain with the program over its lifetime, while others return to the product unit or to another program when the two- or three-year design effort is completed. Although the engineers may come and go, the functions within the product units remain permanent, serving as "functional homes" for them.

Also reporting to the Punto program manager is the Melfi satellite plant. The product units supply components to the Melfi satellite

Figure 13.6. A Global Product-Customer Structure.

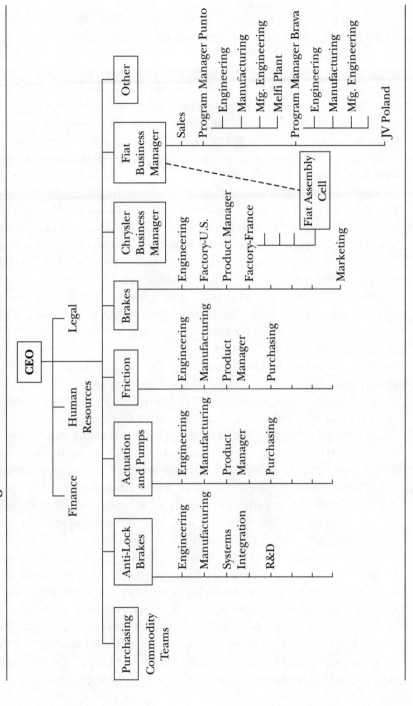

plant, where they are assembled on a just-in-time basis to feed the Fiat assembly line. For the Brava program, the components are assembled at the French factory, with the final assembly process taking place in customer-dedicated cells; a cell-manufacturing manager works for the French plant manager and the Brava program manager (this matrix reporting relationship is another link between the front and the back). Finally, the manager of the supplier's joint venture in Poland, which supplies Fiat's joint venture there, also reports to the Fiat business manager. Thus, all Fiat-dedicated activities are placed in the Fiat business unit.

Through the structural changes discussed, the customer relationship has been transformed from a sales relationship managed by a salesperson to a partnership managed by a business manager. All activities that can economically be dedicated to the customer are aggregated in the customer's business unit. This structure permits strong integration across functions and across borders and thus reduces product-development time. The customer further facilitates the process by granting global volume for a platform to a single partner; thus the volume justifies the overheads necessary to operate the dedicated organizational units.

The customer unit is responsive to the unique needs of the particular customer. All activities necessary to meet these needs report to a customer business manager, who is the single point of contact for Fiat top management. The customer business manager can meet with Fiat management to discuss the strategic decisions of having the supplier invest in a new plant, a new country, a new joint product, and so forth in order to supply Fiat in South America. The Fiat platform-program manager has an equivalent program manager at the supplier, to whom all functions report. This is an organization that is clearly designed to meet the standards of an increasingly demanding automotive customer.

However, not all activities can be placed in customer-specific units. Scale manufacturing of components is shared across all customers, as is the R&D investment to develop the next-generation braking systems, which is placed in product-specific units. The supplier has to continue to develop new technologies and maintain product excellence; the superiority of the product was one of the reasons the supplier was chosen by Fiat in the first place, and continued product excellence augurs well for future platforms.

The factors that cause a multiproduct company to choose the front-back structure are listed below:

1. Customers can buy all products.
2. Customers want a single point of contact.
3. Customers want a sourcing partnership.
4. Customers want solutions and systems, not components and products.
5. Opportunities exist for cross-selling and bundling.
6. Value-added is becoming increasingly customer-specific.
7. Advantage can be gained through superior knowledge about customers and customer segments.

The pressure for a market focus (and a separate structure) starts when customers buy—or can buy—all products. (If products are all purchased by different customers in different countries, there is no pressure for separate customer structures.) When customers can buy all products, the question arises of whether each product group needs its own sales force—all of whom call on the same customer. Would it not be more economical to have one sales force sell all products to the customer? The answer depends, in part, on how the customer wants to do business. Some customers have different buyers purchasing different products from the same vendor; these companies may prefer to have separate, product-knowledgeable salespeople calling on separate, product-knowledgeable buyers. Some products may be sold to the customer end user and not to buyers from purchasing at all. Increasingly, however, customers are pooling their purchases and negotiating a total, single contract with multiproduct vendors. These customers want a single point of contact in the vendor organization for communication, negotiation, and coordination to lower their joint costs; these single interfaces are the beginning of the front-end customer structure.

An increasing number of customers are adopting sourcing policies like those of the auto industry—that is, they prefer to have fewer, closer, and longer-term vendor relationships; they choose one or two vendors for a product and dedicate their entire volume to those vendors, who become their partners. In return, the customer may prefer—and some will insist—that the vendor create a strong local manager or a dedicated organizational unit with whom it can conduct its business (Lewis, 1995); this unit becomes a front-end customer unit.

Some customers want to buy systems rather than products. Wells Fargo Bank is buying products when it orders 250 PCs from IBM, but Wells Fargo may actually want to buy a consumer banking system. A system consists of many products—desktop computers, teller terminals, automatic teller machines, high-volume transaction processors, disk-drive storage—that are all manufactured by different units at IBM. When buying a system, Wells Fargo does not want a collection of products but a banking system that works. As a result, IBM will do the systems integration for customers like Wells Fargo who do not want to do it themselves. Vendors like IBM, therefore, need a systems-integration capability, which also becomes a front-end customer function.

Customers who do not currently buy all a vendor's products may provide cross-selling opportunities for the vendor; by packaging ("bundling") products together for a single price, the vendor may win an increased share of the customer's business. Software companies create "suites" of programs in this way for selected segments. Citibank relationship managers package foreign exchange and cash management for global customers. Cross-selling and bundling usually require a single customer-focused unit in the front end to create and price the package for the customer.

The examples above illustrate that more value-adding activities are being created that are best located in the front-end structure and focused on the local customer or global-customer segment. In the past, sales was the one activity organized around the customer, but more customer-specific services and software are now being added. IBM and Hewlett-Packard, which used to have only sales and after-sales equipment service in their front-end customer organization, have added application software, customer education, consulting, and systems integration, and they will even run a customer's entire information-technology function. PPG used to sell paint to automobile manufacturers; today, it sells paint, provides application software for choosing paints, and runs the entire painting operation for General Motors. As the economies of developed countries become service- and information-oriented, companies will continue to add service and software as a source of growth. These services, which typically require customization for market segments and customers, are being located in the front-end local, or customer, structure.

Many companies are recognizing that a local-customer or customer-segment structure allows them to create superior information and knowledge about customers and to form close relationships with them. If the knowledge and relationships can be converted to superior products and services, the segment focus will become a competitive advantage.

The front-back structure should continue to increase in popularity; as the forces listed above continue to grow, so should the use of global-local, front-back organizations. However, the continued expanding use of the hybrid structure is contingent on its effective implementation. Implementing the front-back hybrid will be one of the challenges facing management over the next decade.

Implementing the Front-Back Hybrid

The challenge of implementing the front-back organization stems from its complexity and the contentiousness it can inspire. This friction arises because the two pieces of the business are first separated and designed to be different (Lawrence and Lorsch, 1967) and are then integrated and expected to work together; this required coordination causes the conflict. In working together, the front and back managers discover that they have different priorities and perspectives. These differences are a natural result of the separation and different designs. The complexity results from having to manage the conflict inherent in the design. Managing conflict is never easy; managing it across cultures, times, and distances takes the challenge to another level. Virtually every issue in the front-back model has the potential to be contentious, so mastering the model means achieving coordination between the two pieces under circumstances that appear to prevent that coordination from ever happening.

Three approaches can be taken to manage the front-back integration. The first is to use management processes to confront the conflict and convert it into communication and coordination. In

order to execute this approach the firm must deal with several issues, which will be discussed in the next section along with some
examples of companies pursuing this approach.

The second approach to linking the front and back is to put a
market mechanism between them and rely on the "invisible hand"
to help sort out the conflicts. Acer, the Taiwanese PC manufacturer,
uses a model based on creating local front ends and then selling
to them. The Acer example is contrasted here with those utilizing
management processes.

The third option is to function only as a front or a back and to
partner with another company to get the missing piece. Corning
could be conceived as a back-end-only company; it creates opportunities through its R&D function and then creates a joint venture that
serves as its front end. Because the best front end varies with the nature of the material and the opportunity is often unknown in advance, the partnering approach provides the necessary flexibility.

Integration Through Coordination Mechanisms

Most companies that institute a front-back model try to coordinate
the pieces themselves. Successful execution of the model requires
answering the following questions:

1. Which functions belong in the front and which in the back?
2. What is the balance of power between the front and the back?
3. What management structures and processes are used to link
   the front and the back?

Management must recognize that dialogue about these questions
is going to take place in a contentious atmosphere. Management
must legitimize the conflict, anticipating that team members coming from the front and the back will probably disagree with each
other initially and that differences are normal, natural, and to be
expected. The leadership should create the expectation that disagreements are desirable—indeed, management will have a bigger
problem if the conflict does not occur—and should provide the
tools for their resolution.

Where Do the Functions Go?

The first contentious issue revolves around the design of the basic structure: Which functions go in the front and which go in the back? Some functions are easily categorized: sales, after-sales service, and customer services are front-end functions; R&D, product design, procurement, and operations are usually back-end functions. The position of marketing, however, is not as clear-cut, and neither are the occasions when product design or parts of operations should be placed in the front end.

The question always arises of whether to put marketing in the customer (or country) unit or in the product unit. As it turns out, marketing goes in both the front and the back. Segment, local, or customer marketing goes in the front end because it focuses on the local market or segmenting the customer population; it concentrates on pricing, channel selection, the bundling of products, unique services for segments, and supporting the sales force. Product marketing goes in the product back-end because it focuses on product positioning, product pricing, new-product development, and product features. The two marketing activities also play key roles in linking the front and back, as will be seen in examples later in the chapter; it is therefore necessary to split marketing and to understand its dual roles.

A debate also arises when traditional back-end activities like manufacturing are proposed as front-end functions. Sometimes there is little choice; a local government may insist on local assembly in order to allow the business in the first place. Similarly, the auto-supplies customer may insist on dedicated product-development resources and on locating them at the customer's site. If an activity is customer-specific and the customer generates a volume greater than minimum efficient scale, a customer-dedicated unit can be effectively located in the front end. For example, IBM's front-end financial-services unit is also responsible for the design and manufacture of automatic teller machines and teller terminals, products unique to this industry segment.

The trend is toward moving activities to the front end; additional services are being provided to the customer who—usually through partnering arrangements—is granting global volumes to meet the scale requirements for customer-specific activities. In most cases, though, there will be a debate about where to locate some of the functions.

What Is the Power Balance Between the Front and the Back?

The issue of power always arises; it is usually indelicately posed as "Who's got the P&L?" The leadership challenge is to end with a power balance rather than a power struggle; there are several ways to approach this goal. One way is to make one of the parts a profit center and the other a cost center. Some of the auto suppliers described previously have moved enough activities to the customer front end to make it the sole profit center; the back end consists of R&D, procurement, and component manufacturing, which are cost centers supporting the customer units.

On other occasions both the front and the back become profit centers, but one of them is given priority. At Citibank the global-customer relationships are profit-measurable, as are the global product lines like structured finance and foreign exchange. As a result of its strategy work, though, Citibank has placed the priority on the customer front end; customers are first and products second. Product lines are to first support the targeted global customers and subsequently to sell outside to get scale and remain competitive. To effectively achieve this balance, the product lines should first be measured on their service to and cooperation with the global relationships, then on their profitability; these soft criteria can be measured through ratings from relationship managers and customer-satisfaction surveys. Thus, the priority needs to be converted into an aligned set of goals; if the product lines see their performance as measured primarily on profit-center earnings, priority disputes between the front and the back will certainly result.

Xerox is trying a balanced approach. Historically, Xerox made more money from sales of supplies and service than from hardware, and as a result the front end was dominant. Now there is a need for faster time-to-market, higher investment in R&D, and a shift to digital technology; the global-product divisions are to become an equal partner. Xerox uses a dialogue between the front and back in order to agree on an aligned set of goals for products and regions.

This dialogue is facilitated by the use of a spreadsheet (Figure 13.7) that displays the whole picture as well as individual relationships.

Figure 13.7. Product-Region Spreadsheet.

	U.K.	France	Nordic Countries	Germany
Large, High-Speed Copiers		*Revenue* *Profit* *Market Share*		
Medium-Range Copiers				
Printers and Fax				

In order to utilize it, the company requires an information system that can account for profits based on both products and regions; sales and profits can then be posted on the spreadsheet, which displays the various product results for each region. In this way, revenues and profits are recorded once and assigned to both the product and the region.

The spreadsheet is completed during the planning process, and the managers from the product divisions negotiate with the regional managers to secure agreement about revenues and profits for each product line in each region. When completed, it results in a consistent set of targets for both sides. It also resolves the differences between the two sides and establishes one target for which the front and back are both accountable; goals become aligned until the next cycle. The process is facilitated by the leaders, who will probably remain significantly active during the first few cycles of the process.

In addition to producing a plan, the process is also intended to be educational: the regions inform the divisions about customers and marketplace trends, and the divisions inform the regions about new products and trends in technology. Japanese companies like Sony use this process in six-month cycles. The process lasts about two weeks, as all regions come to Japan and interact with the product divisions; this dialogue creates the next six-month plan. It is, however, also a time for learning and for social gatherings to build relationships.

When both front and back are profit-measurable, it is also necessary to define roles and responsibilities. The complexity of the front-back model derives from the fact that virtually every issue must be resolved if it is not to become a source of contention. Who sets the price? Who does the forecast? Who is responsible for the inventory? These roles need to be clarified so that managers can spend more time on the work itself and less time arguing about who is responsible. A tool such as a responsibility chart that shows who is responsible for which decision and who should be consulted is valuable (see Galbraith, 1995, p. 146). For complicated decisions, like the pricing of cross-selling, a process map that shows step-by-step role assignments may be necessary for clarity.

It is a role of leadership to continuously balance the power relationships. This balancing can be accomplished through the assignment of top talent, role definitions, control of resources, and how the leaders exert their influence and relegate their own time.

What Are the Links Between the Front and the Back?

Initially, the front and back ends of the value chain are separated and independently optimized; they then have to be recombined in order to deliver the outputs of both halves to the customer. Thus, the separately designed halves of the value chain should not lead to separate companies but to coordinated halves. Linking them can be challenging when there are a large number of countries (or segments) and products; it can be more challenging when the products must be generated and delivered on short time cycles.

Most of the time, the link is directly between the product units and the local or customer units. The link for the Citibank example in Figure 13.3 is shown in detail in Figure 13.8. The front-end customer portion of the automotive segment is organized by customer and then by geography where that customer is present. These team members manage the customer relationship in their country and coordinate across borders. A product-management unit links the automotive segment to the product lines; this unit also customizes and bundles products for the industry. In the early

Figure 13.8. Industry-Product Direct Link.

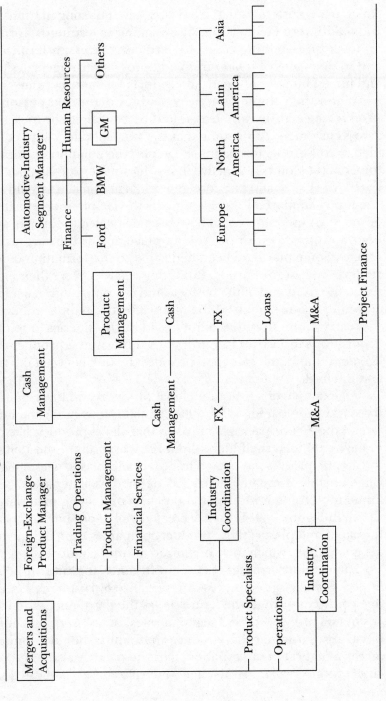

1990s, many customers in the industry were investing in China and India and were facing issues of financing investments, forming joint ventures, getting access to hard currency, transfer pricing, and so on; teams of relationship and product managers designed and priced bundles of financial products for these customers.

When the volume of activity justifies dedicated personnel, product specialists can be assigned to customers or to regions across customers. At the time that the auto suppliers were consolidating in Europe, for example, Delphi, the component supplier for General Motors, was active in buying smaller suppliers. A dedicated M&A specialist and foreign-exchange specialists could have been fully employed for some time by the Delphi merger activity; or the M&A specialists could have been dedicated to Europe, working on all the acquisitions taking place across the various customers. Some may have been dedicated to the formation of joint ventures in eastern Europe. Product specialists bring their expertise to the front end of the business and customize it to meet local-customer requirements; if the M&A activity declines in Europe, they can transfer to auto acquisitions in North America or to other acquisitions industries in Europe. In this way, the product-management unit in the front end provides the link between the front and the back.

An example of a firm with global products and local- or country-market companies is Tetra Pak, which is known for the invention of the aseptic packaging process that allows products like milk to have extended shelf life without refrigeration. In the 1990s, as the aseptic process was copied by others and plastic packaging became a viable alternative, Tetra Pak defined itself as a packager of liquid food using both paper and plastic packaging materials. As shown in Figure 13.9, Tetra Pak created global-product companies for paper and plastic; these product companies supplied the market companies, which were organized around countries.

Each country configures itself differently for sales and distribution. Some large countries can specialize by customer segment; one country shown in the figure serves the dairy, juice, and water customers with specialized segment sales forces. Another country has a large customer that produces both milk and juice and thus merits a dedicated organization, and the country also has several large producers of mineral water, which also have a dedicated sales

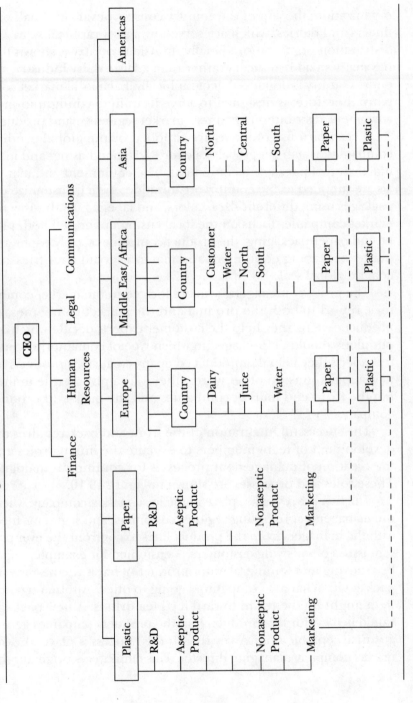

Figure 13.9. Global Products and Local Markets.

organization; the rest of the country consists of various small producers and dairies, which are served by a geographical sales and
distribution organization. Finally, an Asian country is shown that
has many small producers rather than a large dairy industry; the
entire country is organized geographically. Each local-market company, therefore, is designed to serve its unique configuration of
customers, distribution channels, market segments, and products.

These various countries are supplied by the global-product
companies, which get global scale for R&D, purchasing, and manufacturing of packaging equipment. The equipment and materials are supplied to the country organizations, which customize the
packages using different sizes, colors, and labeling. In this way the
market companies focus on the local customer and sell both plastic and paper packaging; the product companies supply paper and
plastic packaging equipment and materials to all countries and
achieve global scale.

The product managers, who are located in the market companies, report to both the product and the market companies. As
product experts they help the customer experts decide which applications should be packaged in which type of container; as country experts they help the product company create new products for
new applications. In other words, they play a pivotal role in linking the front-end market companies and the back-end product
companies.

The successful integration of the front and back requires the
development of team members to execute the linking roles and
the creation of management processes for continuous dialogue.
These roles and processes are shown in Figure 13.10.

The first process takes place in the local-market company, where
the managers representing regions, customers, and segments meet
with the managers from the product lines to confront the ever-pre-
sent issues of satisfying customers. A customer, for example, might
be readying a new mineral-water product. What is the best way to
package it? What are competitors going to offer? Another agenda
item might be the trend toward iced-tea drinks. A new package
would be best for this product. Can the product companies generate an acceptable one? A key role in this process is played by the
market-company managing director. This employee—originally the

Figure 13.10. Key Roles and Processes.

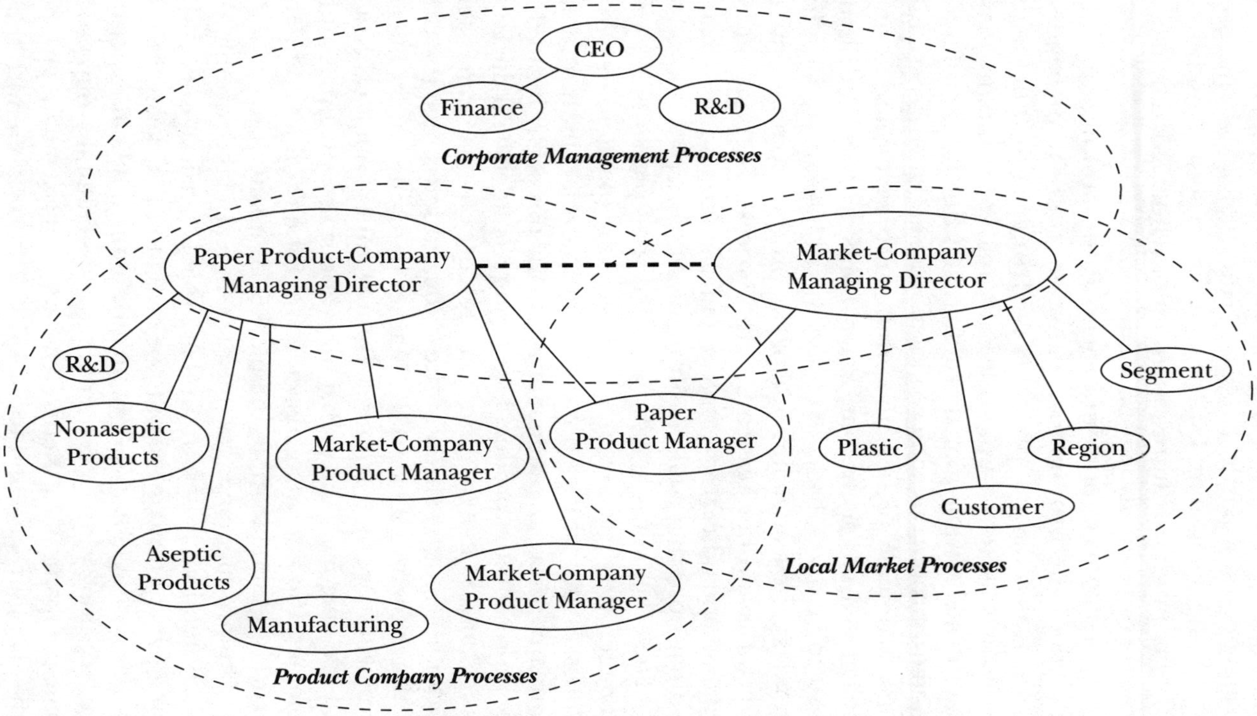

Corporate Management Processes

Local Market Processes

Product Company Processes

CEO
Finance
R&D

Market-Company Managing Director
Segment
Region
Customer
Plastic

Paper Product Manager

Paper Product-Company Managing Director
Market-Company Product Manager
Market-Company Product Manager
Manufacturing
Aseptic Products
Nonaseptic Products
R&D

top salesperson in the country, calling on the biggest dairies and customers—now needs to build a team and lead it in intense problem-solving discussions. Different customer needs must be met with different product features; when there is not a good match, a new-product opportunity may be identified.

The second important process is the product-development process of the product company, wherein the managers from global functions and products confront the product managers from the market companies. Each market company may have unique needs, while global products and functions prefer a single standard product to achieve global scale and lower costs. Like the market-company process, the product process requires team-based problem-solving discussions, which can be intense. The discussions need to be open, frank exchanges, not bargaining with hidden agendas. The leadership role of the product-company managing director is another key feature; the process is dependent on having managing directors who can build teams and then lead them in discussions that could easily tear them apart.

The other key role in these processes is played by the product manager in the market company, who participates in both processes and wears a different hat in each one. In the market company, where the manager is usually physically located, he or she represents the product line, trying to understand the local customers and to match a product's features to a customer's needs. With knowledge gained in these local discussions, the product manager then represents the market in discussions at the global-product company, teaching the global units about local customers and learning from the global units about new materials and technologies; the knowledge gained from the product-company discussions is then taught to the market company.

The product manager must teach, learn, and, overall, resolve the contentious issues; this linking role is a crucial one, and some management thinking should be given to the development of talent to execute it. A mix of formal training and field experience is needed, along with some training in cross-cultural group processes. Some companies, like Xerox, have adopted a standard group-problem-solving process and tools, providing everyone with the same problem-solving language and skills. The ideal background for the product manager is in the marketing or sales unit of a market company, plus experience in the product company. Having thus worked in both the front and the back organizations, the person is positioned to link the two halves. The effectiveness with which the front-back model is executed is contingent on the availability and skill of the person executing this linking role.

The last process shown in Figure 13.10 is the corporate process, described earlier for Xerox; this is the planning and budgeting process that utilizes the spreadsheet of Figure 13.7. The CEO needs the same team-building and team-leading skills as the managing directors need. The managing directors represent their units in discussions at the corporate level; the product- and market-company discussions should have prepared them for the corporate process.

The successful execution of the front-back model using management processes requires the alignment of all policies. Several key structural roles support these processes, and team members with the appropriate skill sets and experiences need to be selected and developed to fill these roles. Creating this aligned package of skills, processes, rewards, information systems, and roles constitutes the challenge to a management that wishes to be global and local.

Integration Through Market Mechanisms

Some companies use market mechanisms rather than coordination mechanisms to link the front and the back. Rather than invest in skills and processes for communication and coordination, these firms reduce the need for coordination through modular product designs and market prices. The Acer Group, the Taiwanese computer and electronics manufacturer, has created a front-back organization that relies on markets for linkage. The front and back portions of the business are shown in Figure 13.11.

The back end is made up of global-product companies called strategic business units (SBUs). These companies produce dynamic random-access memories (originally a joint venture with Texas Instruments called Acer-TI); personal computers (Acer Computer); disk drives, monitors, and other peripherals (Acer Peripherals); and consumer products (Acer Consumer Products), among other products. The SBUs contain the functions for purchasing, product

Figure 13.11. The Acer Group's Front-Back Configuration.

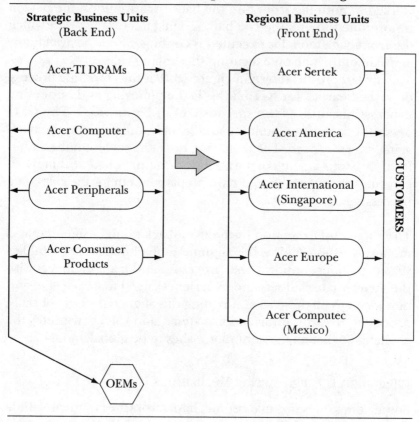

design, manufacturing, product marketing, and product sales to other companies, who put their own brand name on them (OEMs). All these SBUs supply product to all the front-end companies, which are called regional business units (RBUs).

The RBUs supply their local country and regional markets and are responsible for local marketing, sales, distribution, after-sales service, and product assembly. Acer Sertek is the sales and distribution company in Taiwan. Sertek, like most of the RBUs, has Acer as the largest stockholder, with the rest of the stock floated on the local stock exchange and held by the local management. Acer America is preparing for its initial offering, while Acer International went public in 1996 and is listed on the Singapore Exchange. Acer Computec, a joint venture with a Mexican family, has the largest market share in Mexico and is responsible for Acer production in Latin America. This local-ownership and local-management form works for Acer, which has concentrated on the home and small-business market and is the leader in most emerging-market countries. It serves local customers through its local companies and does not focus on global accounts or the cross-border customer.

Acer, like Tetra Pak and Xerox, uses the back-end SBUs for global scale. The purchasing of Pentium chips, power sources, and the like is negotiated by the SBUs. Other scale-sensitive activities—like R&D, component manufacture, product design, and global brand management—are also executed by the SBUs. The front-end RBUs are utilized to attain local responsiveness. Each local PC market is quite different, with markets at different stages of development, different levels of affordability, and preferences for different product configurations. Despite the publicity given to the big players like Compaq, Hewlett-Packard, and IBM, about a third of the PC market is served by small, fast, local players, which are Acer's main competitors.

In order to respond to the local market, Acer uses locally owned and managed RBUs familiar with their markets. The simultaneous achievement of local customization and global scale results from modular product design and product standards. The products are designed for easy local customization, with three different plastic housings that allow for all combinations of motherboards, disk drives, and other boards. The motherboard, which houses the microprocessor, is designed to accommodate several different memory chips and as many as five different Pentium processors. The product is designed to be compatible with industry-standard chips, disk drives, monitors, and so forth. As a result, the product can be assembled locally at the last moment, configured on demand to meet various local preferences. An RBU can buy components—which show considerable price volatility, usually downward—at the last moment, and as new technologies arrive in various local markets, the RBUs can adopt and incorporate them into their products. Thus, an RBU has the flexibility to respond not only to the usual volatility in demand volume but also to variations in preferences for product configuration, prices for components in a price-sensitive business, and new standard technologies.

The RBU has minimal constraints on its actions; constraints are usually placed only on activities that provide scale. The RBU must use the Acer motherboard, which is produced in volume and may contain proprietary chips that give Acer an advantage in some applications. These components are flown by air freight to the RBUs; motherboards are manufactured in Taiwan (where UPS has a hub) and Subic Bay, Philippines (where Federal Express has a hub). The RBU must use the plastic housings, power sources, and keyboards from Acer; these components are not volatile, are purchased or manufactured in volume, and are shipped by low-cost sea transport. The other constraint is the brand; an RBU must use the brand name (the logo), but it can modify promotions coming from Acer for the local market.

An RBU is free to choose the other components at market prices; the first choice would be Acer Peripherals, but if cheaper, new disk drives and monitors are available locally, the RBU is free to buy them. Acer negotiates discounts from Intel and other suppliers, but again the RBU can buy locally if prices fall or new technologies appear. The RBUs are local businesses that respond to the variety of local markets that they serve; the SBUs are global businesses that attain product excellence and global scale in their offerings. A standard transfer price is set for the few required components (like motherboards), but other components must compete for RBU orders. Acer exemplifies using the front-back structure as the way to implement mass customization: the back end is responsible for the mass-produced product platform, the front end for local customization, and both are responsible for the overall design of products and processes for mass customization.

The modular product design and industry standards allow a market to coordinate the independent decisions of the RBUs and the SBUs. The other integrating mechanisms are the energy and attention of Acer founder Stan Shih, who carefully selects the RBU partners and maintains relationships with them. Almost all the RBU partners are Chinese; they are local citizens, but ethnically Chinese. To some degree, the front-back at Acer fits the Chinese family-business model and the network of overseas-Chinese companies. In any case, Acer is a front-back organization designed to simultaneously achieve global scale and local responsiveness as they are needed.

Summary

The front-back structure is an increasingly popular hybrid organization. It results from separating the value chain and organizing the front end around the customer and the back end around the products. The front end is designed to be locally responsive and customer-focused; the back end is designed for product excellence and global scale. In order to be simultaneously global and local, the company must master the challenge of linking the front and back ends. This mastery is attained either through conflict-resolving management processes or through pricing mechanisms.

Chapter Fourteen

A Look Ahead

As the future unfolds with ever-increasing momentum, a moment should be spent speculating about the path of globalization. To begin, though, inevitably a book based on five levels of development will inspire the question, "What will Level VI be?" These issues are addressed in this closing chapter.

A Sixth Level?

The presentation of levels of international development in this book ends with Level V, the transnational form. A natural question is whether the dimension of the customer with its front-back hybrid structure constitutes a new level of international development. My opinion is that the customer dimension and the front-back model fall within the framework of the multidimensional network. The customer dimension is just that—another dimension. The front-back structure is itself a multidimensional network, albeit a complex form: it can exist as a network in which the home country is dominant, as in the Japanese version (Sony and Canon have the product ends in Japan with the customer-focused units located around the world) or it can exist as a transnational with lead product centers and lead customer units located wherever such leadership is best exercised. When perceived only as further dimensionality, the customer dimension with its front-back structure does not appear to be a new level of development. What, then, might be?

The Monoethnic Multidimensional

One candidate for a new form of organization is the monoethnic multinational (Kotkin, 1992). Taking advantage of their own global presences, the overseas Chinese and the overseas Indians are creating multinational enterprises. Each local subsidiary is a local business run by a member of the ethnic group but it attains the scale and presence of a multinational. These companies additionally achieve international integration because of their common values, common language, and high levels of trust. The monoethnic enterprise has some clear advantages, but it does not appear to be a new level of development; it is quite possible to have a monoethnic company at Level I, Level III, or Level V.

Global Consortia

Another form thought to be on the rise is the global consortium (Friedheim, 1998). Whereas a multinational enterprise owns and controls all the subsidiaries, the global consortium is an alliance of local subsidiaries; each subsidiary is a local enterprise with local ownership. This model avoids ownership of local subsidiaries by foreigners, and local ownership and identity are the strengths of the model. The question is whether this form is able to coordinate across borders; in order to be both global and local, it must achieve the global integration of an independently owned collection of companies.

The viability of this model is still being tested; it has been used and reused in telecommunications. These former state-owned monopolies were thought to be unavailable to foreign acquirers, with an integrated telecom multinational thus being a consortium of local enterprises. There have been numerous attempts at multicountry consortia, but they have formed and dissolved like Hollywood marriages. At the end of the 1990s, the big telecom companies like AT&T, Deutsche Telekom, and France Telecom preferred to own and control the subsidiaries.

Another industry, state-owned airlines, has taken a similar approach. State-owned airlines are not usually for sale, so global consortia like the Star Alliance and One World have been formed. These consortia are volatile; the Delta–Swissair–Singapore Airlines combine, for example, has crumbled. However, after some courtship and learning, the airlines may converge in the global-consortium model.

The global consortia will probably constitute a new level of development if they survive. They represent extensive distribution of value-adding activities and power and can clearly be local. The test is whether they can become global by integrating the local units when necessary and thereby become a viable form.

Virtual Clusters

A variation on the global consortium is the global virtual cluster. Clusters have been identified as effective institutions for commerce. Silicon Valley, Hollywood, and the Prado area of Italy have become popular models. A virtual cluster consists of a large network and small specialized companies; it attains scale and specialization through the network, and it attains speed, innovation, and responsiveness through the small companies. These clusters have thus far been geographical, but Hollywood is moving labor-intensive operations to Vancouver, Canada, and the entrepreneurs of Prado are considering moving the spinning and weaving functions to lower-cost Asian countries.

Another model features clusters of businesses, with each participant located in a geography superior for that activity. Each local activity is then integrated through electronic means; these electronic clusters are marketlike; they use prices and market mechanisms to coordinate their activities.

Clusters may find further proliferation through the growth of the Internet. These clusters may also prove to be viable global commercial units.

The Future of Globalization

These speculations about new forms or levels of international development are based on the assumption that the process of globalization will continue. Whether globalization will continue, will stall, or will be reversed is a real question. The financial crisis of 1997 did not precipitate a backlash against globalization; emerging-market countries are continuing in their development.

The demonstrations at the World Trade Organization meeting in Seattle suggested that the developed countries are the ones reacting to globalization; local constituencies plus the NGOs are working to restrict the globalization process. The multinationals have been successful at selling global products like the Sony Walkman, Coca-Cola, and DuPont Lycra; they have been unsuccessful at selling the positive economic consequences of globalization. The NGOs like Greenpeace continue to carry the day with scare tactics that attract the media. If these efforts lead to increased protectionism, the result could be a stall in the process of globalization, with little subsequent pressure to invent new forms of cross-border integration. Leaders of subsidiaries would probably take on a local face and participate more in the selling of the free-trade concept.

If the stall is pronounced or leads to even more protectionism, it is doubtful that a new model will evolve. Multinationals will likely revert to older models; with less cross-border trade and more within-border trade, the country-manager or regional-manager model may reappear. The companies will effect a shift of power back to the geographical dimension and away from the business unit, global customer, and function.

However, regardless of whether globalization continues, stalls, or even reverses, the models described in this book should continue to guide organizing choices. The most likely new level of international development will probably be a consortium or some type of electronic or virtual combination of local companies.

It may no longer be true that "the more things change, the more they stay the same"; the status quo does not exist long with the proliferation of fundamental and far-reaching changes in today's global market. As businesses struggle to compensate and thrive on their ever-expanding journey, the ideas and structures presented in this book can serve as a road map.

The New Global Process of New-Product Development

The process of new-product development forms one of the key networks of functions and subsidiaries; this process is receiving increasing attention for several reasons. First, because competitive advantages at the product level do not last long in most industries, the winners are those who create a *sequence* of short-lived advantages—in other words, those who create the best *process* for new-product development. Second, the process has global capabilities. As product life cycles get shorter, with fewer years to recover the fixed R&D costs, products must be spread across more countries to capture the necessary revenue. The process is becoming a primary means of cross-border coordination and one of the principal drivers for the shift in power from countries to business units. The third attractive feature of the process is its use of new electronic tools and new-product architectures; a product concept in digital form can be worked on from anywhere by anyone, and modular designs permit a task to be decomposed into separate modules that can be worked on independently. The increasing sophistication of the new coordination technologies allows for the increasing complexity of new-product development (Sanchez, 1995).

This appendix begins with a general discussion of the transformation of the process of new-product development. Although entire books have been devoted to this topic (Clark and Wheelright, 1996; Deschamps and Nayak, 1995), the focus here is on the global aspects of the process. The second section addresses the forces necessitating a global process and global products. The next sections describe the new concepts and tools—those that globalize products as well as those that help coordinate the increasing number of workers involved in the product-creation process.

The Evolution of New-Product Development

The process of developing new products has rapidly evolved into one of today's competitive weapons. It has become increasingly complex, and mastering the process is a challenge, but complexity simply means that mastery can become a source of advantage.

Although it did not seem so at the time, the process in the 1960s and 1970s was relatively straightforward: engineers and marketing people agreed on a set of technical specifications for a product that would create value for customers. Engineers set about transforming technology into a product that met those specifications; the manufacturing function designed the fabrication and assembly processes; purchasing started negotiating with vendors; and sales and marketing prepared the launch plans. The process was sequential and long. Because design changes were the major source of disruption and complexity, attempts were made to invest up-front time defining the product, then freezing the design; new ideas generated after the freeze were incorporated in the next-generation product. Performance was measured by how well the product met the specifications, whether the project milestones were met, and whether the project came within the budget targets set for the development effort.

Almost all aspects of the process have changed. Engineers still try to transform technology into features and performance that customers value, but there are an increasing number of "design for" initiatives. The first was design for manufacturability: with the Japanese at the forefront, products were developed not only to meet customer requirements but also to be easily manufactured at the lowest cost. Manufacturing engineers entered the design process early to suggest manufacturable designs before the design concept was frozen. Then came design for reliability, whereby products were designed not to fail or to fail less frequently (although many products still required some maintenance after sales); quality-assurance engineers entered the design process. When customer-service engineers offered suggestions to make products more serviceable—mainly to reduce the demand on field engineers to replace frequently failing parts—design for serviceability began. Then came design for usability: products should not only be easy to use but should look good and feel good to the touch; anthropologists entered the design process, along with artists and designers.

More recently initiatives have centered around design for recyclability; manufacturers are becoming increasingly responsible for their products after their useful life has ended. One personal computer (PC) manufacturer discovered that it cost twenty times as much to disassemble a PC than it did to assemble it in the first place because the product was never designed to be disassembled. So today the process involves designing for manufacturability all the way to designing for disassembly. Each of these "design for" initiatives introduces a new player in the process, and each new player wants to enter as early as possible to influence the original design.

In addition to many new internal players, there are new external players as well. Courses on new-product development all have a section on "early supplier involvement." Learning another lesson from the Japanese, companies are making their suppliers partners in the design process, and the suppliers, of course, want to enter the process early enough to influence the design. Finally there is the customer: when designing the 777, Boeing had customer representatives around the table; they made suggestions along with all of Boeing's internal participants.

One of the effects of the new players has been to convert the process from sequential to simultaneous. Moving sequentially through all these constituencies would take far too long, so all the players are brought into the process from the beginning (before the design freeze) in order to define the product concept. This process is referred to as simultaneous engineering, or concurrent design.

Another reason for concurrent activities is the assault on development time. Instead of meeting the project milestones, the performance measure is now the acceleration of the process and the shortening of milestones as measured by time-to-market. Other measures have also surfaced, such as time-to-volume (the time between project launch and the date of delivery of one million defect-free items per month). One factor driving the shortening of the development cycle is cost; a large project averaging three hundred engineers would save $30 million by reducing development time by a year. The rate of change, however, is the main driver; if it took five years to develop a computer, the market and technology would have changed so significantly during the development time that the product would arrive obsolete. In order to keep pace with the rate of change, the product-development process had to be greatly accelerated. Reduced development cycles and product life cycles are both the cause and the effect of the accelerated pace of change.

The short development and life cycles have two big new impacts. The first is the tightening of the links between all parties involved in the new-product process; not only are an increasing number of parties involved in the design, but their efforts must be more tightly coordinated. Everything must be accomplished at the same time, including having the materials arrive from suppliers, attaining the desired rate in manufacturing, filling the distribution channels, preparing promotional materials and ads, and training the sales force; a well-synchronized organization is required.

The second impact is on capital investments and total life-cycle costs. In the past, an investment with a pay-back period of two years was great; with a product life cycle of one year, it is a disaster. A whole new economic model is needed to manage costs and capital investments. Previously, the project manager looked at development costs, capital investments, and production costs (the cost of goods sold); those costs are still measured but so are costs of warranty, service, support, and, now, disposal. There is a need for financial modeling of the lifetime costs of the product, from start to finish. There are pressures for reuse. To reduce capital investment, can the same equipment be reused? Can some of the parts of the last model be reused? These pressures result in yet another player entering the product-development process, the financial modeler. The modeler's task is to track estimated lifetime costs and to get the other parties to think in those terms.

One of the tools used to communicate these new economics is target costing, whereby a total lifetime cost is estimated and broken down into costs of various components of the product; every team participating in the design effort is then given a target cost to meet. The target cost brings the challenge of the marketplace and the life cycle directly to the design teams.

The target cost is also related to the target price needed to win the customer order. Another task of the financial modeler, therefore, is to understand not just the cost (price) of the product to the customer but the customer's total cost of use. Does the customer have to retrain employees after each new product is introduced? Can features be added or deleted that will decrease the customer's total lifetime costs?

The new total-lifetime-cost economics is one of many factors that makes mastery of product development challenging. In addition to the usual requirement of being technically feasible, new products must also be manufacturable, reliable, serviceable, usable, disposable, and reusable. Plus one more factor: they must be global or salable across borders.

Pressures for Global Products

The forces favoring a move to global products have been mentioned before. This section brings them together and puts them into context. The primary force for global products is the capture of economies of scale. The fixed costs of R&D and product development can be recovered by collecting revenue from many countries; these economies can be considerable. There is also a convergence of preferences and tastes across countries in some product categories, some of it due to the rise of the global customer. Working against globalization of products is the still-considerable number of product differences required in various parts of the world.

At the center of the fixed-cost argument is the role of R&D in the globalization process. Led by the Japanese, most of the developed countries increased the proportion of their gross domestic product invested in R&D; the amount jumped in the late 1970s from around 1 percent to a little less than 3 percent. As wage and exchange rates rose in Japan, labor-intensive manufacturing was shifted to Taiwan and Hong Kong, and subsequently to Thailand, Indonesia, and China. The Japanese then concentrated on technology-intensive products and invested heavily in R&D. Although some increase was due to the military build-up, the United States, Germany, and France matched this R&D increase. Today, companies from developed countries use superior technology as the source of their competitive advantage when entering new geographies. A consequence of this pattern of investment is high fixed costs of R&D; it costs billions of dollars to create a new automobile platform, a new computer architecture, a new Pentium chip, or a new version of Windows. Selling these products in as many countries as possible is the only way to recover costs and profit from the technology; these products must therefore be designed to be global from the beginning.

Compounding the effect of rising fixed R&D costs is the reduction of product life cycles. In the past, a computer system had a useful life of eight to ten years; today it is one to two. Thus, R&D investments that could once be written off over ten years must now be written off in about one; today, one year of revenue from many countries has to cover fixed costs and profit demands that ten years of home-country revenue previously could.

Another benefit of global products is the reduction in fixed costs associated with reducing the number of products, packages, and ads. Black & Decker discovered it had over one hundred different types of motors for its products in 1985; it has gained enormous savings by moving toward five basic types. The move has led to overhead reductions by eliminating multiple design groups, multiple warranty policies, and all types of inventories, and by simplifying transactions. Procter & Gamble has been a leader in simplifying its product lines and moving to global products; it spends billions on new-product development, advertising (about $3.5 billion alone), promotions, packages, and inventories but has also saved billions by standardizing products where feasible. Pringles potato chips has one product, one process, one package, and one ad from one worldwide agency; for Pringles and some other products, the savings have been enormous. These savings are then translated into lower prices for the consumer and higher margins for the retailer and Procter & Gamble.

One of Procter & Gamble's discoveries was that managers were not aware of the costs of variety. When variety is reduced, sales do not necessarily drop if the savings are shared with customers; the amount of savings and the reaction of customers were pleasant surprises.

Managers also lack an awareness of commonalties. One of the legacies of country subsidiaries is a constant emphasis on differences (Yip, 1992, p. 99). Country managers were always quick to point out differences in order to keep employees from headquarters away and thus to remain autonomous, and other country managers quickly supported them. Today, a global mind-set allows managers to put more effort into finding commonalities than into emphasizing differences. To be sure, there are still differences, but firms like Procter & Gamble can account for them by making minor additions late in the process (making Pringles salty or spicy, for example); major commonalities and global savings, however, are captured first.

Another factor enabling the globalization of products is the convergence of preferences and tastes around the world. Although within a country the move seems to be toward mass customization and an increase in the number of market segments, these segments are converging across countries. Several reasons are given. One is that because of the increasing globalization of media and travel, people are exposed to many kinds of products and want the best of the lot. Another is that consumer behavior is determined largely by education and disposable income, and these factors are converging. Finally, there is the global customer. If Procter & Gamble has the same manufacturing process for Pringles around the world, it will buy the same manufacturing equipment at each of its Pringles factories; similarly, Mitsubishi Trading will want the same trading rooms in Tokyo, Singapore, New York, and London.

A Gucci handbag is identical in every identical Gucci retail store. Other products, however, exhibit real differences in various geographical markets. The new global process of product development is designed to capture the commonalities as well as to respond to the real differences.

The Global Development Process

Few global or universal products sell in an unmodified form around the world. For most products, modifications are needed to respond to real differences in geographical markets. These products, however, do not have to be totally redone or modified; over the years, multinationals have been creative in designing products that capture global scale and commonality in some ways yet are easily modified for local differences in others. The key is to use a global or regional product-development process, which designs products to be global from the beginning. This global process employs some or all of the following concepts: platforms, postponement, computer-aided design (CAD), and modularity.

Platforms

Essentially, the product-development team designs a product platform or base on which variations can be made inexpensively. The platform is designed from inception to capture scale among the most expensive components of the product or service. A computer, for example, is designed so that the expensive hardware is nearly the same everywhere, but the software is changed to accommodate local languages; the computer operating system is designed from the beginning to give error messages in other alphabets and in Kanji characters. The discovery, clinical testing, and manufacture of the active ingredient in a pharmaceutical is centrally coordinated through a global process; local packaging then allows the ingredient to be delivered as a powder, tablet, or injection, per local medical practices. Procter & Gamble has been leading the way in consumer packaged goods, and its shampoos have a basic platform character: they contain a single perfume, but less of it is used for Japan (where consumers prefer subtle scents) and more conditioner is added (because Asians have thicker hair).

Savings result from a single design effort; it costs more to design a global product than a product for a single national market, but one global design is a lot cheaper than multiple designs for multiple national markets. One product design allows for one manufacturing process and volume purchases of common components.

Finding a common platform is not always easy. For decades, the auto industry has been searching for a world-car design to replace the three different car designs for North America, Europe, and Japan. These markets have real differences, and attempts at designing a single, easily modified platform have not succeeded. One reason is the size of the cars: Americans still prefer large, roomy cars, while the Japanese and Europeans have to contend with narrow streets; the size of a car cannot be easily changed without significant redesign costs. Honda may have found an answer with its flexible frame, which allows the size of the car to be changed. It introduced a 1997 Accord into the Japanese and North American markets using the same modifiable platform, with another version introduced in Europe in spring 1998. Honda, which is ranked thirteenth in world volume of car sales, cannot afford to match its rivals' R&D spending; it worked for five years trying to discover a way to easily change the size of a car. With the new frame, it may have achieved global volume from a single platform. In the auto industry, where it costs from $1 billion to $6 billion to create a new platform, as well as in other industries, the search continues for platforms that are easily modifiable. The use of modular designs (to be discussed later) has great potential for new platforms.

Postponement

A product platform is usually combined with a postponement strategy in order to fully capture the economies of the design. Postponement can take two different forms: delay in the differentiation of a product for a particular country or customer to the last possible step in the supply chain and delay in freezing the product design or concept until the last moment.

In order to postpone differentiation, the product must be designed to allow it, the manufacturing process must be designed to enable it, and the supply network must be designed to accommodate it. For example, PCs and printers all have power sources that must vary with the voltage used in various countries; typically, these power sources are inside the product and installed early in the assembly process. However, installing a power source early commits the product to a particular country and thus forces the firm to accurately forecast by country and to hold inventories for many country-specific products. Under postponement, a standard product is supplied for all countries and held in a single inventory until ordered. Products can be shipped and transshipped across countries; then, on receipt of a customer order, the differentiating power source is added and the product is shipped within the country. This arrangement may increase the cost of product assembly but significantly decrease the total costs of inventories, obsolete products, duties, and taxes. Additionally, it speeds order delivery to the customer and provides local content for the country.

In order to postpone differentiation, the product and power supply must be designed—and the assembly process altered—to permit last-minute insertion; the distribution system must also be designed to allow last-minute assembly in distribution centers. Postponement also favors a decentralized warehouse structure to fully capture savings; products assembled in country-specific forms benefit from having one global warehouse to minimize inventories and optimize total costs, but the use of postponement and generic products is optimized by having many local distribution points to hold the generic inventory and assemble products to customer order. Thus, product design, process design, and logistics-system design must all be coordinated to postpone differentiating a global, generic platform until the last possible step.

The other form of postponement is delay in freezing the product design or concept until the last moment, as illustrated in Figure A.1. The figure shows the contrast between two variations of a product-development process. Each consists of two phases: arriving at the product definition or concept and the actual design of the product, or implementation, after the concept freeze. In the first model (a) the phases are sequential; implementation does not begin until the concept is frozen, with no subsequent changes to the definition or concept allowed. With this version, all players participate early in the process to achieve products that are manufacturable, reliable, and global; this process works fine when implementation time is short and when there are few changes to the technology, the market, and the internal priorities.

In volatile markets, however, a firm may be presented with too many changes to which it cannot respond after the concept freeze; the "new" products arrive obsolete. Instead, firms in turbulent markets postpone the concept freeze in order to minimize the development window during which they are exposed to market volatility, as illustrated in Figure A.1(b). They have learned to manage the joint evolution of product concept and product design. The process is, in part, one of postponing decisions about the most volatile and costly product components until the last minute, but it also involves frequent, early tests of the concept itself; the customer is brought in from the beginning and exposed to prototypes. This early, frequent testing is key; it means searching for and welcoming changes rather than forbidding them. This form of postponement has been facilitated by the development of the CAD process.

Figure A.1. Two Models of Effective
Product Development with Delay in Freezing.

(a) Traditional Model

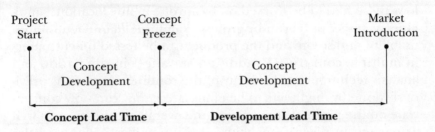

(b) Flexible Model

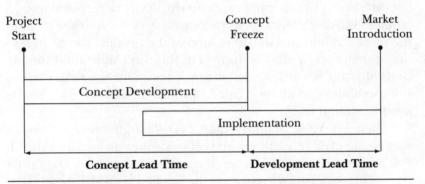

Source: Iansiti, M. Copyright © 1995, by The Regents of the University of California. Reprinted from the *California Management Review,* Vol. 38, No. 1. By permission of The Regents.

Computer-Aided Design (CAD)

The early and frequent testing and modification of product concepts or architectures is possible because of the enormous cost reductions available when the product or service is captured in digital form early in the process; experiments can be conducted on the digital product, and changes are easily made to it. An increased number of players can be accommodated by this process because many alternatives and suggestions can be tested with the digital product. The sophistication of CAD software has made these advances possible.

The current generation of CAD software creates a three-dimensional representation and analysis of the product in files accessible to anyone with a compatible CAD system and a password. The combination of CAD software, groupware, and intranets allows these files to be worked on by anyone in any location: simultaneous tests can be run by groups examining manufacturability, usability, and so on; and the product can be tested on customers in multiple countries. In addition, advances in simulation and analysis techniques allow many of the routine calculations previously done by engineers to be eliminated; they can now concentrate on the product concept and the overall architecture, as well as engage in discussions with all the new participants in the process. Simulations can also answer a lot of questions regarding serviceability or usability. A three-dimensional product file at Boeing can show a virtual employee entering a virtual airplane to fix a part and walking around in the various service areas of the aircraft; the three-dimensional digital version of the product can allow testing of many serviceability designs in this way. Additional simulations of plant layouts, assembly sequences, and the fit of various subassemblies can all be created, with the results fed back to the product-design team.

There is usually an official digital version of the product; copies may be checked out and worked on by various groups, but the official version is not changed until tested and approved. Suggested changes from various groups can be applied via a simulation that tests the integrity of the product concept. Sometimes design changes are created on one continent, then simulated and tested on another; use of round-the-clock design processes is increasing.

Technologies are also emerging that allow rapid prototyping. A three-dimensional digital product can be downloaded to machines that create and assemble parts; it takes just a few hours to create a new Hewlett-Packard (HP) printer prototype. A central file can then be downloaded into prototyping machines in Japan, Europe, and North America. These prototypes can be shown to customers and suppliers to solicit their input; customer opinions from different geographies can be collected and analyzed before a decision is made on the architecture and design of a global platform.

The increased complexity of the product-development process is being matched by the increased power of the CAD software. Players can all test their ideas, and data can be used to resolve conflicts among them more rapidly than debates over biased opinions; much of the increased coordination required by the large number of players can be embedded in the software.

Modular Product Architecture

The use of platforms and postponement is also facilitated by the increasing use of modular product architectures (Sanchez, 1995). A PC hardware platform, for example, can be designed for use throughout the world while also allowing for the last-minute attachment of power source, keyboard, monitor, software, voice-recognition chip, and manuals for country-specific versions. Modular PC design, in fact, allows for different amounts of memory, different CD-ROM drives, disk drives, external disk drives, microprocessor speeds, and so on; the PC can be assembled to order and meet the various requirements of different markets in different countries. The product, however, must be designed from the beginning to be modular and capable of postponement.

The design of a product or software package typically begins with the decomposition of the product into subsystems, the subsystems into components, components into parts, and so on, depending on the complexity of the product. An automobile, shown in Figure A.2, can be divided into sections for the chassis, power train, interior, and exterior; the chassis can be divided into the suspension system, the braking system, and so on. The specifications for how all the components work together translate this work-breakdown structure into an architecture. This architecture, in turn, describes how all the interfaces of subsystems and components will work. These interfaces define how components will be joined together, how power will be transmitted, and what electrical signals will pass.

Traditional product design tries to optimize the performance of the product, with all components functioning together in a highly integrated manner. Because the components are tightly integrated, the teams designing the components must also be tightly integrated; a high volume of communication within and across teams is necessary. This traditional process will still be used for high-performance products; a space capsule going to Mars will need unique components that fit tightly together and minimize weight and space.

Figure A.2. Architectural Structure of an Automobile.

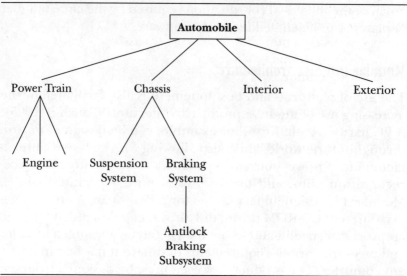

But for many other products modular architectures have been adopted in various forms to minimize complexity, allow for reuse, provide variety for different markets, and reduce costs. According to modularization expert Ron Sanchez (1995, p. 309), "Rather than seeking a design optimized to some cost or performance constraint, the objective of modular product design is creation of a modular product architecture that can serve as the basis for a number of product variations with different performance and cost characteristics."

Modularity is achieved by specifying the interfaces and standardizing them, so that any module that meets the standards can be used. The standards use the same global architecture but allow a mixing and matching of modules to meet the different demands of geographical markets (as with the PCs described above). Because modular architectures greatly reduce the costs of variety, many industries are converting to them. The software industry talks about objects rather than modules; software objects are ways to connect groups of objects, or modules, easily and without having to rewrite commonly used code. The auto industry, consumer electronics, major appliances—all are searching for ways to get scale from a platform and variety for market segments.

In addition to providing affordable variety for different local markets, modular architectures have other positive effects: certain modules may be reusable, and modules subject to rapid change can be replaced frequently. Modularity also transforms the relationships of the organizational units designing the modules; in contrast to the tight integration of traditional product design, the modular approach encourages relatively independent units, as long as they meet the interface standards. This independence has several consequences. First, the rate of innovation increases because each unit can independently experiment with its module while adhering to the standards. Second, once the architecture is decided on, each unit can implement the design concurrently; this independent and concurrent design implementation speeds product-to-market and reduces implementation time (which is minimal because of postponing the commitment to an architecture). Third, with the greatly reduced need for communication across groups, a company can locate design efforts in the best places globally. With CAD tools, the designs of modules can be distributed around the world; coordination is imbedded in the architecture and the software.

An example of this point is found in an engineering and construction firm that designs and builds oil refineries. Winning the contract for a refinery in the Philippines, the firm located project management and several modules in the Calgary office (the Canadian government makes financing available at favorable rates if work and leadership are located in Canada); the module for the catalytic cracking unit is based in the southern California office, where the expertise is located; and the Houston office, which was just finishing a project and needed new work, houses a few modules. The project manager in Calgary visits the other offices but generally controls the design through simulations and observation of the digital three-dimensional representation. Most of the high-level design is done in North America; when completed, it is sent via satellite to the Philippine office, where three hundred Filipino engineers complete the work by creating the fifteen thousand detailed isometric drawings that guide the construction effort—this last step performed at a much lower cost than is possible in North America. Thus the modular design and digital three-dimensional software allow this company to move the work to the "best" place in the world for its execution.

These four practices form a package for implementing global-product designs: platforms from modular architectures are completed by postponing the final attachment of local modules until the last minute; the CAD systems and rapid prototyping allow early and frequent testing of product ideas with customers around the world; this testing allows postponement of the final architecture decision to the last moment; and modular design and CAD allow independent and concurrent design to speed the product to market. These practices also permit the introduction of new players into the process in its initial stages. To be a player in the global-product-development game, a company—in addition to developing capabilities for platforms, postponement, modularity, and CAD—must also master the design of the product-development organization.

Product-Development Organization

The product-development organization varies over the development cycle; it starts as a few people from multiple disciplines in the concept-definition launch and becomes many in the detailed implementation. The detailed implementation phase is of interest here. There are two organizational-design issues: the design of the implementation team and the power base of the project leader.

Team Design

Implementation teams have progressed beyond the standard cross-functional team; global products also require cross-border teams. Today's product-design efforts require a hierarchical complex of teams, with the complexity of the team structure defined by the complexity of the product and its architecture plus the number of distinct geographical markets for which it is intended. For example, the Boeing 777 had a work-breakdown structure similar to the automobile structure shown in Figure A.2. The 777 was broken down into tail, fuselage, wing, and so forth, with the wing itself divided among twenty cross-functional teams managing the design. Boeing used about 250 teams for the whole design effort and also brought its launch customers—British Airways, All Nippon Airways, and United Airlines—into the process. Each customer had a team of ten to twenty-five people on-site over the development time, and these representatives also attended the cross-functional team meetings. Resolution of all issues was attempted at the first-level team, but many issues became major and were driven up the hierarchy of teams, with some reaching the top team, known as the megateam. A similar structure was created for vendors. Thus, customers, vendors, and functions all participated in the 250-team complex.

Although all organizations do not have a product as complex as an airplane or an automobile, many do have their own complexities. For example, HP launched a new desktop electronic instrument under the guidance of a core team—a cross-functional, cross-border team headed by an engineer as project manager plus an architect. Members of the core team were leaders of subteams, which were created for hardware design, software design, manufacturing-process design, marketing and sales, and localization. Figure A.3 illustrates some of the complexity (each dot represents an employee). The hardware group designed the platform, which itself consisted of several modules; these modules required their own cross-functional teams for manufacturability, as shown in the figure.

The other key team was the localization team, which designed the software and local hardware modules that are attached to the platform in the geographical areas; this team was both cross-functional and cross-border. Some members of the localization team were dedicated, while others performed linking roles. Some engineers were members of both the hardware platform team and the localization team; they provided the links and carried on negotiations between the two groups. The joint members of the sales and marketing subteam and the localization team were product managers from Europe, Japan, and Singapore; the localization team members who also participated on the hardware, software, and manufacturing teams came from the site in France where European manufacturing is performed. As shown in the figure, there was also a localization subteam to decide which product features should be in hardware or chips and which should be in software.

The HP product team, like that for the 777, was multilevel. The module manufacturability team was first-level and cross-functional, while the functional subteams were second-level, cross-border teams. The localization team was a hybrid second-level team, both cross-functional and cross-border; it was the key team for creating a global platform and both local modules and local software for

Figure A-3. Team Complex for Designing a Global Product.

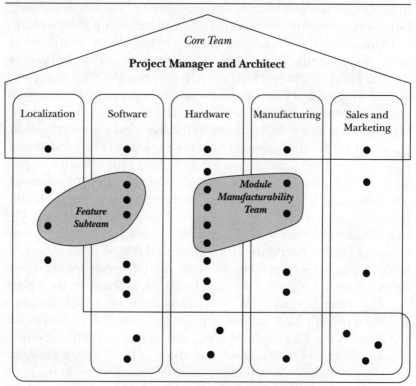

market differentiation. The overall program was guided by the third-level, core team; this cross-functional, cross-border team was the conflict-resolving body for the whole effort and was the highest in the hierarchy.

On occasion, companies like HP also create commodity teams, which focus on certain standard parts like power source, plastic housing, keyboards, or liquid-crystal displays. The objective is to see whether multiple products can use the same part or, at least, the same vendor in order to cut the costs of these standard items by concentrating as much volume as possible in a single vendor. These teams are made up of hardware engineers from the product teams and purchasing specialists; these commodity teams are also cross-functional and cross-border and may include the vendor's engineers.

Implementation teams for global products have progressed quite a bit beyond the cross-functional model. All the coordination requires intense communication, even for modular products. Multi-level teams with multiple links across functions, products, and borders are becoming the norm. One function provided by multiple levels is the timely resolution of conflicts among the parties; the top, or core, team, led by the project manager, is the final court of appeal. The power base of this manager is the other organizational issue to be addressed.

Project-Leader Power

The leader of the core team must have sufficient power to resolve conflicts and to integrate cross-border and cross-functional activities. This leader is given strength in proportion to several factors: the newness of the product, the type of product, the cycle time, the complexity of the effort, and, to some degree, the duration of the project.

New Products

New products vary in how really new they are. The greater the degree of a product's authentic newness, the more power the leader will require. In Figure A.4, a range of newness is shown for various types of "new products." The further to the right on the scale that the product program is located, the newer the product and the greater the power required by the leader to coordinate the efforts of different groups. The farther to the right, the greater the magnitude of changes, learning, risk, uncertainty, disruptions, resources, and difficulty in communicating about unknown issues. More strength will be needed for a leader to maintain integration and resolve conflicts under these circumstances.

Figure A.4. Types of New Products.

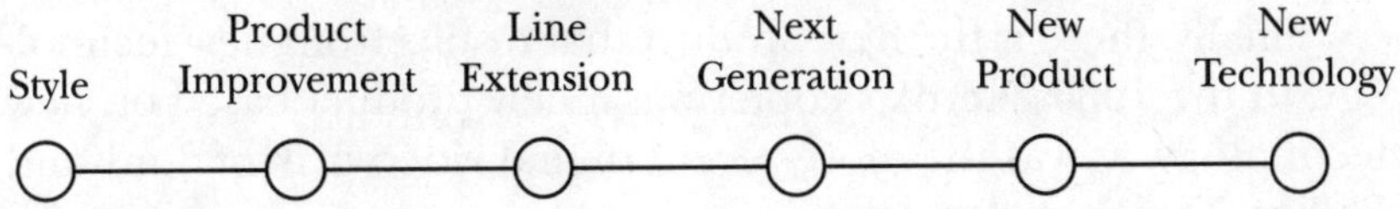

Style	Product Improvement	Line Extension	Next Generation	New Product	New Technology
O	O	O	O	O	O

The least authentically new—and the easiest to coordinate—is the style change. Often a product is relaunched and given new color schemes and packaging; it is largely a marketing effort rather than a true innovation. A more multifunctional effort occurs when improvements are made in a product; the effort is still centered around an existing product, but some new features or new ingredients are added. These improvements are often combined with style changes.

A greater change results from line extensions. Still an existing product, it has been changed sufficiently to appeal to a new market segment. For example, an automobile manufacturer that has introduced a new-model car may then, using the same platform, extend the product line with a convertible version. These extensions require some changes in design, manufacturing, and marketing and thus need more coordination than simple product improvements.

The next generation is a major update of an existing product; it combines many improvements and style changes and usually introduces new technologies. When a new generation of memory chip comes on the market, the next generation of electrical products becomes feasible, and Intel introduces its next P6 or P7 microprocessor. The auto companies introduce next generations of their line every five to eight years; BMW introduces the latest version of the 3 series, then of the 5 series, and possibly also new platforms or new engines. These efforts are major updates and require major changes in all functions.

The next degree on the scale of change is the genuinely new product. Chrysler's minivan was a new product, as was Apple's personal computer; there were no products like them on the market when they were introduced. These products used existing technologies but combined them in new ways. A product may be new for a company but not for the market, such as Black & Decker's flashlight. Even so, the company has to make many changes in all functions. More uncertainty is involved but not as much risk as might be expected because the company can learn from others.

Finally, there is the new product that results from new technology. In the 1960s Xerox's copier was a new product based on new technology, as was the more-recent digital video disk of Sony and Philips. These products require the most change and learning, and the uncertainty and risk are greatest. Under these circumstances, communication across functions and countries is most difficult, and the highest level of power must be supplied to the leader.

Type of New Product

Any of the new products discussed above could be local, regional, multiregional, or global. A product improvement solely for the United States is an example of a local new product. A regional product is a new auto platform for Europe. Ford is trying multiregional platforms for North America and Europe; the cars are not yet intended for Latin America or Asia. Clearly, a global product is one, like Levis or Coke, that is meant for all countries.

The greater the number of countries or regions in which the company intends to sell the product, the greater the coordination and communication effort needed in the new-product-design process and the greater the opportunity for differences and conflict. Hence the greater the power the leader needs to maintain integration and resolve conflicts.

Speed

The faster the product-development effort is relative to the normal cycle time, the more coordination that is needed. Efforts of all parties must be closely synchronized, conflicts must be resolved quickly, and decisions must be made in a timely fashion. The faster the relative cycle time, the stronger, again, the project leader must be.

Complexity

As the number of specialties and the number of modules increase, the coordination task increases. A style change may involve only marketing, but as products are designed for manufacturability and for recyclability, they become increasingly complex. Clearly, designing a computer system requires the coordination of more specialties and groups than does the design of a flashlight. As can be expected, the greater the complexity of the total effort, the stronger the leader needs to be.

Duration

The duration of a project can have different impacts on the desirable strength of a leader. The longer a project, the more likely and more feasible it usually is to have the core team report directly to the project leader; it may also be feasible to co-locate the team. For projects such as the design of new automotive platforms, which last between two and four years, it is feasible to change reporting relations and physical location; for projects of three to six months, people should remain in their functions and countries.

Another variation is life-cycle management. With the life and development cycles of PCs, printers, and copiers now running between eighteen months and two years, the leader and core teams are assigned to manage the product over its life cycle. The same team designs, launches, manages the product to maturity, and then manages the exit; ideally it achieves a profit and retains no inventory. It is feasible to maintain core teams for life cycles of about two years, with development cycles averaging six or eight months.

The above factors have led to stronger and stronger project leaders. As more players enter the process, as products become more global and cycle times collapse, the project leaders have grown from coordinators to experienced line-business managers. Figure A.5 details the choices of power base for the project leader. The product in question is cross-border—regional or global. As the newness of the product increases, so does the power base of the project leader; for new-product projects up to the next generation, the leader has an integrating role (described in Chapter Eight). The power base is increased by selecting more experienced integrators, setting product goals for functions and countries, and giving a budget to the project leader. For new products and new technologies the project becomes the line organization, run by the "heavyweight" product managers discussed by Clark and Fujimoto (1990); the functions and countries still have influence, but the decision-making power is in the hands of the product team. These teams quickly resolve conflicts, integrate efforts, and reduce product-development cycle times.

Summary

The new development process for global products is one of the key organizational capabilities that a firm must master when evolving into a multinational company. Even without the global challenge,

Figure A.5. Power Distribution for New Products.

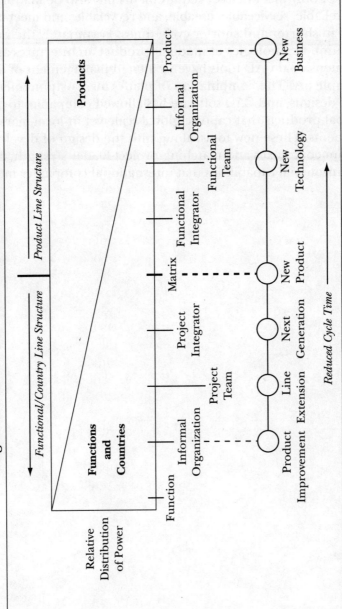

the product-development process has become complex; products have to not only meet market requirements but also be manufacturable, reliable, serviceable, useable, and recyclable, and meet target costs in shorter and shorter cycle times. Fortunately the new coordination technologies of modular product architectures and three-dimensional CAD tools have facilitated management of the new complexity. The combination of platforms, postponement, modular designs, and CAD software has allowed companies to design global products that capture global scale yet fit local-market requirements. These new tools, along with the design of development-team complexes and matching project-leader strength, are the organizational capabilities that international companies must develop.

References

Ackenhusen, M., Muzyka, D., and Churchill, N. "Restructuring 3M for an Integrated Europe: Part One." *European Management Journal,* 1996, *14,* 21–36.

Ashby, R. *Design for a Brain.* London: Chapman and Hall, 1952.

Baliga, B., and Jaeger, A. "Multinational Corporations: Control Systems and Delegation Issues," *Journal of International Business Studies,* Fall 1984, pp. 25–40.

Bartlett, C., and Ghoshal, S. *Managing Across Borders.* Boston: Harvard Business School Press, 1989.

Bleeke, J., and Ernst, D. *Collaborating to Compete.* New York: Wiley, 1993.

Buechele, E. "Key Success Factors in Transnational Teams." Speech given at the Center for Effective Organizations, University of Southern California, Apr. 1997.

Campbell, A., and Goold, M. *Synergy.* Oxford: Capstone, 1998.

Chandler, A. *Strategy and Structure.* Cambridge, Mass.: MIT Press, 1962.

Clark, K., and Fujimoto, T. "The Power of Product Integrity." In K. Clark and Wheelwright (eds.), *The Product Development Challenge.* Boston: Harvard Business School Press, 1990.

Clark, K. B., and Wheelwright, S. C. *The Product Development Challenge.* Boston: Harvard Business School Press, 1996.

Cohen, S. "Teams and Teamwork: Future Directions." In J. R. Galbraith and E. E. Lawler (eds.), *Organizing for the Future: The New Logic for Managing Complex Organizations.* San Francisco: Jossey-Bass, 1993.

Contractor, F., and Lorange, P. (eds.). *Cooperative Strategies in International Business.* San Francisco: New Lexington Press, 1988.

Corey, E., and Star, S. *Organization Strategy: A Marketing Approach.* Boston: Harvard Business School, 1970.

Davidson, W. *Global Strategic Management.* New York: Wiley, 1982.

Davidson, W., and Haspeslagh, P. "Shaping a Global Product Organization." *Harvard Business Review,* July-Aug. 1982, pp. 125–132.

Deschamps, J.-P., and Nayak, P. R. *Product Juggernauts.* Boston: Harvard Business School Press, 1995.

299

Doz, Y. *Government Control and Multinational Strategic Management*. New York: Praeger, 1988.

Doz, Y., and Hamel, G. *Alliance Advantage*. Boston: Harvard Business School Press, 1999.

Doz, Y., and Prahalad, C. K. "Controlled Variety: A Challenge for Human Resource Management in the MNC." In V. Pucik, N. Tichy, and C. Barnett (eds.), *Globalizing Management*. New York, Wiley, 1992.

Dyer, W. *Team Building: Issues and Alternatives*. Reading, Mass.: Addison-Wesley, 1988.

Eccles, R., and Crane, D. *Doing Deals*. Boston: Harvard Business School Press, 1988.

Edstrom, A., and Galbraith, J. "Transfer of Managers as a Coordination and Control Strategy in Multinational Organizations." *Administrative Science Quarterly*, 1977, *19*, 493–506.

Egelhoff, W. *Organizing the Multinational Enterprise*. New York: Ballinger, 1988.

Eisenhardt, K. "Making Fast Strategic Decisions in High-Velocity Environments." *Academy of Management Journal*, 1989, *3*, 543–575.

Eisenhardt, K., and Galunic, D. C. "Coevolving: At Last, a Way to Make Synergies Work." *Harvard Business Review*, Jan.-Feb. 2000, pp. 91–101.

Eisenhardt, K., Kahwajy, J., and Bourgeois, L. "How Management Teams Can Have a Good Fight." *Harvard Business Review*, July-Aug. 1997, pp. 77–85.

Eisenhardt, K., and Tabrizi, B. "Accelerating Adaptive Processes: Product Innovation in the Global Computer Industry." *Administrative Science Quarterly*, 1995, pp. 84–110.

Encarnation, D. *Rivals Beyond Trade*. Ithaca, N.Y.: Cornell University Press, 1993.

Fouraker, L., and Stopford, J. "Organization Structure and Multinational Strategy." *Administrative Science Quarterly*, June 1968, pp. 57–60.

Franko, L. *The European Multinationals*. Greenwich, Conn.: Greylock Press, 1976.

Freidheim, C. *The Trillion-Dollar Enterprise*. Reading, Mass.: Perseus Books, 1998.

Galal, H., Stoddard, D., Nolan, R., and Kao, J. *Verifone: The Transaction Automation Company*. Harvard Business School Case 9–195–088. Boston: Harvard Business School, 1994.

Galbraith, J. *Designing Complex Organizations*. Reading, Mass.: Addison-Wesley, 1973.

Galbraith, J. *Organization Design*. Reading, Mass.: Addison-Wesley, 1977.

Galbraith, J. "Strategy and Organization Planning." *Human Resource Management*, 1983, *22*, 63–77.

Galbraith, J. *Competing with Flexible Lateral Organizations.* Reading, Mass.: Addison-Wesley, 1994.

Galbraith, J. "The Value-Adding Corporation." In J. Galbraith, E. E. Lawler, and Associates, *Organizing for the Future: The New Logic for Managing Complex Organizations.* San Francisco: Jossey-Bass, 1993.

Galbraith, J. *Designing Organizations: An Executive Briefing on Strategy, Structure, and Process.* San Francisco: Jossey-Bass, 1995.

Galbraith, J. "Linking Customers and Products." In S. A. Mohrman, J. R. Galbraith, and E. E. Lawler (eds.), *Tomorrow's Organization: Crafting Winning Capabilities in a Dynamic World.* San Francisco: Jossey-Bass, 1998.

Galbraith, J., and Edstrom, A. "Transfer of Managers in Multinational Organizations." *Columbia Journal of World Business,* Fall 1976.

Galbraith, J., and Kazanjian, R. *Strategy Implementation: The Role of Structure and Process.* (2nd ed.) St. Paul, Minn.: West, 1986.

Galbraith, J., and Nathanson, D. *Strategy Implementation: The Role of Structure and Process.* St. Paul, Minn.: West, 1978.

Garud, R., and Kumaraswamy, A. "Technological and Organizational Designs for Realizing Economies of Substitution." *Strategic Management Journal,* Summer 1995, pp. 93–110.

Ghoshal, S., and Bartlett, C. "The Multinational Corporation as a Differentiated Network." *Academy of Management Review,* 1990, *15,* 603–625.

Ghoshal, S., and Nohria, N. "Horses for Courses: Organizational Forms and Multinational Corporations." *Sloan Management Review,* Winter 1993, pp. 23–35.

Graber, D. R. "How to Manage a Global Product Development Process." *Industrial Marketing Management,* 1996, *25,* 483–489.

Haeckel, S., and Nolan, R. "Managing by Wire." *Harvard Business Review,* Sept.–Oct. 1993.

Hofstede, G. *Culture's Consequences: International Differences in Work-Related Values.* Thousand Oaks, Calif.: Sage, 1980.

Iansiti, M. "Shooting the Rapids: Managing Product Development in Turbulent Environments." *California Management Review,* 1995, *38*(1), 37–58.

Jaeger, A. "The Transfer of Organizational Culture Overseas." *Journal of International Business Studies,* Fall 1983, pp. 91–114.

Johanson, J., and Valne, J. "The Internationalization Process of the Firm." *Journal of International Business Studies,* Spring-Summer 1977, pp. 23–32.

Johanson, J., and Wiedersheim-Paul, F. "The Internationalization of the Firm: Four Swedish Case Studies." *Journal of International Business Studies,* Oct. 1975, pp. 305–322.

Killing, P. *Strategies for Joint Venture Success.* New York: Praeger, 1983.

Kogut, B., and Singh, H. "The Effect of National Culture on Entry Mode." *Journal of International Business Studies,* Fall 1998, pp. 411–432.

Kotkin, J. *Tribes: How Race, Religion, and Family Determine Success in the New Global Economy.* New York: Random House, 1992.

Laidler, N., and Quelch, J. "Bausch and Lomb: Regional Organization." Harvard Business School Case 9–594–056. Boston: Harvard Business School, 1993.

Lawler, E. E. *Strategic Pay.* San Francisco: Jossey-Bass, 1990.

Lawrence, P., and Lorsch, J. *Organization and Environment.* Boston: Harvard Business School Press, 1967.

Lewis, J. *The Connected Corporation.* New York: Free Press, 1995.

Lorenz, C. "Lean Regime for a Fitter Future." *Financial Times,* May 6, 1992.

Malknight, T., and Yoshino, M. "Citibank (A): European Strategy." Harvard Business School Case 9–392–021. Boston: Harvard Business School, 1992a.

Malknight, T., and Yoshino, M. "Citibank (B): European Organizational Challenges." Harvard Business School Case 9–392–022. Boston: Harvard Business School, 1992b.

Martinez, J., and Jarillo, J. "The Evolution of Research on Coordination Mechanisms in Multinational Corporations." *Journal of International Business Studies,* Fall 1989, pp. 489–514.

Melin, L. "Internationalization as a Strategy Process." *Strategic Management Journal,* Winter 1992, pp. 99–118.

Mohrman, S., Galbraith, J., and Lawler, E. E. (eds.). *Tomorrow's Organization: Crafting Winning Capabilities in a Dynamic World.* San Francisco: Jossey-Bass, 1998.

Nohria, N., and Eccles, R. *Networks and Organizations.* Boston: Harvard Business School Press, 1992.

Nohria, N., and Ghoshal, S. *The Differentiated Network.* San Francisco: Jossey-Bass, 1997.

O'Hara-Devereaux, M., and Johansen, R. *Globalwork: Bridging Distance, Culture, and Time.* San Francisco: Jossey-Bass, 1994.

Porter, M. *Competition in Global Industries.* Boston: Harvard Business School Press, 1986.

Porter, M. *The Competitive Advantage of Nations.* London: MacMillan, 1990.

Prahalad, C. K., and Doz, Y. *The Multinational Mission.* New York: Pergamon Press, 1987.

Pucik, V. "Joint Ventures with the Japanese: Implications for Human Resource Management." In F. Contractor and P. Lorange (eds.), *Cooperative Strategies in International Business.* San Francisco: New Lexington Press, 1988.

Pucik, V. "Strategic Alliances, Organizational Learning and Competitive Advantage." In V. Pucik, N. Tichy, and C. Barnett (eds.), *Globalizing Management*. New York: Wiley, 1992.

Ruigrok, W., and van Tulder, R. *The Logic of International Restructuring*. New York: Routledge, 1996.

Sadtler, D., Campbell, A., and Koch, R. *Break Up!* Oxford: Capstone Press, 1997.

Sanchez, R. "Strategic Flexibility in Product Competition." *Strategic Management Journal*, Summer 1995, pp. 135–160.

Simon, H. *Hidden Champions*. Boston: Harvard Business School Press, 1995.

Slywotzky, A. *Value Migration*. Boston: Harvard Business School Press, 1996.

Snow, C., Davison, S., Snell, S., and Hambrick, D. "Use Transnational Teams to Globalize Your Company." *Organization Dynamics*, Spring 1996.

Stoddard, D., Donnellon, A., and Nolan, R. "Verifone (1997)." Harvard Business School Case 9–398–030. Boston: Harvard Business School, 1998.

Stopford, J., and Strange, S. *Rival States, Rival Firms: Competition for World Market Shares*. Cambridge: Cambridge University Press, 1991.

Stopford, J., and Wells, L. *Managing the Multinational Enterprise*. London: Longmans, 1972.

Treacy, M., and Wiersema, F. *The Discipline of Market Leaders*. Reading, Mass.: Addison-Wesley, 1995.

Tsurumi, Y. *The Japanese Are Coming*. New York: Ballinger, 1976.

Ulrich, D. *Human Resource Champions*. Boston: Harvard Business School Press, 1996.

Wall, S., and Wall, S. *The New Strategists*. New York: Free Press, 1995.

Wernerfelt, B. "A Resource-Based View of the Firm." *Strategic Management Journal*, 1984, *5*, 171–180.

Winter, M., and Steger, U. *Managing Outside Pressure*. New York: Wiley, 1998.

Yetton, P., Davis, J., and Craig, J. "Redefining the Multi-Domestic: A New Ideal Type." Working Paper 95–016. New South Wales: Australian Graduate School of Management, University of New South Wales, Sept. 1995.

Yip, G. S. *Total Global Strategy*. Englewood Cliffs, N. J.: Prentice Hall, 1992.

Yoshino, M., and Rangan, U. *Strategic Alliances*. Boston: Harvard Business School Press, 1995.

Yu, Y.-S. "The International Transferability of the Firm's Advantages." *California Management Review*, 1995, *37*, 73–88.

Index